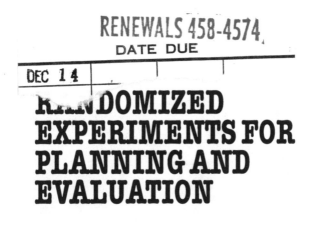

RANDOMIZED EXPERIMENTS FOR PLANNING AND EVALUATION

Applied Social Research Methods Series
Volume 44

APPLIED SOCIAL RESEARCH METHODS SERIES

Series Editors
LEONARD BICKMAN, Peabody College, Vanderbilt University, Nashville
DEBRA J. ROG, Vanderbilt University, Washington, DC

Other volumes in this series are listed at the back of the book

RANDOMIZED EXPERIMENTS FOR PLANNING AND EVALUATION
A Practical Guide

Robert F. Boruch

Applied Social Research Methods Series
Volume 44

SAGE Publications
International Educational and Professional Publisher
Thousand Oaks   London   New Delhi

For information address:

SAGE Publications, Inc.
2455 Teller Road
Thousand Oaks, California 91320
E-mail: order@sagepub.com

SAGE Publications Ltd.
6 Bonhill Street
London EC2A 4PU
United Kingdom

SAGE Publications India Pvt. Ltd.
M-32 Market
Greater Kailash I
New Delhi 110 048 India

Printed in the United States of America

Library of Congress Cataloging-in-Publication Data

Boruch, Robert F.
    Randomized experiments for planning and evaluation / Robert F. Boruch.
        p.   cm. — (Applied social research methods series ; v. 44)
    Includes bibliographical references and index.
    ISBN 0-8039-3509-9 (acid-free paper). — ISBN 0-8039-3510-2 (pbk.: acid-free paper)
    1. Social sciences—Methodology. 2. Evaluation research (Social action programs) I. Title. II. Series.
    H61.B6276 1997
    300'.72—dc20   96-25315

98 99 00 01 02 03 10 9 8 7 6 5 4 3 2

Acquiring Editor:	C. Deborah Laughton
Editorial Assistant:	Eileen Carr
Production Editor:	Michèle Lingre
Production Assistant:	Karen Wiley
Typesetter/Designer:	Danielle Dillahunt
Cover Designer:	Lesa Valdez
Print Buyer:	Anna Chin

To Dorothy

Contents

1

Introduction

*Man is naturally metaphysical and arrogant and
is thus capable of believing that the ideal creations of his mind,
which express his feelings, are identical with reality. From this, it
follows that the experimental method is not really natural to him.*

—Claude Bernard,
Introduction à la médecine expérimentale, 1865

A GENERAL PROBLEM

Estimating the effect of a new social or educational program requires comparing the condition of the individuals who have received the new service against the condition they would have been in had they not received the service. At times, their condition in the absence of the service is predictable; often, however, predicting how a group of individuals would have fared without the new service is difficult or impossible. A forecast of a group's behavior would, for example, have to take into account ordinary growth, cyclical or seasonal variations in behavior and the environment, and ordinary random fluctuations. Such a forecast also would need to determine whether the group might have received no services or services other than the new one, then somehow predict the effect of these unreceived services or alternative services.

In the absence of reliable predictions about a group's behavior, it is natural to construct a comparison group that has not received the new service. For a comparison to be fair, the comparison group must not differ systematically from new service recipients in any respect that would affect their future state. That is, the groups must be such that an unbiased estimate of the relative effect of the service is possible. More precisely, a fair comparison requires that the characteristics of individuals who receive services, or those who do not, be independent of the response variable used to make judgments about relative effectiveness. In other words, how people are selected for groups, or select themselves into groups, must not depend on factors that could influence outcome.

A SPECIFIC EXAMPLE

Consider, for example, a police study that compares the recidivism rate of individuals who were arrested for misdemeanor violence against the recidivism among those who were not arrested, the object being to establish whether arresting an offender reduces his or her subsequent violence. In an uncontrolled or observational study, particular police officers will prefer to arrest some offenders and not to arrest others, choosing instead to mediate the dispute. This *selection*, born of police officers' preferences, leads to two offender groups that are likely to differ systematically in ways that are observable. Arrestees may, for example, have a higher unemployment rate. The groups may also differ in unobservable ways. For example, offenders who were not arrested may have been motivated to lie about their employment status or to talk about the dispute in such a way as to generate more lenient treatment by the police officer. These factors arguably are relevant to the outcome of primary interest, recidivism.

The differences between the groups that evolve from the natural processes will be tangled inextricably with the actual effect of arrest, if there is an effect. A simple difference in recidivism between the two groups, one composed of individuals who were arrested and one composed of those who were not, will not then register the effect of arrest alone: It will reflect the effect of arrest and the combined effect of all selection factors, including police officers' preferences, unmeasured motivational differences among offenders, and so on. As a consequence, the estimate of the effect of arrest based on a simple difference in the recidivism rate between the groups is equivocal at best. It may also be misleading. Recidivism in the arrested group, for example, may be higher, making it appear that arrest increases assaults when, in fact, arrest has no effect. It is the selection factors that produce the difference. Thus, a simple observational study of arrested and nonarrested offenders, which merely compares recidivism rates after the police encounter, will yield a result that cannot be interpreted easily.

Eliminating selection factors in evaluations that are designed to estimate the relative effectiveness of alternative approaches to reducing a problem is difficult. Selection factors affect nonrandomized studies, such as those based on passive surveys that purport to assess the impact of manpower training programs, health care systems, compensatory education efforts, and innovation in civil and criminal justice. They also affect studies that purport to match individuals in each group to the extent that matching is imperfect or incomplete in ways that are unknown or unknowable.

The fact that many studies cannot take into account the selection factors or other competing explanations for a difference between treatments does not mean that such studies are useless. It does, however, imply that when appropriate and feasible, one ought to exploit sturdy methods for estimating the relative effects of initiatives, methods that are not vulnerable to selection problems and do not lead to estimates that are equivocal or biased in unknown ways. The approach covered in this book, employing randomized field tests, is far less vulnerable to such problems than are other methods.

RANDOMIZED EXPERIMENTS
FOR PLANNING AND EVALUATION

In the simplest randomized experiment, individuals are randomly assigned to one of two or more treatment groups. This is in the interest of determining which treatment works better relative to some outcomes. The groups so composed are, roughly speaking, equivalent. They do not differ systematically. The treatments may eventually produce a systematic difference among the groups, the experiment being employed to discern such a difference.

In more complex experiments, individuals or entire jurisdictions may be matched first, then randomly assigned to treatment groups. For example, schools from a sample of schools have been matched into pairs, members of the pair being similar. Each member of the pair was then randomly assigned to either a control group or a group that received resources for a schoolwide substance abuse prevention program (Ellickson & Bell, 1992). Matching—and other strategies discussed later—enhances the precision of the experiment; the randomization again ensures that unknown influences on behavior are equalized across the treatment groups.

The first of two principal benefits of randomized tests is that they permit a fair comparison. Estimates of the relative differences among the treatments being compared will be unbiased; that is, the estimates of their effect will not be tangled inextricably with competing explanations of what caused the difference in observed outcome. This is because the groups being compared will not differ systematically, as a result of the random allocation. The virtue in the idea of a comparison that leads to clearly interpretable results was recognized more than a century ago by Jastrow and Pierce in psychophysical laboratory experiments (Stigler, 1978). It is a virtue that has been recognized in evaluating programs in the social arena, judging from the increased use of the method in policy research.

The second benefit, developing a statistical statement of one's confidence in the results of the experiment, depends on the idea that the results are subject to ordinary variability in human behavior and that this variability can be taken into account. The ability to make such a statement is important on scientific grounds. We know that we will err, at times, in judging a treatment's effectiveness simply because ordinary chance variability in human and institutional behavior can be substantial. Understanding the character of the random variation and delimiting its magnitude is then important. The construction of formal statistical tests about the relative differences among treatments in a randomized experiment, based on the randomization procedure, is attributable to Sir Ronald Fisher (1935) and to his colleagues and students such as Oscar Kempthorne (1952).

DISTINCTIONS

Randomized experiments are to be distinguished from *observational studies*, in which there is no opportunity to assign individuals to alternative treatments in accord with a randomization plan or rule and in which the object is to estimate relative treatment effectiveness (Cochran, 1983). The causal connection between tobacco use and cancer, based on survey samples rather than controlled experiments, exemplifies the genre. Such studies cannot always sustain defensible analyses of the relative effects of different treatments but can be very persuasive when done well. (For an illuminating state of the art monograph on this topic, see Rosenbaum, 1995.)

Randomized field tests are also different from *quasi-experiments*. The latter research designs have the object of estimating the relative effectiveness of different treatments that have a common aim, just as randomized experiments do, but they depend on methods other than randomization to rule out the competing explanations for the treatment differences that may be uncovered. Quasi-experiments and related observational studies then attempt to approximate the results of a randomized field test (Campbell & Stanley, 1966; Cook & Campbell, 1979; Cochran, 1983).

A variety of important statistical approaches have been invented to try to isolate the effects of treatments in observational studies and quasi-experiments. They attempt to recognize all the variables that may influence outcomes, including treatments and possible selection factors. Contemporary advances in this arena often fall under at least three rubrics: *structural models*, *selection models*, and *propensity scoring*. Antecedents to these approaches include covariance analysis and matching methods. Some of these techniques are reviewed in Coyle, Boruch, and Turner (1991) in the context of disease prevention.

Quasi-experiments, observational studies, and other approaches have been useful in science and policy research. This is partly because it is not possible or desirable to employ controlled experiments in all settings in which estimates of the relative effectiveness of different programs must be produced. They can be useful, and have been, when used in conjunction with randomized experiments for a variety of reasons. A randomized test, for example, may be undertaken with a modest sample of individuals to evaluate a set of practices. A quasi-experimental framework might be used simultaneously to try to estimate the effect of a policy on the entire population from which the subsample is drawn.

The phrase "randomized controlled experiment" will be used hereafter interchangeably with other terms that have roughly the same meaning and are common in different research literatures. These terms include "randomized controlled test" and "randomized social experiments," used frequently during the 1970s and 1980s, and "randomized clinical trials," a term often used to describe the same design for evaluating the effectiveness of medical or pharmaceutical innovations.

ILLUSTRATIVE EXPERIMENTS
FROM DIFFERENT FIELDS

The illustrations described here have been chosen to characterize the range of settings in which randomized tests have been undertaken. Some of the examples focus on small components of larger programs, for example, enhancing the well-being of maltreated children who are involved in preschool centers. Others involve comparative tests that are larger in scope. Many are used later in this book to help explain issues in design, execution, and analysis of randomized field tests.

Education

In education, as in other arenas, individuals, institutions, and other entities may be allocated randomly to different treatments in order to produce good estimates of the treatments' relative effectiveness. For example, entire schools have been randomly assigned to alternative regimens to understand whether intensive schoolwide campaigns could delay or prevent youngsters' use of tobacco, alcohol, and drugs (e.g., Ellickson & Bell, 1992). Classrooms have been allocated randomly to different teacher-based approaches to enhancing children's cognitive achievement (Porter, 1988). Individual students have been the targets in controlled tests of computer-assisted instruction, compensatory education, dropout prevention, and other programs.

Randomized controlled experiments have been mounted at the preschool level to learn whether early educational enrichment programs would lead to enhanced academic achievement of economically deprived children (McKay, Sinisterra, McKay, Gomez, & Lloreda, 1978). Because the relative impact of magnet schools is hard to estimate, experiments have been undertaken to produce good evidence. Crain, Heebner, and Si (1992), for example, analyzed data from New York City's Career Magnet schools, to which a sample of eighth grade students were assigned randomly, to learn whether the schools did in fact reduce the likelihood of dropout and increase reading achievement levels. At the high school level, randomized tests have been undertaken in numerous schools to assess dropout prevention programs (Maynard, 1991) and to evaluate the effects of Upward Bound programs on level of education and achievement (U.S. Department of Education, 1991b). There have been experiments at the college level to test programs that were thought to enhance the performance of high-risk students, to increase comprehension, to improve the efficiency of instruction, and to achieve other goals (e.g., Light, Singer, & Willett, 1990).

Employment and Training

The Rockefeller Foundation has supported randomized controlled field tests of integrated education and employment programs under its Minority Female Single Parent Program. The objective was to understand whether a program involving a constellation of child care, job skills training, general education, and counseling would enhance the economic well-being of single mothers with low education and low employment skills.

The research was mounted in collaboration with community-based organizations. It involved randomly assigning eligible women to either the integrated program or a control group whose members had access to employment, training, and other services generally available in the community. The organizations employed randomized experiments in order to ensure that the new resources yielded data that could withstand harsh criticism in scientific and public policy forums.

The experiments, for example, eliminated the problem of creaming, that is, selecting superior applicants in the interest of making a training program look good. The problem was chronic in evaluation of many employment programs of the 1960s and 1970s. Further, the randomization feature helped to avoid a major problem encountered in earlier attempts to evaluate such programs. That is, it is often difficult or impossible to disentangle the average effect of a new program from the characteristics of individuals who elect (or do not elect) to enter a new program unless a controlled experiment is performed (Cottingham, 1991; Rockefeller Foundation, 1990).

Related examples include multistate evaluations of work-welfare initiatives (Gueron & Pauly, 1991; Hollister, Kemper, & Maynard, 1984) and regional tests of new programs designed to retrain and employ workers displaced by technology and competition from their jobs (Bloom, 1990). These form part of a substantial effort to generate good evidence for policy and administration and the economic sciences.

Tax Administration

The interests of the U.S. Internal Revenue Service (IRS) and of tax agencies in other countries lie partly in understanding how citizens can be encouraged to pay the proper amount for their taxes. For example, delinquent taxpayers identified by the IRS have been assigned randomly to different encouragement strategies, then tracked to determine which strategies yielded the best returns on investment. One set of strategies tested has focused on varying the characteristics of letters to tax delinquents; the letters varied in their frequency and severity of tone (Perng, 1985). Other experiments have been undertaken to determine how tax forms could be simplified and how taxpayer errors could be reduced through various alterations in tax forms (e.g., Roth, Scholz, & Witte, 1989).

Such research extends an early experiment by Schwartz and Orleans (1967) to learn how people might be persuaded to report thoroughly certain taxable income. This study compared the relative effectiveness of appeals to moral conscience, threats of legal action, and information about the socially embarrassing consequences of failure to report the income. Which strategy worked best depended on income level. Appeals to conscience produced better reporting among low-income individuals, and the possibility of social sanction affected those with higher incomes. This study was small, and it is not clear whether similar results would be found in other settings.

The random allocation of taxpayers into the various treatment groups ensures that the groups are equivalent apart from chance differences that can be taken into account. For example, if the contents of letters sent to delinquent taxpayers in the Perng (1985) study had been determined by individual IRS staff members, the effect of factors such as frequency and severity of the letters would have been mixed inextricably with the effect of the staffers' preferences (i.e., a selection factor). Developing a defensible estimate of the relative effectiveness of letter strategies independent of such preferences would have been impossible.

Civil and Criminal Justice

The Minneapolis Domestic Violence Experiment was designed to understand how misdemeanor domestic violence cases could be better handled by police officers (Sherman & Berk, 1984). Within the limits set by the police departments and legal counsel, such cases were allocated randomly to three different police handling tactics: arrest of the offender, mediation of the dispute, or immediate temporary separation of the offender and victim. The object was to determine which of these treatments produced the lowest level of subsequent domestic violence in households.

The integrity of the results depended heavily on the random allocation of cases. That is, the cases in each treatment group were statistically equivalent as a result of the random assignment. Competing explanations that were common in earlier nonrandomized studies could then be ruled out. Such explanations included differential police preferences for one or another way to handle the violence complaint. The Minneapolis experiment helped to inform a 15-year debate on handling such cases, in that arresting an offender was found to work better than other strategies tested (Sherman & Hamilton, 1984). Similar experiments were then undertaken by six other police departments to determine whether arrest would prove more effective in other cities and to test other methods of reducing violence (Garner, Fagen, & Maxwell, 1995).

There have been two substantial reviews of randomized field experiments in civil and criminal justice. Dennis (1988) analyzed the factors that influenced the quality of 40 studies undertaken in the United States. His dissertation updated Farrington's (1983) fine examination of the rationale, conduct, and results of randomized experiments in Europe and North America. The range of treatments whose effectiveness has been evaluated in controlled tests is, to judge from each review, remarkable. They have included appeals processes in civil court, telephone-based appeals hearings, victim restitution plans, jail time for offenders, diversion from arrest, arrest versus mediation, juvenile diversion and family systems intervention, probation rules, bail procedures, work-release programs for prisoners, and sanctions that involve community service rather than incarceration.

Mental Health

Federal agencies such as the National Institute of Mental Health have supported a variety of multisite experiments to understand the effectiveness of different approaches to mental illness. One such trial involved the random assignment of people who were seriously depressed (from a pool of volunteer patients) to one of each of three promising treatment approaches: a specialized brief form of cognitive behavior therapy, pharmacotherapy with clinical management, and placebo with clinical management. The object was to estimate the relative effectiveness of treatments so as to ensure that estimates would not be contaminated systematically by unknowable extraneous influences such as physician or patient preferences and beliefs (Collins & Elkin, 1985). The groups being compared did not differ systematically, by virtue of randomization prior to treatment. More recent experiments have been mounted; for example, to produce unbiased estimates of the relative effectiveness of consumer case managers (Solomon & Draine, 1995a) and programs for mentally ill individuals who are released from jail (Solomon & Draine, 1995b). Regional experiments have been executed by Vinokur, Price, and Schul (1995) to learn whether a specialized program reduced the mental depression of dislocated workers and enhanced the likelihood of re-employment (it did).

Abused and Neglected Children

One object of research in this area has been to understand how to enhance positive behaviors of withdrawn, maltreated preschool children. A randomized field test was undertaken by Fantuzzo and others (1988) to evaluate the effectiveness of an innovative approach to the problem, notably the selection and training of highly interactive and resilient preschoolers in playing with their maltreated peers. The program involved children initiating activity and sharing during play periods with children who had been withdrawn and timid.

The field test involved comparing the withdrawn children who were randomly assigned to this approach against children who had been randomly assigned to specialized adult-based activity. The results from blind on-site observations and school records showed remarkable increases in positive behaviors and decreases in problem behaviors among withdrawn children who were engaged by their peers. The initial study was small.

Larger-scale tests have been undertaken by Fantuzzo and his colleagues in Head Start Centers in Philadelphia, partly on the basis of the results from the initial effort.

A different stream of controlled experiments has been undertaken to understand how to prevent out-of-home placement of neglected and abused children. In Illinois, for example, the studies involved randomly assigning children at risk of out-of-home placement, such as foster care, to either the conventional placement route that included foster care or to a Family First program that leaves the child with the parents but provides intensive services from counselors and family caseworkers. Related research has been undertaken by other agencies involved in child care in California, Utah, Washington, New York, New Jersey, and Michigan (Schuerman, Rzepnicki, & Littell, 1994). The need to produce good evidence in this arena is driven partly by political and professional interest in learning whether foster care can be avoided.

Nutrition

The U.S. Department of Agriculture's Food and Nutrition Service is responsible each year for a $12 billion Food Stamps Program, a $4 billion School Lunch Program, and a $2 billion food program for Women, Infants, and Children (WIC). Each program directs attention to individuals who are economically vulnerable and, on this account, also likely to be nutritionally at risk. The poor, including infants, often do not have an adequate diet.

Evaluation and analysis units at the Food and Nutrition Service have mounted randomized controlled tests of different approaches to improving service since the early 1980s. Among these are multisite experiments that compare strategies for securing employment for able-bodied food stamp recipients who would otherwise be unemployed. The objective was to understand which of more than a dozen strategies worked, and in what sense, to increase the recipients' earnings and reduce their dependence on the Food Stamp Program (Wargo, 1989). Others are identified elsewhere in this book.

ELEMENTS OF A
RANDOMIZED EXPERIMENT

Consider the following question: How can police officers best handle a case in which police are called when a male has assaulted his female partner? Where there is serious injury, police action usually is direct. The alleged offender would be arrested and charged with a felony. Where there is no evidence for assault or threats, then the action will also usually be direct. Police will usually explore the case, determine that there is no probable cause evidence to believe that the woman has been hurt, and leave the home.

When the woman has been threatened or assaulted but the level of injury is not sufficient to justify a felony charge, matters are often less clear. The majority of assaults lie between the two extremes just described; that is, the crime is a misdemeanor. Some observers have argued that, in this gray area between extremes, issuing a warning to the offender and providing information to the victim about shelter services and their rights are all that reasonably can be expected from the police. Advocacy groups concerned about both current and future injuries to women, on the other hand, have argued that arrest is the most appropriate approach to handling the assailant. A misdemeanor crime has been committed; therefore, arrest is justified. Others have argued that police restoration of order followed by counseling for the couple is a sensible way to reduce further disputes. Still others have argued that arresting an offender on a misdemeanor charge will lead to further assaults because the offender will be angry.

Until the 1990s, evidence was insufficient to determine the effects of any course of action. Learning about their relative effectiveness in reducing recidivism arguably is important for managing police resources, reducing injuries, and administering justice. The ambiguity of evidence and the importance of the problem invite considering controlled tests, including randomized field experiments.

Broad elements of a randomized test for learning what works better in this scenario are outlined in Box 1.1 and discussed briefly in what follows. Each element is discussed in a separate chapter of this book. The description is based mainly on major controlled field tests sponsored by the National Institute of Justice on police handling of domestic violence, the Spouse Assault Replication Program (SARP). Other substantive examples, such as tests of manpower projects, are used to reiterate the fundamental character of the elements.

Questions

Put bluntly, the questions best addressed by randomized controlled tests are, What works better and in what sense? For whom? and At what cost? The primary question must, of course, be framed for the specific case. Secondary questions are often important for science or policy, and their lower priority needs to be made plain.

BOX 1.1
Elements of a Randomized Field Experiment

The questions: What works better? With whom? For how long? At what
    cost?
Ensuring ethical propriety
The experiment's design
    Target population, statistical power, and the pipeline
    Treatments
    Random assignment
    Observation and measurement
    Analysis
    Reporting

In the Spouse Assault Replication Program, for example, the *primary*
question was, Does arrest for the misdemeanor domestic violence reduce
recidivism relative to conventional police handling of such cases? The
question was determined by the sponsoring agency, the National Institute
of Justice, based on earlier policy research and the counsel of its advisers.

It was also based in part on a theory. The theory is that arrest has a
specific deterrent effect. The rationale for the question was based on the
need to understand whether arrest is more effective in a variety of settings
than are conventional police attempts to restore order and mediate domestic
disputes. The primary outcome variable of interest in all cases was recidivism, or a repeat event involving the same couple.

Secondary questions also were posed by principal investigators in each
site in which the experiments were run. Omaha's police department, for
example, examined the question of how to handle cases in which the
alleged offender was not present when police arrived. In collaboration with
researchers at the University of Colorado, police designed a randomized
test to understand whether issuing warrants on offenders who were "gone
on arrival" resulted in lower recidivism relative to the usual practice.
Warrants are not issued in many jurisdictions when the alleged offender in
a misdemeanor domestic case is not present when police arrive (Dunford,
1990).

The technology of controlled experiments, when applied well, yields the
least ambiguous evidence possible on the questions, Does it work? and
What works better? It is not usually designed to address other questions

that lie behind these questions, such as What is the nature and scope of the problem? and Which programs are planned and actually put in place?

Answers to these latter questions are a prerequisite to designing a good experiment. For example, understanding the incidence of domestic cases in various neighborhoods of a police jurisdiction is necessary to determine where and how a controlled experiment for testing new police services can be deployed. Learning that there are a variety of existing victim services apart from those offered by the police is, at times, essential to designing field tests of new police approaches and interpreting the results of an experiment. These topics are discussed in Chapter 2, which deals with the context of experiments.

Ensuring Ethical Propriety

Whether an experiment is ethical can be judged by a variety of criteria. The medical, social, and behavioral sciences and education have been vigorous in producing ethical guidelines for research and monitoring adherence to them. Two kinds of standards are outlined here and discussed in Chapter 3.

The first set of standards, developed by the Federal Judicial Center, involves general appraisal of the ethical propriety of randomized tests. The Federal Judicial Center's threshold conditions for deciding whether an experiment ought to be done involve addressing the following questions:

- Is there need for improvement?
- Is the effectiveness of proposed improvements uncertain?
- Will a randomized experiment yield more defensible evidence than alternatives?
- Will the results be used?
- Will the rights of participants be protected?

Affirmative responses to each question invite consideration of a randomized test.

The second set of standards relevant to the behavioral and social science are those operationalized by institutional review boards (IRBs). In any institution receiving federal research funds, IRBs are responsible for reviewing the ethical propriety of research, including field experiments. The principal investigator for an experiment is responsible for presenting the field test's design to an IRB. This investigator also has the responsibility for capitalizing on the IRB's counsel and tailoring the experiment's design to meet good ethical standards.

In the Spouse Assault Replication Program, for example, discussions of each of the Federal Judicial Center's threshold questions in effect were undertaken at the federal level, notably by the National Institute of Justice and its advisers, and at the local level, for example, by the Milwaukee City Council and the police department. The principal investigator also had the duty of explaining the research to an independent IRB so as to develop a design that met local concerns about the ethical appropriateness of the experiment.

The Experiment's Design

The design of a controlled field experiment involves specifying the study population and units; sampling method and sample size; the interventions and methods for their observation; the method of random assignment and checks on its integrity; and response or outcome variables and their measurement, analysis, and reporting.

Target Population,
Statistical Power, and the Pipeline

For an experiment on police handling of domestic violence, one might specify the *target population* in any given site to be all cases involving males who cohabit with a female partner, married or not. This definition depends on several of the numerous *eligibility criteria* used to specify the target in the SARP.

Exclusions from the target population are as critical in social and educational field experiments as they are in medical clinical trials. For example, explicit exclusions in the SARP include brothers and sisters who are involved in a violent domestic dispute, fathers and sons, and so on. Attention focused on spouselike relationships. The rationale for choice of eligibility criteria and, in effect, the target population are discussed in Chapter 4.

The way that the target population is defined and the sample obtained, of course, determine the generalizability of the experiment's results. Usually, the object is to ensure that a generalizable conclusion is possible. For example, in the Atlanta SARP, the number of domestic violence cases was large. The principal investigator drew a random probability sample of cases in two police zones to generate cases for the experimental test. In Charlotte

(North Carolina), the case flow was lower and *all* eligible cases appearing during a 2-year period were used in the experiment.

In each case, the sampling method addressed cases normally handled by police, so generalization to such cases is legitimate. In each case, the sampling was bound by time. Generalizations to future conditions then are limited by obvious concerns, for example, that local social, economic, and cultural conditions may change.

The sample size usually is chosen so that one can be confident that important differences among regimens will be detected. The calculation of necessary sample size (i.e., statistical power analysis) depends on, among other things, the heterogeneity of responses and the size of effects produced by the treatments. These matters are discussed in Chapter 4.

Treatments

"Treatments" here refer to the programs or projects, program components, or program variations, the relative effectiveness of which is of primary interest. It is obvious that one ought to know what activities characterize the program, how they are supposed to work, and how one can verify that they occur.

In the SARP experiments, for example, the two interventions to which each case was randomly assigned were arrest and mediation. That an arrest occurred (or had not) when it was supposed to occur was determined by relying on police reports. Understanding what "arrest" means is not so easy if one recognizes that in some jurisdictions, the process may involve a few hours at the police station, whereas in other jurisdictions, it may involve more than a few hours in a very unpleasant holding tank.

Programs, of course, are not always delivered as they are supposed to be. Establishing that people who should have been arrested in the SARP actually were arrested was important. Consequently, the experiments involved careful attention to departures from the treatments assigned. Fertility control devices designed to reduce birth rate, for example, have not been delivered. Manpower training projects have not been put into place, in the sense that appropriate staff have not been hired. Drug regimens have been prescribed for tests, but individuals assigned to a drug do not always comply with the regimen.

More generally, one ought to know whether and how programs are implemented in an experiment. The interventions, including control conditions, need to be understood. Absent such understanding, a field experiment is useless at best. With such understanding, clear statements of what works, or what works better, are far more likely. The topic is discussed in different ways in Chapters 6, 7, and 8.

Random Assignment

Well-designed experiments involve matching or using related strategies to increase the power of the experiment; randomly assigning units of people (or institutions) to treatments to ensure statistical unbiasedness and a legitimate statement of one's confidence in results; and checking continuously on the integrity of random assignment procedures. These topics are not considered deeply in statistical texts on design of experiments. Nevertheless, each is difficult and important. They are discussed in Chapter 5.

For example, various options were open to police in early tests of ways to handle domestic violence (Sherman & Berk, 1985). Officers might flip a coin, for example, to determine which of the two regimens would be employed. The coin flip process was recognized as imperfect, as indeed it can be, in producing a random sequence and, moreover, it is easily subverted.

The option chosen in one site of the SARP experiments hinged on the time that the case was telephoned into the police department. The times were automatically registered by computer to the second (e.g., 10:37:03 p.m.). The determination made, roughly speaking, was to assign all cases with an even-numbered second to the arrest condition and all odd-numbered cases to the mediation regimen. In another site, the approach involved generation of a list of random assignments, having a competent statistician analyze the list for possible pseudo-randomness or special kinks, inserting each assignment into a sealed envelope numbered sequentially, and determining that each case in the sequence would be assigned in accord with the contents of the next sealed envelope.

Observation and Measurement

In the SARP experiments, at least two measures of recidivism, indexing the effect of police handling of domestic violence, were available. One measure relied on a victim's (or others') call to police after the initial encounter. Another approach employed interviewers to do surveys periodically after the initial incident to determine whether the female partner had been assaulted again.

Complicating matters is the need to understand the quality of measurements. Telephone calls to police are tape-recorded routinely in many police departments, for example, but women whose partners are arrested may become too frightened to call. Personal interviews with women who have been assaulted may avoid the problem of variations in women's willingness to call the police, especially if interviewers are well trained and persistent, as indeed they can be. Victims, however, disappear. They may stay with Mom for a while, find a new partner, or go to another city with or without their companions. Tracking victims and eliciting their cooperation is difficult and can lead to errors in measurement, just as police records might. In the absence of any good information about which approach works better, *both* methods were adopted in the SARP randomized field experiments. This can, and does, lead to some potential disagreements.

The measurement issues in evaluations of programs in criminal justice, manpower training, education, and other areas are complex. Practical aspects of the problems and solutions are given in Chapter 7.

Management and Operations

At least two features of the management structure of experiments are important in the execution of field tests. The first involves identifying and recruiting competent institutional partners. The SARP experiments, for example, involved joint efforts between the Milwaukee Police Department and the Crime Control Institute of Washington, D.C. The Omaha Police Department and the Behavioral Research Institute at the University of Colorado made a similar contract.

A second feature of structure that is important in medium- and larger-scale efforts involves advisory groups. The purposes of advisory committees in any such effort vary. One may choose a committee whose members help to ensure that the experiment is run well locally, or to resolve technical issues, or to address naive as well as informed attempts to attack the experiment.

Analysis

The analysis of data generated from an experiment depends critically on the experiment's design. The perspective emphasized here is, "Analyze them as you randomize them." That is, the analysis is such that all individuals (or entities) assigned randomly to a regimen are handled as a group regardless of whether some individuals actually received the prescribed services. Failing to adhere to this rule, for example, by analyzing data on the basis of regimen actually received versus regimen actually assigned, subverts the usefulness of the experiment.

The analysis also must recognize that there are departures from design. Consequently, simple analysis plans usually have to be augmented. Just as designs must be tailored to suit the setting, analyses have to be fitted to the data at hand. Chapter 9 covers a variety of classes of analysis that seem sensible.

Reporting

Reporting well on an experiment is not easy. The standards for good reporting are discussed in Chapter 10. Its topical coverage includes the audiences for reports and how reporting method depends on them, the contents of interim and final reports, and the issuance of public use data sets that are generated by the experiment, handling matters related to individual privacy, and conflict of interest.

2

Experiments in
the Context of Evaluation

*You remember what Quetelet wrote ". . . put down what you expect
from such and such legislation, after . . . see where it has given what
you expected. But you change your laws and your administration of
them so fast, and without an inquiry after results past or present, that it
is all . . . see-saw, doctrinaire, a shuttlecock between two battledores.*

—Florence Nightingale, Letter to Sir Francis Galton (1891)

This chapter puts field experiments into the broad context of evaluation
policy. The events that lead up to such controlled tests are reviewed first.
The section that follows summarizes basic questions that are addressed
in contemporary evaluation policy and describes how each question
bears on the use of randomized tests. The last section describes briefly
how various government agencies and private foundations in the United
States have employed controlled experiments.

A COMMON SCENARIO

The able civil servant, scholar, or public representative recognizes that
it is difficult to translate a potentially good idea into law or regulation. They
know also that the law, when enacted, generates activity that may or may
not accord with its aims. Apart from this, the creation of a law and activity
that may ensue carries rewards for the proponents. A new publicly supported program that appears to address a serious problem will be viewed
positively by the public as "doing something," as "taking action," and as
"making decisions." Regardless of whether the initiative produces any
durable and positive effect, the acclamation is important.

This sequence of events often is followed by thoughtful questions about
the actual effects of the activity. Critics, sponsors of the innovation, or

19

disinterested observers ask, Did the projects work to reduce the problem? How well did they work? and What evidence can be produced? Evidence bearing on these questions has been useful for legislative or administrative decisions about whether to change (U.S. General Accounting Office [U.S. GAO], 1988a, 1988b). Consider two illustrations of the process. The Centers for Disease Control (CDC) was responsible, beginning in 1988, for allocating more than $200 million each year to AIDS-prevention projects, including school-based and media-based public education campaigns (Turner, Miller, & Moses, 1989). Most of these efforts were designed initially as demonstration projects to assist individuals who were thought to be at risk of AIDS. For example, a school district or a community-based organization might propose an idea for an AIDS-prevention project to the CDC. The proposals were screened, and those deemed most worthy of support were funded under the assumptions that projects could be implemented and would reduce individuals' exposure to AIDS.

Any serious requirement by the CDC to evaluate the programs, in the sense of documenting activities attentively or estimating their relative effects, was absent during the 1980s. The National Academy of Sciences Committee on AIDS Research urged the CDC to get beyond the products usually generated in such demonstration projects, to document the activities of the projects, and to estimate the effects of a few projects using controlled field tests (Turner et al., 1989; Coyle et al., 1991). The CDC undertook evaluative work, including controlled field experiments, partly in response to this counsel.

Consider next the evaluation of manpower training programs in the United States during the early 1980s. The Youth Employment Development Program Act (YEDPA) led to more than 300 projects designed to alleviate the problems of unemployed young men and women, school dropouts, and young people who were, and continue to be, at economic risk. Less than a dozen projects produced defensible evidence of whether their efforts actually reduced unemployment or increased wage rates (Betsey, Hollister, & Papagiordiou, 1985). Independent reviews of these projects' evaluations resulted in a shift in the policies of sponsoring organizations (Stromsdorfer & Farkas, 1980; Cottingham, 1991). For example, more resources for designing better evaluations, including controlled field experiments to estimate project effects, were developed by the U.S. Department of Labor and the Rockefeller Foundation. Examples of the experiments are given elsewhere in this text.

FUNDAMENTAL QUESTIONS THAT UNDERLIE
EVALUATION POLICY AND PRACTICE

The federal government spends roughly $200 million each year on evaluating domestic programs that are supported by a $400 billion annual investment (U.S. GAO, 1987). The actual expenditure is probably greater, in that much of what is designated as applied research in health services, education, and so forth is, in fact, evaluative in function. Similarly, evaluations are supported at times at the state and local level and by some private foundations; this is independent of the federal investment.

Evaluation activity in the United States is complex. At the federal level alone, it involves more than 200 distinctive evaluation units in 30 major government agencies. The bureaucratic support for the enterprise varies considerably from the cases in which the word "evaluation" is invoked honorifically, and without substance, to those in which there is conscientious professional investment in evaluation design, execution, analysis, and reporting. Much of the actual work may be contracted to research firms and universities, with contracts issued by the U.S. Departments of Education, Health and Human Services, Agriculture, and others. The work also may be done within an agency, as in the case of the U.S. General Accounting Office.

Evaluation is a small industry but a sturdy one. It is characterized by high-quality professional journals, such as *Evaluation Review, New Directions for Program Evaluation, Evaluation and Program Planning*, and *Educational Evaluation and Policy Analysis*; by the production of reports by government evaluation agencies and foundations; and by active professional organizations, such as the American Evaluation Association. These journals, reports, and association activities supplement reports on surveys and field studies covered by the journals of the older academic disciplines, notably the American Economic Association, American Public Health Association, American Sociological Association, American Psychological Association, American Educational Research Association, and American Society for Criminology, among others.

The field is characterized by textbooks that often recognize the technical, managerial, political, and other problems that the competent evaluator may encounter. Such texts include Campbell and Stanley's (1966) now classic volume, Riecken and colleagues (1974), Cook and Campbell (1979), and Rossi and Freeman (1989). Others are identified elsewhere in this monograph.

The lexicon in the evaluation arena is elaborate partly because evaluative activities are diverse and cut across disciplines that each have a specialized vernacular. There are neologisms, as in other disciplines, that are at times vague but useful. Phrases such as "meta-analysis," "summative and formative evaluation," and "illuminative" evaluation are, at worst, confusing. At best, they focus efforts and serve as convenient labels for an assemblage of good ideas, processes, and issues.

The Questions

Despite this complexity of the evaluation enterprise in the United States, the questions that form the core of evaluation policy can be put simply:

- What is the severity, scope, and nature of the problem? How do we know?
- What programs, projects, and/or practices are being implemented to reduce the problem? How do we know?
- What are the effects? For whom? How do we know?
- What programs work better? How do we know?
- What are the relative costs and benefits of alternatives? How do we know?

The question "How do we know?" implies the need for high-quality evidence in each instance. Implicit in each question is another: "Who poses the question?"

What Is the Severity, Scope, and Nature of the Problem? How Do We Know?

Examples of high-quality work to address the question are not difficult to find. Claims that the homeless in Chicago, for example, numbered more than 25,000 were not uncommon until Rossi, Wright, Fisher, and Willis (1987) undertook sample surveys to produce a scientifically credible estimate closer to 2,500. Similarly, journalistic reports and advocacy groups maintained, for a time, that the U.S. "underclass" included more than 8 million individuals. Efforts by the Urban Institute, relying on defensible U.S. Census data and thoughtful definition of the characteristics of the underclass, put the number in the range of 0.5 million to 2.5 million (Ricketts & Sawhill, 1988). At times, the number of individuals who are eligible to participate in a government-funded assistance program is unknown. For example, until the U.S. Department of Agriculture's Food and

Nutrition Service sponsored independent well-designed surveys, the department, the U.S. Congress, and the public had no substantial understanding of how many women and infants could benefit from the program for Women, Infants, and Children (Wargo, 1989).

In such cases, well-designed probability samples, rather than convenience samples, were essential to meet ingenuous claims about the national severity of a problem. They have been instrumental in better allocation of resources to those with identifiable needs.

Single-time surveys or new record systems such as those just described have produced results that have been useful in policy formulation. In the long run, a coherent system of surveys for producing policy-related data over time is a natural option. At the U.S. Department of Education, for example, considerable responsibility for evaluation lies with the Planning and Evaluation Service (PES) of the Office of the Assistant Secretary for Policy and Planning. This office depends on data collected by statistical agencies, such as the National Center for Education Statistics (NCES), and on contracts for special data collection efforts.

The NCES's Schools and Staffing Survey, for example, is used by PES and other evaluation groups to analyze teacher supply and demand, critical shortages and turnover in specific disciplines and regions, local practices in control of turnover and shortages, and characteristics of teachers such as qualifications. Household surveys also have been conducted by NCES to illuminate issues in preschool education, family support for and involvement in education, and other topics. A regular Fast Response Survey System, based heavily on telephone surveys, has been used to obtain data quickly to produce information on new and fast-developing topics such as business-school partnerships. The National Assessment of Educational Progress is conducted to understand students' educational achievements and what the achievement levels imply about the educational needs of youth.

Surveys of these kinds illuminate phenomena thought to be important in policy. Further, they often serve as the antecedent to evaluations that are designed to address questions *other* than severity of a problem. In particular, surveys arguably are a prerequisite to any effort to estimate the effects of programs that purport to remedy a problem.

In the foundation arena, for example, the Rockefeller Foundation's field experiments on the Minority Female Single Parent Program were designed to estimate the program's effects on employment and earnings for women with very low education levels and income. Data were obtained prior to and during the experiments to ensure that the proper target population was indeed addressed by the program (programs often miss their targets), to gauge the scope and severity of the women's problems, and to understand the contexts in which the programs operated (Burghardt & Gordon, 1990). These data also allowed comparison of those served in the experiments with the national low-income population.

Similarly, Schuerman et al. (1994) designed both qualitative and quantitative methods to study the effects of Illinois family preservation programs. In particular, they used frequent unstructured interviews to learn how staff and management viewed the new program, its goals and operations, and how decisions were made. This was done in the context of a randomized field test in which eligible families were randomly assigned to the family preservation program versus conventional services to produce statistical estimates of the new program's effects.

What Projects or Programs Are Being Implemented? How Do We Know?

Once said, it is obvious that no policy, program, or project is ever delivered as planned. There are large, sometimes formidable, variations in individuals' capacity, willingness, and understanding of how to implement a regimen. There are remarkable variations over time in any given project in level and character of implementation.

Examples of failure to implement school programs that were heartily supported by influential principals, parents, and teachers are not hard to locate. For Ralph Tyler (1991), a statesman in this area, they include progressive education of the 1930s, activity schools of the 1940s, and open classrooms of the 1960s.

Education is not the only enterprise in which program form, at times, is accompanied by no serious function. With some exceptions, the early couneling and testing programs for those at risk of AIDS in the United States were documented badly. During the late 1980s, it was not clear who delivered services to whom, when, and how. Virtually nothing was known of quality control (Coyle et al., 1991).

Asking questions about the implementation of a project, policy, or program is fundamental to evaluation policy. Efforts to address the questions include demonstration projects that focus on learning how projects are put into the field. The best of such efforts have produced good evidence on:

- *how* to specify goals and actualize plans,
- *whether* and how a plan is implemented (e.g., whether pregnancy prevention services for adolescents can be delivered well), and

- the flow of clients through the system (e.g., a *pipeline study* on how individuals become involved in a program, the various services they receive, dropouts, and so forth).

Goals of social ameliorative programs are often framed plainly but ambiguously in law. In Illinois, for example, the Family Preservation Act states that the act's objective is to prevent the placement of at-risk children in substitute care (e.g., into foster care), in order to preserve the integrity of the family. The ambiguity lies partly in determining what "at-risk" means, what the standards for prevention should be, and what service mix would best meet the objectives. For example, Littell, Schuerman, and Rzepnicki's (1991) evaluative studies focused on how these goals were translated by the executives and line staff who were responsible for implementing a new prevention program and by contracted service providers. The translation often was made in ways that did not always accord with law. The target identified in law (i.e., children at risk of placement) had been broadened to include children who were arguably not at risk of placement but whose needs included the types of services that were being offered under the new program. That is, the goal had become handling children at risk not of placement, necessarily, but of abuse or neglect that was sufficient for a social worker to justify intensive services.

At the core of most implementation studies is serious attention to the nature of the target group and the services its members receive. Intensive monitoring of program implementation was supported by the Rockefeller Foundation, for example, in controlled experiments on special training and support programs for female single parents. Hershey's (1988) report, for example, covers each site's program model, the delivery system, the program structure and operations, differences and similarities among sites, recruitment and retention practices, types of remedial education provided by each site and levels of students' participation in the education, duration and level of training, level and type of child care including financial subsidy, day care utilization, job development, and placement of people in jobs. The data helped to inform judgments about the program's implementation and to illuminate the result of subsequent impact evaluation. In particular, one local program achieved remarkable effects relative to services ordinarily available in the community. The implementation data make it possible to try to duplicate the program in other locations (Cottingham, 1991).

Pipeline studies of client flow are not common in studies of program implementation. They are nevertheless important insofar as they describe how children or families are involved and not involved in particular programs, the various routes they may take through the system, dropouts and persistence, exits from and returns to the system, and how decisions are made at each point. Partial examples of pipeline studies are not difficult to find. It makes sense to build on these to uncover actual and potential decision points in the system and the import of the points in adjusting the flow. Studies of decision making in statewide systems for the care of abused and neglected children represent one approach. Schuerman et al. (1994), for example, employed administrative records, interviews, and case analysis to produce a detailed description of what decisions made, when, and by whom led to what services. Proposals for data systems that integrate information from different sources, such as child welfare agencies, juvenile justice and mental health service providers, and others, have been made by Goerge (1991) and Goerge, Osuch, and Costello (1991), among others, to ensure that children at risk of abuse and neglect can be tracked properly and to evaluate components of the systems. Partial pipeline studies are a basic feature of many formal controlled tests of new programs, tests of the kind described in the next section of this chapter. Illustrations include Schuerman et al.'s (1994) efforts to learn why teenage parents who were invited to participate in new service programs often fail to do so (the takeup rate was 25% in one such test).

The major benefits of the well-done implementation study, to judge from McLaughlin's (1987) review and the examples cited here, are substantial. They include sophisticated understanding of variability in project imple- mentation, the tension between micro- and macrolevel implementation issues, the contextual influences on implementation, and the critical need for local negotiation in implementing a project. Evidence about program implementation commonly is in demand and used in policy forums (see Ginsburg, McLaughlin, Pliska, & Takai, 1992, and references therein) regardless of whether the program has a detectable effect on its target individuals.

Implementation studies alone do not answer the question, "Does it work?" because they commonly include no provision for understanding how individuals would have fared without the program. That is, they often include no credible comparison group. One could not then determine whether the activity had an effect regardless of its ostensible worth. The thoughtful public servant, practitioner, or scholar need not be content with demonstration projects that involve no systematic attempt to estimate effects. This leads naturally to controlled randomized field tests.

Does It Work? How Do We Know?

The question "Does the project, program, or practice work?" often is framed in other ways, such as "Does the innovation or intervention have an effect?," "What difference did the investment make?" and "For whom does the service work best?"

Regardless of how the question is framed, the answer depends on what would have happened to the program's target individuals if the program had not been implemented or if the services had not been provided. For example, determining whether an activity that is designed to prevent students from dropping out of high school does indeed reduce the dropout rate requires understanding how the adolescents would have behaved in the absence of the activity. This understanding comes about by either predicting students' behavior in the absence of the program or representing how students would behave in the absence of the program by using a control group. Some of the choices that are engendered by the question are considered next.

New Versus Existing Programs

The feasibility of producing good evidence based on a randomized field study depends heavily on whether the treatment for which the effect is of interest is new or already in place in most settings. For new programs, projects, and practices whose effects are uncertain, formal randomized tests usually are recommended (Coyle et al., 1991). The test of the new program against a control group to which the new services are not provided is more easily justified, for example, when resources for the new program are scarce and cannot be provided to everyone, and the results will be used to enlarge the new services if, indeed, the services are shown to be effective. Consider three examples.

In testing new variations on Head Start at seven sites, researchers initiated efforts to learn whether new programs based on the home environment could engage economically disadvantaged parents and lead to better achievement for their children (Gottfried, 1984). It was important to produce high-quality evidence on effectiveness of the new programs in view of the debatable quality of evidence on effectiveness of earlier related Head Start projects. At one site, the project was evaluated using a longitudinal experimental design in which half of each of six cohorts was randomly assigned to the new program versus a control group whose members availed themselves of conventional services.

Randomly assigning families to alternative regimens ensured that there were no systematic differences between the families who received special services and those receiving conventional ones, apart from the effect that special services may have. The procedure also generated a legitimate statistical statement of confidence in the results, the statistical characterization being important in science and policy debates about home-oriented programs.

Hawkins, Catalano, Jones, and Fine (1987), for example, tested new school-based parent training to understand whether such an approach could, when applied in first and second grades, reduce children's subsequent aggressiveness and increase parents' skills. The available evidence suggests that it can. Hawkins, Jenson, Catalano, and Wells (1991) similarly have tested skills training for high-risk adolescents to learn whether such training would reduce the likelihood of delinquent behavior, again using randomized experiments. The evidence suggests that, relative to control group members who were not provided the new service, program participants are more likely to avoid drugs and alcohol and to have a larger behavioral repertoire in dealing with problematic situations. See Tremblay et al. (1991) for related work.

It is not common for state agencies to formally test innovation in the child abuse and neglect arena. Nevertheless, some agencies have had the forbearance and the resources to do so. The Illinois Department of Children and Family Services, for example, sponsored tests of innovative approaches to providing service and stipends to families with children whose level of mental illness and developmental disability put the children at risk (Goerge et al., 1991). The field tests were undertaken with the Chapin Hall Center for Children at the University of Chicago (Schuerman et al., 1994). Similarly, conscientious tests have been undertaken to estimate the effects of Illinois' Young Parent Program. The program's targets, teenage parents, were randomly assigned to new special services in the interest of producing reliable estimates of the effect of services on the teenagers' dependence on public assistance, on their family planning, and on other outcomes (Schuerman et al., 1994).

Existing Programs

Determining the effect of an existing program generally is a more difficult problem. Random allocation of individuals to a group whose members do not receive the program services may be illegal or regarded as unethical. This is despite the fact that the program's effects are uncertain. The National Academy of Sciences Panel on Evaluation of AIDS Interventions, for example, recommended against using randomized field tests to evaluate counseling because it was ordinarily provided in centers that provide blood tests for HIV exposure. Counseling was and is an integral part of HIV testing, is thought to be valuable, and is required by law. Randomly depriving individuals of counseling was deemed unethical (Coyle et al., 1991). For similar reasons, the federal government has abstained from estimating the effects of certain Head Start programs and other ameliorative programs using studies that include a randomized, "no program" control group.

Evaluation designs other than randomized tests can, at times, yield credible estimates of the effects of ongoing programs. They require strong theory or important assumptions, notably about how people behave in the absence of the service. The assumptions are, at times, untenable and untestable (Campbell & Stanley, 1966; Meier, 1972). More important, perhaps, these assumptions can lead to evaluations that have invidious statistical biases (Campbell & Boruch, 1976). Nonrandomized approaches nevertheless are critical to advancing understanding as to the conditions under which they might be employed, and they are considered next.

*Criteria for Choosing
a Nonrandomized Approach*

General conditions for seriously considering approaches to estimating treatment effects *other* than randomized tests apply mainly to the new program setting. Coyle et al. (1991) set out five conditions in query form for evaluation in health. They are pertinent to decisions about evaluation of other program areas.

The first is whether the decision maker can tolerate serious ambiguity in estimating the effect of the new program or project (Coyle et al., 1991, p. 183). The tolerability may be a function of the perceived importance and cost of the program itself: Producing a high-cost estimate of the effect of a low-cost or low-importance treatment is unwarranted. The tolerance for ambiguity may stem from the fact that the evidence need not be defensible in public forums; rather, the decision is a private one. The ambiguity may be tolerable and often must be in public policy research because the randomized test is not feasible for one reason or another. Finally and perhaps most important, the ambiguity level may be low and tolerable, despite the absence of random assignment, because alternative methods, whose underlying assumptions are accessible, yield good estimates. This condition leads naturally into the next. For discussions and empirical research on whether theory and data suffice, see Fraker and Maynard

(1987), Heckman and Hotz (1989), Holland and Rubin (1988), LaLonde (1986), and Moses (1995).

Coyle et al.'s (1991, p. 184) second question is whether competing explanations for the project's effect reasonably can be assumed to be negligible. The distinctive contribution of Campbell and Stanley's (1966) work on quasi-experiments to understanding whether a program works, for example, is their focus on identifying factors other than the program that might produce the effects that are observed. The randomized experiment equates these factors across groups and presumes that researchers are ignorant of their magnitude. The quasi-experiment's designer seeks to identify settings in which the magnitude of such factors' effects can be assumed to be negligible or ruled out through thoughtful design of the evaluation. For example, a simple before-after approach to estimating the effect of a highly visible police program for ticketing speeders might safely assume that the rate at which drivers speed prior to the program would persist in the absence of the program; the defensibility of the analysis would be enhanced using time-series data to take seasonal variation into account.

A third question suggested by Coyle et al. (1991) is whether the program must be deployed to all relevant individuals or institutions that are eligible. Bangser (1985), among others, reiterates the point that, as a matter of evaluation policy, it is inappropriate to employ a randomized experiment at a site where all eligible recipients of a service are engaged in the service. Rather, alternative methods must be used to estimate service effects even where these programs are new. State statutes that require all schools to produce school report cards, for example, generally are enacted to improve school performance. Whether the performance actually improves as a consequence of a school report card program and by how much may be discoverable, but usually not through randomized tests. Similarly, entitlement programs at the federal or state level—in education or social services, criminal or civil justice, and so forth—cover all eligible individuals. The construction of a randomized "no program" comparison condition is then likely to be ethically unacceptable.

A fourth question concerns whether a nonrandomized experiment will meet standards of ethical propriety in cases in which a randomized experiment will not (Coyle et al., 1991, p. 185). Standards of propriety are discussed in Chapter 4 of this book. Suffice it to say here that when the treatment already is known to be beneficial or when methods other than randomized tests yield arguably unbiased estimates of treatment effect, then field studies that involve randomized control groups are not justified.

Finally, Coyle et al. (1991, p. 185) suggest asking whether theory-based or data-based predictions of effectiveness are so strong that nonrandomized studies will suffice. Available evidence, for example, suggests that work-related behavior of young women who receive Aid to Families With Dependent Children is more predictable than related behavior of young unemployed males. One implication is that evaluation of programs directed toward employment of the latter cannot rely on evaluation designs that rely heavily on prediction; rather, they must depend on randomized tests. More generally, this criterion depends on empirical research to learn about when estimates of program effect based on nonrandomized studies can approximate those of a randomized experiment. It is not difficult to find examples of efforts to make this kind of comparison. Indeed, such efforts are part of the history of statistics and of science in medicine, nutrition, and agriculture. A tidy and informative summary of related work in evaluating training programs is given in Bell, Orr, Blomquist, and Cain (1995).

What Works Better? How Do We Know?

The first question implies that two or more different approaches might be employed to resolve the same problem but that their relative effectiveness is unknown. The answer to the question depends on how individuals would have fared had they not received the particular regimen that they did, in fact, receive. The evaluator might then assume or try to forecast how individuals who received service A would have fared had they received service B. The evaluator also would have to forecast how those who turned out to receive service B would have fared had they received service A.

If those who receive services A and B are equivalent, as in a randomized study, then the matter is simple: Formal and statistically valid comparisons can be made. Consider, for example, high-quality work on a currently important topic: tutoring children in high-risk environments. Few hard data are available to begin with. Further, there usually is little structure to the tutoring enterprise as employed in the field. Recognizing the potential weaknesses of unstructured tutoring, Fantuzzo and his colleagues (1988) devised reciprocal peer tutoring interventions in which students alternate between student and teacher roles (i.e., they are trained in each), follow a structured format to facilitate academic progress, and are rewarded based on the pairs' attainment levels.

The evaluators undertook controlled field tests of structured tutoring in high-risk areas of Philadelphia, conventional tutoring programs being used as the basis for comparison. Fourth and fifth graders were randomly assigned to the structured and unstructured tutoring. Results based on these randomized field tests suggest that reward was remarkably effective in improving math performance and that this effect was enhanced remarkably when the tutoring enterprise was structured.

More generally, the B regimen may be an augmented version of a new A regimen. For example, more intensive parole supervision might be compared to conventional, less intensive supervision. There also may be several levels of B, as in comparisons among an array of taxation plans in the negative income tax experiments. B also might entail a version of A that involves a different or smaller service package, as in comparison of alternative service strategies for assisting dislocated workers. Regardless of particulars, the comparison is made in the interest of discerning differences among two or more distinct regimens.

In fact, B also may be a control condition. The question "Does it (A) work, relative to a control?" then is equivalent to the question "Does A work better than B?" The distinction between the two questions is drawn here to highlight the more general case of competing treatments in contrast to testing a new regimen against often ill-defined conditions and the different implications of each question. Generally, it is more feasible to mount randomized tests that address a question about competing treatments than to mount tests that ask politically more threatening questions such as "Does it work?" relative to a no-treatment control condition. Comparing two or more distinct programs engenders other difficulties, including ensuring that resources are available for implementing and monitoring each program and that the flow of individuals into each is large enough to sustain high statistical power. These and related issues are discussed later in this book.

What Are the Relative Costs
and Effectiveness of Alternatives?
How Do We Know?

Developing a defensible cost-effectiveness analysis is difficult partly because such analyses depend heavily on one's ability to address the four questions just examined. A cost-effectiveness analysis of arrest versus conventional police handling of misdemeanor violence cases requires data on the problem, the relative effectiveness of the programs established (perhaps through an experiment), and reliable estimates of various kinds of costs.

This is not to say that questions about cost-effectiveness analysis are absent from the evaluation portfolio. Virtually all contemporary field experiments in employment and training, for example, include cost-effectiveness analyses. This is partly because economists have a substantial role in such experiments and their expertise in doing such analyses is substantial. Specific examples of such analyses are given later. For competent handling of the topic of cost-effectiveness in areas apart from training and employment, see Levin (1991), Gramlich (1990), Yates (1996), and Rossi and Freeman (1989).

CONTEMPORARY INTEREST IN RANDOMIZED FIELD EXPERIMENTS

Interest in using controlled experiments to plan and evaluate government-supported domestic programs emerged strongly during the late 1960s. The reasons for this attention include massive federal investments in antipoverty programs, the political debates that the investments engendered, and the need for better evidence on the programs' performance. The period also was marked by remarkable efforts among social scientists to bring good research methods to bear on understanding social problems.

Indicators of Interest

The Social Science Research Council, for example, was asked by the National Science Foundation to take stock of the evaluations of programs that were purported to ameliorate problems and to develop a state-of-the-art monograph on randomized experiments and high-quality quasi-experiments that would assist in generating better evidence. This effort was in turn based on the work of the President's Science Advisory Committee and the Brookings Institution, among others. See Riecken et al. (1974) and the references therein.

This interest built on a substantial statistical technology that had been developed earlier. The mathematical statistics that underpin randomized experiments had been articulated by Sir Ronald Fisher (1935), Oscar Kempthorne (1952), and William Cochran and Gertrude Cox (1950), among others. It also was based on methodological advances in designing field studies so as to reduce ambiguity in the interpretation of their results, notably Campbell and Stanley's (1966) work on quasi-experiments.

More recent interest in using experiments to plan or evaluate can be marked by a variety of indicators. They include textbooks on the method and monographs and journal articles that report the results of field tests. For community-based mental health, Fairweather and Tornatsky (1977) produced a textbook on how, when, and why randomized tests of rehabilitative programs could be run. In the economic arena, Ferber and Hirsch (1982) produced a monograph on the conduct of experiments in the welfare arena; the work was extended by Hausman and Wise (1985). The Federal Judicial Center's (1981) effort directed attention to the ethical propriety of experiments in the courts, building on earlier work by Bermant, Kelman, and Warwick (1978), among others. The Federal Judicial Center work is generalizable to other settings and is exploited later in this book.

Friedman, Furberg, and DeMets (1985), and Meinert (1986) served the medical research community by generating monographs on how clinical trials could be employed to understand the relative effectiveness of different approaches to surgery, therapy, and drug treatment. Textbooks, such as Wegman and DePriest's (1980), have been written to explain the design of randomized tests in cloud-seeding and other weather-control environments. These have been based partly on analyses by Neyman (1977), among others, to understand whether weather can indeed be influenced so as to enhance crop production or decrease crop damage.

The thoughtful reader will doubtless recognize that the production of textbooks about randomized field experiments does not necessarily mean that institutions will take seriously the idea of fair tests of programs or projects. The consideration of the idea, one may argue further, might well be rejected often by governments or agencies. In fact, there have been major changes in the way government agencies and others view randomized experiments.

Federal Government Agencies: United States

To judge from reports issued by the U.S. General Accounting Office prior to 1976, few if any members of the GAO staff relied much on evidence generated in controlled experiments. Afterward, to judge by reports of the GAO's Human Resources Division and the GAO's Training Institute, this investigative agency has relied heavily, where it could, on the less equivocal data generated by such tests. See, for example, the U.S. GAO (1986) report on federally supported programs for preventing teenage pregnancies and U.S. GAO (1992) and Droitcour, Silberman, and Chelimsky (1993) on cross-design synthesis.

The U.S. Department of Agriculture's Food and Nutrition Service has dedicated resources to randomized tests when that has been feasible and desirable. For example, field experiments reported by St. Pierre, Cook, and Straw (1981) contributed to the agency's understanding of the effectiveness of education and training in nutrition. The department also has undertaken evaluations of various approaches to decreasing nutritional and health risks of women and their children under the Women and Infant Care program, decreasing the costs and increasing effectiveness of food stamp programs, and meeting other goals (e.g., Puma et al., 1989; U.S. Department of Agriculture, 1992).

As mentioned earlier, the U.S. Internal Revenue Service (IRS) periodically has mounted controlled tests of ways to reduce costs, identify tax delinquents, and improve the agency's performance. Roth et al. (1989) reviewed the IRS efforts and developed a research agenda in a National Academy of Sciences Committee dedicated to tax administration and other topics.

Over the last decade, randomized field tests have become part of the research armamentarium of the U.S. Department of Justice. One research arm of the department, the National Institute of Justice, has supported controlled tests of intensive supervision for parolees; electronic monitoring of offenders who are assigned to arrest in their home, school, or work environments rather than to prison; alternative methods for police to handle domestic violence; and drug testing of arrestees. The Spouse Assault Replication Program, among other experiments cited in this text, was sponsored by the institute.

As part of a larger agenda for reinvigorating the quality of evidence in education-related evaluations, the U.S. Department of Education (USDE) has undertaken controlled randomized tests (Ginsburg, 1992). These include evaluations of Even Start programs for poor families and their children, Upward Bound projects for at-risk youth (USDE, 1991a), and dropout prevention programs in schools (Maynard, 1991). Encouragement to undertake well-controlled tests has been provided at times in reports to the department and to Congress by committees of the National Academy of Sciences (e.g., Meyer & Fienberg, 1992) and independent research groups (Boruch & Cordray, 1980).

It is not easy to establish the benefits of employment and training programs. The U.S. Department of Labor sponsored controlled experiments to generate fair comparisons and good evidence. Rossi, Berk, and Lenihan (1980), for example, set a precedent for evaluating the effects of income supports for released offenders. The more recent work by Bloom (1990), involving tests of employment programs for displaced workers, is part of the product and is exploited in this volume.

State and Local Agencies

State, county, and local government agencies collaborate, at times, in controlled tests of initiatives. Their investment of resources has been notable, to judge from the commitment of eight state governments to collaborative randomized tests of work/welfare plans (Gueron, 1985). The investment is apparent in Tennessee's undertaking of remarkable experiments on the relative effects of classroom size on student achievement (Finn & Achilles, 1990). It is evident in the contribution of police departments in Charlotte, Atlanta, Metro-Dade County, Colorado Springs, Milwaukee, and Omaha to experiments on police handling of domestic violence (Garner et al., 1995).

Multiagency coordination often is essential. Texas's Department of Community Affairs developed and provided partial support for randomized tests of programs for assisting dislocated workers, all in concert with the Texas Employment Commission (Bloom, 1990). California's tests of welfare to work programs engaged six county departments of social services in cooperation with the State Department of Social Services (Ricchio & Friedlander, 1992). California's randomized field tests on the effectiveness of intensive supervision of probationers involved three county probation departments (Petersilia & Turner, 1990).

Community-Based Organizations

Community-based organizations have contributed remarkably to randomized tests. The Rockefeller Foundation's Minority Female Single Parent Program, for example, engaged the Center for Employment in San Jose, the Atlanta Urban League, and Washington, D.C.'s Wider Opportunities for Women, among others. Randomized field tests undertaken by Fantuzzo and Stevenson (1993) to understand how to enhance the well-being of families and children participating in Head Start, studies of new work and welfare programs (Gueron & Pauly, 1991), and research on delinquency prevention efforts (Hawkins et al., 1991) have each depended heavily on community groups for their execution.

Legislatures

Legislatures often are not regarded by the public or the press as a vehicle for generating high-quality evidence about the effectiveness of innovative educational programs designed to ameliorate special problems. Nevertheless, lawmakers do, at times, provide the opportunity to develop better evidence. At the state level, for example, California's GAIN legislation was explicit in authorizing controlled tests of training and employment programs for poorly educated and unemployed citizens (Ricchio & Friedlander, 1992). The Tennessee legislature, for a variety of reasons, committed more than $3 million to the controlled experiments on class size reported by Finn and Achilles (1990). Such activity often is accompanied by debate and controversy; nevertheless, it signals a distinct interest in a reliable scientific basis for decisions.

Private Foundations

The Russell Sage Foundation appears to have been among the first to support randomized controlled tests of ameliorative programs. Meyer and Borgotta's (1959) experiment on work-related rehabilitation of the mentally ill, for example, was supported by the foundation and appears to have set a precedent. During the 1980s, the Rockefeller Foundation underwrote, among other evaluations, the development and tests of programs for minority female single parents (Cottingham, 1991) described earlier elsewhere in this text. Over a 20-year period, the Ford Foundation supported large-scale multisite randomized experiments in the welfare reform arena. These tests, involving more than 65,000 service recipients in 20 states, were designed to discover what approaches work best to enhance skills and wage rates of individuals, the stability of families, and the well-being of children (Gueron & Pauly, 1991). In health services, the Robert Wood Johnson Foundation has at times sponsored controlled randomized field studies (Robert Wood Johnson Foundation, 1992). These evaluations have been designed to learn about improving hospice care, dental services, and health education, among other services (Aiken & Kehrer, 1985). The William T. Grant Foundation has supported innovative augmentations of large experiments and small-scale field tests driven by theory. The New Chance experiments, for example, were designed originally to understand how to enhance the self-sufficiency of teenage mothers. The foundation augmented the experiments by investing resources in understanding the impact of the self-sufficiency efforts on the young mothers' children (Zaslow, 1995). Such examples suggest that private foundations take seriously the task of evaluating their efforts, as do some public agencies, and they are likely to continue to do so.

3

Ethics, Law, and
Randomized Experiments

Advances in the exact sciences and the achievements in invention . . .
in large measure . . . have been due to experimentation. . . . It is one of
the happy incidents of the federal system that a single courageous State
may, if its citizens choose, serve as a laboratory; and try novel social
and economic experiments without risk to the rest of the country. This
Court has the power to prevent an experiment. . . . But in the exercise of
this high power, we must be ever on our guard, lest we erect our
prejudices into legal principles. If we would guide by the light
of reason, we must let our minds be bold.

—Justice Brandeis, *New State Ice Co. v. Liebmann*

The contention that a randomized field test of alternative treatments is unethical, illegal, or immoral is not an uncommon one in volatile settings. Regardless of volatility, it behooves the experiment's designer to ensure that certain proprieties are met, for if they are not, the test may, indeed, abridge ethical or other standards.

As a practical matter, experiments must be vetted to ensure that they meet ethical standards by a legally mandated institutional review board (IRB). The procedures, conditions, and use of IRBs are discussed in this chapter. A broader framework for making decisions about the social ethics of randomized tests has been developed by the Federal Judicial Center. The framework is also described, using an example from the training and education arena.

In most social research, including experiments, prospective participants are assured that the information they provide about themselves will, as a matter of good ethics, remain confidential. At times, the assurance has some legal standing. Testimonial privilege statutes, for example, have been created to ensure that records on identifiable research participants cannot be used for nonresearch purposes. These and other relevant laws are important in meeting ethical standards and therefore are described here.

The chapter concludes with brief consideration of related topics. They concern the idea that a lottery is a fair basis for allocating scarce resources, how the courts have viewed randomized experiments, and an empirical basis for justifying the fairness of such tests.

ETHICS AND FEDERAL LAW

Federal law requires that one attend to good ethical standards in biomedical and behavioral research involving human subjects. In particular, the Health Research Extension Act of 1985 (Public Law 99-158) obligates the Secretary of the U.S. Department of Health and Human Services (DHHS) to require all research organizations receiving federal funds to create an institutional review board to assess the ethical character of the research that is done under the organization's auspices. The Secretary is further enjoined to develop procedures for responding to alleged violations of ethical standards and for providing guidance on ethical issues. In meeting these obligations, DHHS developed regulations that summarize how ethical matters must be handled (*Federal Register*, *58*(117), June 18, 1991, pp. 28003-28031). They are promulgated formally in the *Code of Federal Regulations* (45 CFR 46, Parts 1-199, 10/1/92).

Not all federal agencies that sponsor research are governed by a similar law. Nevertheless, many of them have agreed to abide by the relevant section of the *Code of Federal Regulations* in order to protect individuals who are the subjects of research. Such agencies include those that have sponsored the randomized experiments described in this text, notably the U.S. Department of Education, the Department of Agriculture, the Department of Justice, and the Department of Health and Human Services.

Despite the brevity of the *Code of Federal Regulations*, it is remarkably thorough in its coverage. It includes basic definitions, the code's applicability to certain research endeavors and its exemption for others, the constitution and operation of IRBs, and requirements for ensuring informed consent. There are special requirements for research on especially vulnerable individuals, such as pregnant women. Because ethical issues can be complex and change in character, a variety of monographs have been produced to educate researchers and other stakeholders about the code's requirements and other standards. Among these are specialized books, for example, on women's participation in clinical trials in medicine (Mastroianni, Faden, & Federman, 1994), on experiments in civil and criminal justice (Federal Judicial Center, 1981), on psychological field research (Sieber, 1992), and on research on children and adolescents (Stanley & Sieber, 1992).

An Illustration

To illustrate application of the *Code of Federal Regulations*, consider an experiment undertaken by the U.S. Social Security Administration—Project NetWork. This study focused on disabled individuals who receive Social Security Disability Insurance payments and Supplemental Security Income payments (Rupp, Bell, & McManus, 1994). Its object was to learn whether the quality of the lives of those individuals could be improved by assisting them in job training, finding jobs, and independent living. Eligible volunteers from the pool of payment recipients were randomly allocated to special programs with these objectives or to a control condition that involved continued receipt of payments with no special assistance.

Applicability of the Code

The *Code of Federal Regulations* is applicable to any grantee or contractor sponsored by DHHS engaged in research on human subjects, as well as to DHHS employees. Furthermore, it applies to research conducted within the United States and outside the United States; a special waiver for the latter is possible. Project NetWork was a research effort engaging potentially vulnerable human subjects, the disabled in the United States. The Social Security Administration, a part of the DHHS, then appears to fall within the ambit of the code.

The code contains important exemptions. Studies of special instructional strategies in educational settings and on educational testing of achievement, for example, are excluded, as are surveys and statistical analyses in which respondents are anonymous. More relevant to the case at hand, there is an explicit exemption for research that is approved by DHHS and designed to evaluate programs under the Social Security Act. Studies that attend to changing methods and levels of payment fall within the ambit of the exemption.

Technically, then, Project NetWork need not have been governed by the code's regulations. The origins of an exemption for this and similar studies lies partly in the theory that government must periodically improve its operations. To impose special requirements on improvement efforts, such as an IRB review, arguably is neither desirable nor feasible on managerial grounds.

Despite the exemption, the Social Security Administration decided to use the *Code of Federal Regulations* as a guide to conducting the experiment. A major justification for this decision lay in the fact that individuals in the target sample—disabled people—could be regarded as especially vulnerable. Moreover, the ethical implications of encouraging the disabled to work instead of accepting disability payments were sufficiently unclear that formal review of the matter seemed warranted.

Assurances

Under the *Code of Federal Regulations*, organizations that conduct research must provide written assurances that they will comply with the regulations, identify procedures to be followed for initial and continued review of the research, and constitute an IRB to review the study. In the case of Project NetWork, major responsibility for this fell to a contractor—Abt Associates, Inc.—selected through ordinary competitive bidding processes to conduct the experiment. Abt has a standing IRB, as do many such organizations. The company has filed assurances and procedures with the DHHS.

In this project, as in other experiments, special procedures usually have been invented so as to meet the particular needs of the target sample in the study. For example, the SSA's operating procedures include guidance to staff about handling threats of suicide or violence made by an applicant or client (Social Security Administration, 1992, 1994). Although not common, such threats are sufficiently important to make sure that responsive procedures were understood and employed in the experiment by the research staff.

Institutional Review Board Criteria

The standards that IRBs must consider in judging the ethical appropriateness of research are given in Section 46.111 of the *Code of Federal Regulations*. They cover research risks and the balance between risks and benefits, the selection of individuals for the research, informed consent, and other matters. The criteria are put into question form in the code and the text that follows.

Are Risks Minimized? Training and employment program participants are unlikely to encounter life-threatening risks. The programs can, however, affect quality of life because a worthless program wastes their time. In any event, the natural approach to minimizing risk is to minimize the number of persons who have to participate in the experiment. Technology is available for minimizing the number of participants in a controlled field test, and it was used in Project NetWork (Kulik & Bell, 1992). The matter falls under the rubric of "statistical power analysis" and is discussed later in Chapter 4.

Furthermore, where control group members—those not offered a specialized program—are thought to be at risk, then the size of this group also can be minimized. For example, an experiment can be designed in which three individuals out of four are randomly assigned to the new, purportedly more effective program, and the remaining individuals are assigned to the control group. The standard is not sensible insofar as the major reason for the randomized controlled test lies in the fact that the effectiveness of the program is uncertain. It is sensible insofar as local practitioners who deliver services also believe that the new treatment ought to be provided to as many individuals as possible regardless of its effectiveness relative to scientific standards.

Beyond this, risk minimization depends heavily on the treatments that are compared in an experiment. In Project NetWork, the handling of both control group members and individuals in the treatment group included procedures designed to avert problems. Individuals who were assigned to receive job counseling, related services, and jobs could, for example, withdraw at any time over the course of the study if the treatment proved sufficiently discomfiting. They were so informed. Case managers operated under rules that directed attention to such matters.

Are Risks Reasonable in Relation to Benefits? The potential benefits of the Project NetWork treatment for the disabled were viewed as a successful return to work for those who wished to be productively employed. A risk, incurred if the program was ineffective, was that Project NetWork program participants would have wasted their time in talking to interviewers and counselors, receiving training, capitalizing on support services, and so on. This might put them at a disadvantage relative to control group members, whose activity was confined largely to receipt of disability payments.

Risks to the control group members, those who were not assigned to the Program NetWork employment program, are real only if the program works. Whether the program would work was unknown when the experiment was initiated. This latter uncertainty justifies experimenting. Control group members nevertheless might feel deprived of a potential benefit of employment assistance, regardless of the fact that actual benefits could not be known until the experiment was completed. Feelings of deprivation are counted by some as a cost or burden to control group members. On the other hand, the benefit of being a control group member arguably lay in the fact that it incurred little time investment and no risk out of the ordinary. The IRB judged risks to be reasonable relative to benefits. This criterion for approval of the research was met.

Is the Selection of Individuals Equitable? This criterion was incorporated into the *Code of Federal Regulations* to ensure that certain eligible individuals would not be put at a disadvantage relative to other eligible individuals. For example, an attractive program might be assigned almost exclusively to relatives, friends, and acquaintances of the program staff. Generally speaking, a randomized experiment meets this standard simply because eligible individuals are assigned randomly to alternatives. There is no opportunity for favoritism in assignment or unfair selection, unless special favors are defined explicitly as part of an exclusionary category in the experiment.

In Project NetWork, there was no written provision for admitting certain individuals to the new employment program absent randomization. All eligible volunteers were assigned randomly to the alternatives. Selection, in this crude sense, was then equitable.

Eligibility normally must be determined prior to the randomization process. This screening is itself a selection mechanism. It is designed to ensure that the program alternatives are appropriate for the target individuals. In Project NetWork, screening was such that only a few kinds of individuals were ineligible. In particular, individuals who did not volunteer, were employed, were under 16 years of age, or were not receiving disability payments were excluded from consideration. Furthermore, if otherwise eligible participants declined to agree to Project NetWork operating rules, they were excluded (Social Security Administration, 1992).

Is Informed Consent Given? Section 46.111 of the *Code of Federal Regulations* requires that "informed consent be sought from each prospective research subject or from the subject's legally authorized representative" and that the consent be documented. The purpose of this criterion is to minimize the possibility of undue influence or coercion. The code further specifies general requirements for informed consent and exemptions that might be permitted.

Project NetWork informed eligible individuals about the new program and the fact of the experiment. A reproduction of the consent form and the information provided is given in Box 3.1 and Box 3.2. Judging from these exhibits, most of the code's requirements for information are met. That is,

---

BOX 3.1
Project NetWork Informed Consent Form

Applicant's Name: _____ SSN: _____-_____-_____

I understand that Project NetWork (the Project) is a Social Security
Administration (SSA) research study testing different ways to help people
with disabilities get the services and items that they need to get and keep
a job. I have been told about these services, that the services and the use
of equipment are free, and I want to join this Project.

The case manager explained the requirements for getting into the Project.
I understand that I may be picked to be in either a group that may receive
services or in a group that only answers questions from time to time, and
that both groups are eligible for special incentives to work. I understand
these groups are picked at random.

The case manager told me that the information SSA collects about me is
confidential and will be protected under the Privacy Act. SSA will share
the information with Abt Associates, Inc., a private organization under
contract to the Social Security Administration, to evaluate this Project and
to learn how well the Project worked and the best way in which to help
people with disabilities to find and keep work. SSA will share it with
organizations involved in this Project to help me get a job and, as required
under the Social Security Act, with State agencies that make disability
decisions. I know how this information and my work can affect my
application for Social Security disability benefits and/or Supplemental
Security Income payments, or my continuing eligibility. I know about the
special benefits of trying to work under this Project.

I know that I do not have to take part in Project NetWork. There is no
penalty for not volunteering or dropping out whenever I choose. I know
that, at any time, I may apply for vocational rehabilitation services from
the State, instead of the services offered in this Project. I can ask my case
manager questions about the Project at any time.

The case manager explained my rights and responsibilities under the
Project to me, and gave me a copy. I want to be part of the Project.

_____   _____
Applicant's Signature   Date

_____   _____
Parent/Guardian/Payee (if applicable)   Date
                                                                   (____)_____-_____
_____
Street, City, State, Zip Code   Telephone

I have read the informed consent materials to the applicant, and I believe that (s)he (or the guardian, if signed) understands it.

_____   (_____)_____-_____   _____
Case Manager   Telephone   Date

Privacy Act Language—Informed Consent

Social Security is allowed to collect the information asked for while you participate in Project NetWork under the Social Security Disability Amendments of 1980, Public Law (P.L.) 96-265, section 505, as amended by P.L. 99-272, section 12101 and P.L. 101-239, section 10103, and section 1110(b) of the Social Security Act (the Act). We use the information to decide what case management services would best help you. You do not have to give us this information. However, if you do not, we cannot decide how to best help you to get and keep a job and will be unable to offer you services.

We release the information you give us on this form without your consent only in certain situations. We release the information to a congressional office in response to an inquiry that office may make at your request, or to Abt Associates, Inc., a private organization hired by the Social Security Administration to evaluate Project NetWork.

We may also use the information you give us when we match records by computer. Matching programs compare our records with those of other federal, state, or local government agencies. Many agencies may use matching programs to find or prove that a person qualifies for benefits paid by the federal government. The law allows us to do this even if you do not agree to it.

Explanations about these and other reasons why information you provide us may be used or given out are available in Social Security Offices. If you want to learn more about this, contact any Social Security Office.

individuals or the representatives were informed in writing and orally by case managers. The information, required by the code and supplied in the consent form, included descriptions of

- The research, its conduct, and duration
- Potential benefits

BOX 3.2

Project NetWork Informed Consent Materials

PURPOSE OF PROJECT NETWORK

Project NetWork (the Project) is a Social Security Administration research project. The purpose of the Project is to test different ways to help people with disabilities get the services that they need to get and keep a job. These services, overseen by a case manager, may include reviews of your capabilities and rehabilitation, training, and employment service needs. The services are free.

VOLUNTARY PARTICIPATION

You do not have to join Project NetWork, and you may drop out at any time without penalty. You can apply for vocational rehabilitation services from the state instead of those offered in the Project.

You may not be chosen to receive services. Instead, from time to time, we may ask you about your efforts to work. This is an important part of the Project.

Volunteers who meet the requirements below will be picked at random to answer questions (control group) or to be assessed for services (treatment group). The case managers have no control over who is selected for either group.

REQUIREMENTS FOR
ACCEPTANCE INTO PROJECT NETWORK

To get case management services, you must:

1. Agree to the rules of Project NetWork and sign the Informed Consent Form, *and*
2. Live in the area served by one of the Social Security Case Management Units taking part in this Project, *and*
3. Be unemployed and not receiving employment services, *and*
4. a. Be receiving Social Security Disability Insurance (SSDI) benefits, *or*
   b. Be at least 16 years old and receiving Supplemental Security Income (SSI) blind or disability payments or be applying for SSI blind or disability payments and waiting for a final medical decision.

YOUR RIGHTS UNDER PROJECT NETWORK

You have certain rights and protections under Project NetWork. Many of these are:

A. Your participation in the Project is completely voluntary. You may drop out without penalty at any time.

B. Potential benefits of the Project.

1. If you are picked to get services (treatment group):

   a. The services are free.

   b. The equipment that you need for rehabilitation and/or to get and keep a job are provided for you to use at no cost. You may be able to keep them under the following conditions:

      *you complete the Individual Employment Plan, *or*

      *you, with good cause, are unable to complete the Individual Employment Plan (e.g., health reasons, job opportunity no longer exists, etc.).

   c. You have a say in setting up your own Individual Employment Plan to help you get the services that you need to get the job that best fits your abilities and goals.

   d. You will be sent to qualified sources by Project NetWork. SSA will monitor the services to make sure they are appropriate, adequate, and timely.

   e. We will tell you what we learn from the examinations and reviews that you have. If you ask, either you or a representative that you name may be given copies of these reports. This may help you to better understand your limitations and abilities, whether or not you are picked to receive services from the Project.

   f. You will be involved in making the decisions about your participation in the Project.

   g. If you are not satisfied with aspects of your participation in the Project or decisions we make, you may request a review. You may contact your case manager and, then, his or her supervisor to request a review.

2. As long as you take part in the Project:

   a. *For SSDI*—work incentives are extended—you can test your ability to work for a longer time—12 consecutive months—before your earnings affect your current monthly benefits.

   For SSI—your work and earnings will not cause a medical review for 12 consecutive months (if you now get SSI disability).

continued

BOX 3.2
Continued

b. Your earnings from work may be higher than your current monthly benefits.

c. We will use the information about people who volunteer for the Project to learn how well the Project worked and the best ways to help people with disabilities to find and keep a job.

d. The information we get about all volunteers is confidential and is protected under the Privacy Act. We will not disclose it without written permission. However, we will share it with: Abt Associates, Inc., a private organization hired by SSA to evaluate the Project; Social Security offices; the organizations working with Social Security on this Project to help each volunteer get a job; and, as required under the Social Security law, to make disability decisions.

e. You can apply for services, at any time, from the State Vocational Rehabilitation Agency instead of Project NetWork.

f. You can ask for information about advocacy groups who may help you.

YOUR RESPONSIBILITIES
UNDER PROJECT NETWORK

A. If you are chosen only to answer questions, you must tell us about your efforts to work by answering written or telephone questions the best you can.

B. If you are chosen to be assessed for case management services:

You know you have to do your part to be successful. You must carry out the case manager's instructions quickly and completely. You must consider the services of Project NetWork to be a full-time job. Some of the duties you agree to do are:

1. attend and be on time for scheduled meetings, evaluations, examinations, services;

2. call your case manager ahead of time, if you cannot attend an appointment so that another can be scheduled;

3. carry out home assignments, such as reading pamphlets, visiting training sites or contacting friends and relatives for information;

4. be available for rehabilitation, training, and work for up to 40 hours a week;

5. give maximum effort in any medical or vocational testing or work evaluation program;
6. give information and answer questions to the best of your ability so that accurate estimates may be made about your vocational abilities and services needed;
7. consider all vocational goals suggested by your case manager;
8. file appropriate forms with Project NetWork, service providers, insurance companies, and employers;
9. answer calls from your case manager and report any return to work, address and/or telephone change;
10. return equipment purchased for your use if you no longer qualify for the Project and it is determined you do not meet the requirements, in B.1.b. under Your Rights Under Project NetWork, to keep the equipment *and*

YOU MUST CONTINUE TO REPORT TO SOCIAL SECURITY ANY CHANGES WHICH MAY AFFECT YOUR SOCIAL SECURITY AND/OR SUPPLEMENTAL SECURITY INCOME DISABILITY BENEFITS OR APPLICATION. THESE REPORTS SHOULD BE MADE TO SOCIAL SECURITY.

_____   _____
Applicant's Name   SSN

_____
Parent/Guardian/Payee (if applicable)
_____ (____)____-____   _____
Case Manager   Telephone   Date

- Alternative procedures available to individuals
- Confidentiality of records
- Contact persons for further inquiry or complaint, and
- The voluntary nature of participation

There is no description of foreseeable risks or discomforts, however, a topic to which the code requires attention. Why the description is absent from Project NetWork's consent form is not clear.

Are the Data Monitored? The *Code of Federal Regulations* requires that, when appropriate, the research plan makes adequate provision for monitoring the data collected to ensure the safety of subjects (Section 46.111(6)). Project NetWork employed procedures that monitored data and operations so as to detect problems of numerous kinds (Abt Associates, 1992). The procedures were revised during the course of the experiment as new problems emerged, notably an instance of suicide (M. Hess, internal memorandum at Abt Associates, May 11, 1993; Y. Leiter, memo to Leo McManus and Kalman Rupp, 1993).

Generally, safety monitoring provisions are developed in clinical trials in medical and pharmaceutical studies when the negative effects of a treatment can be nontrivial. The safety issue normally has been innocuous in social and educational experiments; however, controlled field tests in potentially volatile contexts and with especially vulnerable target individuals have increased over the last decade, mainly in the interest of learning what works better and for whom. Consequently, systems for monitoring for safety are likely to be integrated more frequently in social experiments. For example, the experiments on police handling of domestic violence described earlier included provisions for both. Such procedures are likely to be articulated better and improved in future experiments of this sort.

Are Privacy and Confidentiality Assured? When the research requires that individuals be identified and that their records be maintained in identifiable form, both the *Code of Federal Regulations* and related laws guide the handling of records. The code, for example, requires that in an experiment, such as Project NetWork, the confidentiality of identifiable records must be maintained. In the case at hand, the Privacy Act of 1974 (PL 93-579) provides protection of privacy for individuals on whom records are collected or maintained by a federal agency, and it specifies the conditions under which records can and cannot be disclosed. The statute is referred to in Project NetWork's consent material. The Privacy Act and other relevant statutes are described in Duncan, Jabine, and de Wolf (1993) and Cecil (1993).

The Social Security Administration, like a number of other federal units, has no statutory protection against research records being used in nonresearch settings. Consequently, the consent information provided to prospective participants in the Project NetWork experiment says that records may be supplied to a congressional office in response to the office's inquiry. Because research records must be linked with administrative records in the research, individuals were informed about this linkage in the consent materials.

Maintaining the confidentiality of information on a given research subject is, in some contexts, sufficiently important that laws have been enacted to present the information's use in nonresearch settings. In criminal justice research, for example, an individual's report on the commission of a crime is sensitive and may invite attention from a law enforcement agency. To remove the information from such an agency's purview, Congress has enacted special laws. They are described later.

ETHICAL PROPRIETY:
FEDERAL JUDICIAL CENTER GUIDELINES

The Federal Judicial Center's (1981) book on the ethics of experimentation offers threshold conditions that must be met if randomized field tests are to be undertaken. Cast into question form, the conditions are the following:

1. Does present practice or policy need improvement?
2. Is there "significant uncertainty about the value of the proposed regimen"?
3. Are there no other practical and scientifically defensible means to determine the value of the proposed regimen?
4. Will the results of the experiment be used to improve practice or policy?
5. Will the rights of individuals be protected?

Affirmative answers justify serious consideration of randomized experiments to evaluate a purportedly good intervention.

The center's report does not concern statutory characterization of ethics of the sort examined earlier, nor does it concern regulations that facilitate adherence to law. Rather, it directs attention to larger questions. The questions are considered here using, as an example, multisite experiments sponsored by the Rockefeller Foundation on how to enhance the self-sufficiency and well-being of economically disadvantaged minority female single parents (Cottingham, 1991; Rockefeller Foundation, 1990; Hollister, 1990). Neither the Rockefeller Foundation nor any other private entity is obligated by specific law to adhere to any system or statement of ethics.

Whether the circumstances of minority female single parents are satisfactory has been a matter of considerable public debate. These women vary considerably as to their needs. Given the evidence available, the Rockefeller Foundation determined that there was a critical need for training over an extended period, child care, and support services. Community-based organizations that might be able to meet these needs were invited to implement programs and to participate in controlled tests of their programs. The evidence on the character and severity of the purported problem, the vulnerability of minority single women with children, was sufficient for the foundation to justify investing in new programs and to consider research on their relative effectiveness.

Whether there is "significant uncertainty" about a proposed innovation is often a matter of much debate. The innovators may, for example, be persuaded that their manpower training works better based on *their* evidence and on thoughtful speculation. Competitors will hold an opposing view, especially in the absence of independent evidence.

In the Rockefeller Foundation experiments, there was an expectation that community-based organizations could construct an effective program for poor single women with children, but the difficulties uncovered in federally supported evaluations of earlier human resources programs justified caution and a willingness to try to understand whether, and how well, the innovation worked (Betsey et al., 1985). In making a decision to acknowledge the uncertainty about program effectiveness, the foundation met the second Federal Judicial Center standard.

The question of whether good alternatives to randomized experiments exist rarely is easy to answer. Recall that the random assignment produces groups that are theoretically equivalent in the long run. Groups that are constituted in ways other than through randomization usually differ in known and unknown ways. These differences are inextricably tangled with the effects of the treatment that each group receives. This may make ineffective variations look good and effective variations appear worthless, and they can make harmful variations appear merely worthless. For example, reviews of 4 randomized and 47 nonrandomized trials on portacaval shunt surgery showed only 1 of the former and 34 of the latter to result in significant effects. According to Friedman et al. (1985), the reviewers recommended against routine use of the new surgery; randomized trials since then appear to have borne out the review. Similarly, work on the Salk vaccine, enriched oxygen for premature infants, anticoagulant drug therapy for acute myocardial infarction, as well as other studies in which both randomized and nonrandomized trials have been conducted, usually shows differences in outcomes depending on whether the experiment was randomized or not.

At the time the Rockefeller Foundation's research was initiated, two technologies of research methods, quasi-experimentation and econometric modeling, had been developed to understand how good estimates of a program's effect can be produced without random assignment. Both, however, depend heavily on prior data, strong theory, or both. Data and theory usually are absent, or at least imperfect, for "new" target groups and for new programs. Women with children and with few financial and educational resources are properly classifiable as a "new" target group in the sense that little good data or theory exists on their number, willingness and ability to participate in programs, and so forth. This helps to justify a formal field test of the proposed intervention, so meeting the third Federal Judicial Center guideline.

Will the results of the field test be used? No one can guarantee that good evidence will be used in any public forum. Indeed, bad evidence has been used, at times, in various societies. Recall, for example, Lysenko's genetics in Russia and the use of laetrile, organ boxes, and other useless medicines in the United States. Merely because some people depend on poor evidence does not mean, however, that good evidence will not be used or that it should not be collected. In fact, evidence from randomized experiments in the social sector has become increasingly important over the last decade. The U.S. General Accounting Office, for example, often discriminates explicitly between trustworthy and untrustworthy studies in its reports, for example, on teenage pregnancy (U.S. GAO, 1986). Committees of the National Academy of Sciences and the National Research Council take the quality of evidence seriously and consider it in their reports, for example, on AIDS prevention programs (Turner et al., 1989). Each entity informs Congress, and part of Congress, at least, attends to good evidence. Case studies that present evidence on the policy use of results from experiments have been developed by Greenberg and Mandell (1991) in economics and Sherman and Cohn (1989) in police research, among other analysts. The probable use of the results of the Rockefeller Foundation's experiment met the fourth Federal Judicial Center standard.

The fifth threshold condition for doing experiments is that special attention be paid to the mandatory character of the criminal justice system. This is in contrast in the "voluntary" character of social and biomedical systems. The experiments sponsored by the Rockefeller Foundation engaged volunteers who had the freedom to agree to participate in the experiment or to decline and to exit the program at any time. The Federal Judicial Center's fifth threshold condition is not directly relevant, then, to the case at hand.

STATUTORY PROTECTION OF PRIVACY

A number of federal laws prevent the appropriation of research information on identifiable respondents for nonresearch purposes. The laws facilitate the researchers' adherence to a promise of confidentiality in controlled field tests of programs that focus on sensitive topics in mental health, civil and criminal justice, delinquency, substance abuse, and other areas. They make explicit the researcher's legal responsibility to ensure confidentiality and provide legal support for meeting it. To the extent that prospective research participants view legal protection as necessary, these laws may also enhance individuals' cooperation rates in randomized field tests.

The relevant statutes are described briefly here, and their provisions are summarized in Table 3.1. Boruch and Cecil (1979) suggest ways to evaluate these laws. Their guidelines, reiterated in other forms by Duncan et al. (1993), are used in what follows. In particular, the following evaluative questions are addressed:

- Is immunity automatic rather than authorized separately for each research project?
- Does immunity refer to administrative, judicial, or legislative agencies seeking to appropriate records?
- Is all information in an individual's record protected, or only the identification of the individual?
- Are there provisions that permit independent statistical analysis of the data by outside researchers?

Public Health Services Act

Two sections of the Public Health Services Act provide legal mechanisms to ensure that sensitive information provided by a research participant will not be appropriated for use against the participant. In the first section, the Secretary of the U.S. Department of Health and Human Services is permitted to:

[a]uthorize persons engaged in research on mental health, including research on the use and effect of alcohol and psychoactive drugs, to protect the privacy of individuals who are subjects of such research by withholding from all persons not connected with the conduct of such research the names or other identifying characteristics of such individuals. Persons so authorized to protect the privacy of such individuals may not be compelled in any federal, state, or local civil, criminal, administrative, legislative, or other proceedings to identify such individuals.

This section of the Act (42 U.S.C.A. §242a (1982)) can be of considerable importance in that the identity of participants in controlled field tests can be protected legally. Moreover, the reference to "other identifying characteristics" ensures that the researcher can prevent deductive disclosure. A specific illustration of the certification is given in Box 3.3.

The law's requirement that researchers be engaged in mental health research and so forth means that it pertains directly to field experiments on treating depression and other illnesses, alternative approaches to preventing or treating substance abuse, and to mental health components of criminal justice programs and AIDS research. For example, research trying to understand the effects of attempts to reduce the depression of AIDS victims or their families, social support systems, risk reduction behavior of those vulnerable to the disease, and the way it conflicts with other behaviors is common and is relevant to mental health. Projects with these aims arguably fall within the ambit of the act.

Three limitations of the statute are important. First, if a legally empowered government agency already knows the identity of a participant in an experiment, then the researcher can be compelled to disclose the research record on that individual. The privilege covers only identification. Gray and Melton (1985) remind us that this limitation had not been confronted by the courts up to the early 1980s. There appears to have been no direct judicial interpretation of the provision since then.

A second limitation is that the privilege must be conferred by the Secretary; it is not activated automatically when an experiment or any other research project is put into the field. Consequently, research groups that investigate politically controversial topics, such as the special programs to reduce sexual behavior related to AIDS, may be at risk of not obtaining the grant of immunity or of having it rescinded. Third, there are no provisions for disclosure of research records to independent researchers for reanalysis.

A second section of the law that concerns privacy is given in Section 308(d) of the Public Health Services Act. Put simply, Section 308(d) bears on work undertaken by the National Center for Health Statistics (NCHS) and its grantees or contractors. In the late 1980s, NCHS was reorganized under the Centers for Disease Control (CDC). CDC legal counsel maintain that the relevant protection applies to CDC more generally (Ladine Newton, personal communication, 1988). The CDC, for example, sponsors controlled tests of innovation in preventing high-risk behaviors related to AIDS, substance abuse among children and adolescents, and other problems. Consequently, the legal protection of respondents in a study is important.

The explanations of the protection, given in documents such as the *NCHS Staff Manual on Confidentiality* (National Center for Health Statistics, 1984), are ample. Section 308(d) says:

TABLE 3.1

Statutes Providing Grants of Qualified Immunity for Research Information and Their Provisions

Statute	Protects Identification of Research Data	Protects Identifiable Information	Automatic, Rather than Authorized	Immunity from Administrative Inquiry	Immunity from Judicial Inquiry	Immunity from Legislative Inquiry	Provisions for Secondary Analysis, in Regulations or Law
Public Health Services Act, Sections 303(a) and 308(d), Public Law 91-513, 42 U.S.C.A. §242a(a)	Y	N	N	Y	Y	Y	Y
Crime Control Act of 1973, Public Law 93-83, 42 U.S.C.A. §3771	Y	Y	Y	Y	Y	N	Y
Juvenile Justice and Delinquency Prevention Act of 1977, Public Law 95-115	Y	Y	Y	Y	Y	N	Y
Controlled Substances Act, Section 502(c), Public Law 91-513, 21 U.S.C.A. §872c	Y	N	N	Y	Y	Y	N
Drug Abuse Office and Treatment Act, Public Law 92-255, Amended, Section 408, Public Law 93-282, 21 U.S.C.A. §1175a	Y	Y	Y	YC	N	YC	Y

Alcohol Abuse Act, Public Law 93-282, 45 U.S.C.A. §4582a	Y	Y	YC	N	YC	Y
Hawkins-Stafford Act, Public Law 100-297	Y	Y	Y	Y	N	Y
Confidentiality of Federal Statistical Records Act	Y	N	Y	Y	Y	Y

Y = Yes, covered explicitly.
N = No, not covered explicitly.
YC = Court order required for disclosure.

BOX 3.3

Sample Confidentiality Certificate

(Public Health Service
Alcohol, Drug Abuse, and Mental Health Administration
Rockville, MD 20857)

No. AA-85-05

Issued to:

RESEARCH PERSONNEL

conducting research known as:

ALCOHOL AND OTHER DRUG INVOLVEMENT
IN SERIOUS TRAFFIC ACCIDENTS

In accordance with regulations at 42 CFR Part 2a, this Certificate is issued in response to the request by Roy E. Lucke, The Traffic Institute, Northwestern University, P.O. Box 1409, Evanston, Illinois 60204, to protect the privacy of research subjects by withholding their identities from all persons not connected with subject research. Mr. Lucke is primarily responsible for the conduct of this research.

Under the authority vested in the Secretary of Health and Human Services by Section 303(a) of the Public Health Service Act (42 U.S.C. 242a(a)), all persons who:

1. are involved in the research conducted by the Traffic Institute, Northwestern University, P.O. Box 1409, Evanston, Illinois 60204; and,

2. have, during the conduct of that research, access to information which would identify individuals who are subjects of the research on alcohol and drug abuse which is being conducted in the study referred to as "Alcohol and Other Drug Involvement in Serious Traffic Accidents."

are hereby authorized to protect the privacy of the individuals who are the subjects of that research by withholding their names and other identifying characteristics from all persons not connected with the conduct of that research.

The proposed research involves using portions of urine and/or blood samples of injured drivers. All injured drivers will be asked for urine samples, but blood will only be obtained if the hospital deems it necessary for medical purposes. The research involves conducting tests on these samples (not normally conducted by the hospital) to determine the presence and quantity of drugs and alcohol. The results will be matched with accident reports filed by the investigating agency in order to determine accuracy of such reports and to assess the role of the drug(s), and/or alcohol in the accident.

As provided in Section 303(a) of the Public Health Service Act (42 U.S.C. 242a(a)): "Persons so authorized to protect the privacy of such individuals may not be compelled in any Federal, State or local, civil, criminal, administrative, legislative or other proceedings to identify such individuals."

This authorization is applicable to all information obtained which would identify the individuals who are respondents in the study conducted by Mr. Roy E. Lucke, Research Analyst, The Traffic Institute, Northwestern University, and whose research has been supported by the Anheuser Busch Foundation, St. Louis, Missouri.

This certificate does not represent an endorsement of the research project by the Department of Health and Human Services.

The Certificate is effective upon date of issuance through September 30, 1986. The protection afforded by this Confidentiality Certificate is permanent with respect to subjects who participate in the research during any time the Certificate is in effect.

(signed)   (dated 12/9/85)
Robert G. Niven, M.D.
Director
National Institute on
    Alcohol Abuse and Alcoholism

No information, if an establishment or person supplying the information in it is identifiable, obtained in the course of activities undertaken or supported (under research sections) . . . may be used for any purpose other than the purpose for which it was collected unless such an establishment or person has consented. (NCHS, 1984, p. 1)

The NCHS's (1984) staff manual lays out rules for employees and contractors, legally mandated assurances that must be given to survey respondents, operational guidance on physical security of records, and proscriptions against disclosure without consent. Its coverage of these topics and about topics rarely considered in privacy debates, such as deductive disclosure, is remarkable. Although the law itself does not have an explicit provision for reanalysis of data collected under a confidentiality assurance, the staff manual contains provision for disclosure of nonidentifiable statistical records.

Omnibus Crime Control and Safe Streets Act

Doing high-quality research on illegal activity, such as domestic assaults, sale and intravenous use of controlled substances, and prostitution, is difficult. To the extent that statutory protection can be offered to individuals who are enrolled in programs whose purpose is to reduce such activity, the research arguably will be more feasible and of higher quality.

Enacted in 1968 and amended in 1973, Section 524(a) of the Crime Control and Safe Streets Act (28 CFR Part 11) says:

> Except as provided by Federal law other than this title, no officer or employee of the Federal Government, nor any recipient of assistance under the provisions of this title, shall use or reveal any research or statistical information furnished under this title by any person and identifiable to any specific private person for any purpose other than the purpose for which it was obtained in accordance with the title. Copies of such information shall be immune from legal process and shall not, without the consent of the person furnishing such information, be admitted as evidence or used for any purpose in any action, suit, or other judicial or administrative proceedings.

This law concerns the researcher employed by government or the researcher who receives a federal grant or contract for research on crime-related behavior. Each is prohibited from disclosing the information provided by the identifiable research participant. Each is protected, to a point, from being compelled to disclose the information from a participant's record to the courts or to administrative agencies. Researchers who are not supported by the federal government receive no protection under the statute. The experiments covered by the statute and discussed in this book include the Spouse Assault Replication Program (Garner et al., 1995; Sherman et al.,

1992; Dunford et al., 1990; Hirschel et al., 1991) and supervision of status offenders (e.g., Land, McCall, & Williams, 1991; Petersilia & Turner, 1990). The statute and implementing regulations are laid out in a monograph issued by the U.S. Department of Justice (National Institute of Justice, 1978). The regulations make it plain that individual respondents in research are covered, but not institutions. For example, then, the responses of individual police officers to questions about how they handle domestic assailants would be protected, but information about the police department's policy or general practices would not be protected.

Under this law, records are not immune to a subpoena by Congress, but they are protected from subpoena from more likely agents—local or state prosecutors or courts. The immunity is automatic in the sense that the U.S. Attorney General, for example, cannot prevent or retract it, at least not without legal complications.

In the interest of independent analysis of data generated through sponsored research, the National Institute of Justice regulations permit the transfer of research data from one researcher to another. The secondary researcher who receives the data is bound by the confidentiality rules governing the original researcher. Such independent analysis can be critical in research on controversial topics; see Chapter 10 on reporting.

Controlled Substances Act

The Controlled Substances Act (21 U.S.C.A. §801-904 (1982)) authorizes the U.S. Attorney General to permit persons engaged in research on controlled substances to withhold identification of research participants from legislative, administrative, criminal, or other proceedings. The authority conferred by the statute is broad, insofar as it bears on all branches of government. This statute is important for researchers who are engaged in comparative tests of programs, practices, and projects in which clients are at risk of substance abuse.

As for the Public Health Services Act, this law's grant of immunity depends on the discretion of a federal executive. It is then subject to the problem that pressure to refuse or rescind a grant on political grounds, rather than scientific grounds, can be exercised. Like the Public Health Services Act, the Controlled Substances Act does not protect research data on identifiable individuals if the research participant's identity already is known. Furthermore, there are no provisions for disclosure of identifiable records for research purposes.

Drug Abuse Office and Treatment Act

This act (21 U.S.C.A. §1175(a) (1982)) protects "records of patients maintained in connection with drug abuse prevention programs assisted by the federal government." The implementing regulations cover records that are maintained for research purposes.

Unlike the Controlled Substances Act, this law is broad, covering both the contents of identifiable records and the identification of the research participant. Furthermore, the law is automatic rather than being dependent on a federal executive's discretion.

The immunity is limited, however. A court is entitled, for example, to subpoena the identification of a research participant and identified records. In *People v. Newman*, the court affirmed the drug researcher's right to refuse to disclose a respondent's identification under the immunity grant of the Controlled Substances Act, despite the exemption of the Drug Abuse Office and Treatment Act (Boruch & Cecil, 1979; Newman, 1977). Furthermore, Gray and Melton (1985) maintain that the law's protection of individuals applies only in delivery of prevention program services. The law also provides for the release of identifiable records for legitimate researchers without the respondent's consent and only for research purposes.

A variety of controlled experiments in related fields do have a prevention mission and so would be covered by the act. For example, McLellan, Arnat, Metzger, Woody, and O'Brien (1993) executed randomized experiments to test the relative effectiveness of minimum methadone services, minimum services plus counseling, and enhanced services. Each service had reduction of opiate use as an objective.

Hawkins-Stafford Act

The Hawkins-Stafford Act (PL 100-297) is the most recent privacy protection law enacted by the federal government. It covers research data obtained by the U.S. Department of Education's National Center for Education Statistics. The statute, modeled after provisions that govern the U.S. Bureau of the Census, improves on them. It attends to research in education, an area that has been ignored for such legislation.

Put briefly, Section M4(a) says that except as provided, no person may:

1. use any individually identifiable information furnished under . . . this section for any purpose other than statistical purposes for which it was provided,

2. make any publication whereby the data furnished by any particular person . . . can be identified, or

3. permit anyone other than the individuals authorized by the Commissioner to examine the individual reports.

Furthermore, Section B requires that "copies of . . . reports . . . shall be immune from legal process, and shall not without the consent of the individual concerned, be admitted as evidence or used for any purpose in any action, suit, or other judicial or administrative proceedings."

The law thus provides a limited testimonial privilege to government employees and to government contractors. The level of protection matches most that of similar statutes in providing protection against judicial or administrative action but not (specifically) a legislative subpoena.

Part of the merit of the statute lies in the fact that it is automatic. A commissioner of education statistics could not withhold such protection from a project that covered controversial topics. Merit also lies also in covering all information collected on an individual, not simply identity. The law covers information elicited from teachers, students, administrators, or other individual persons (Section F) and is thus broad in its protection at the person level. There is a specific exclusion of entities; for example, the names of states, local education agencies, or schools are not regarded as "persons" under the act.

The educational researcher or educator who does work on potentially volatile topics, such as substance abuse among students or dropouts, and who is *not* sponsored by the National Center on Education Statistics (NCES), is not protected under this law. Protection might then be sought under the other statutes described here. The NCES does not sponsor controlled experiments on programs, so the statute might be thought irrelevant. The NCES does, however, sponsor methodological research, including randomized experiments to discover better ways of asking questions. Participants in such work are covered under the law.

Advantages of Statutory Approaches

The federal laws that help to preserve the confidentiality of research participants' records are not uniform. Each statute focuses on a different area and differs in the nature of protection. Insofar as the courts are formally responsible for interpreting law, any interpretation must be tentative.

Despite the statutes' complexity, they have some advantages over the contemporary statistical and procedural devices used to ensure confidentiality of data. Most procedural devices, such as eliciting anonymous information, limit the quality of experiments. The statutes have the benefit of protecting both narrative case study information and quantitative data. They are applicable to small and large samples, a distinct advantage in that distinctive methods of statistical protection, such as randomized response, are relevant only to large samples (Boruch & Cecil, 1979). The statutes also have the virtue that they are specific enough to discourage if not prevent legal harassment of researchers.

The Courts and the Power of Subpoena

How have the courts treated privacy of individuals who participate in legitimate social research, including comparative field experiments? In general, the courts rarely handle the matter. That is, the courts have only infrequently considered cases in which research records are relevant and, even less frequently, have compelled disclosure of research records on identifiable participants.

Knerr's (1982) surveys of researchers in the United States revealed less than 20 clear cases of subpoena over the preceding 10 years. Searches by Boruch and Cecil (1979) and Cecil and Boruch (1988) help to confirm the point that the probability of a court subpoena is extremely low despite the controversiality of topics examined in applied social research.

Some of the reasons for the courts' disinterest in a researcher's records are obvious. Information that is more relevant to a court case typically is available from police or corporate records. Furthermore, if data are pertinent to a court case, nonidentifiable records or other *statistical* summaries often are sufficient for the courts' interest (Cecil & Boruch, 1988).

However infrequently the courts compel disclosure of identifiable research records, the fact remains that the courts are empowered to do so unless the power is restricted by law. The restrictions are of the sort specified in immunity statutes discussed earlier.

THE LAW AND
RANDOMIZED EXPERIMENTS

Debates about the ethics of testing innovations usually involve collision of different ethical systems. Cotton Mather, for example, introduced trial inoculation for smallpox in the 18th century and attempted to introduce it on a larger scale to stem the epidemic disease. To judge from one historian, Mather and his allies believed that presenting good evidence based on limited-scale pilot tests would inform a decision to adopt inoculation on a larger scale (Cohen, 1982). Their opponents regarded the pilot evidence as irrelevant, arguing that any novel program, such as inoculation, interfered with God's wishes. There were also those who maintained that evidence showed that inoculation was ineffective. Those interested in evidence eventually exploited theological arguments as well as evidence to make their cases.

Challenges to the legality of randomized experiments have been based partly on constitutional guarantees that the rights of citizens will be recognized. The guarantees invoked in court settings have included the Fifth and Fourteenth Amendments to the Constitution of the United States.

The Fifth Amendment, which became effective in 1791, declares, among other rights, that individuals may not be "deprived of life, liberty, or property, without due process of law," referring specifically to criminal cases. The Fourteenth Amendment, made effective in 1868, declared that states could not abridge the rights of U.S. citizens, nor could they "deprive any person of life, liberty, or property, without due process of law, nor deny persons within its jurisdiction the equal protection of the laws."

The history of debates on the morality and legality of tests of innovations, with some exceptions, appears not to have been well explored. Since the 18th century, what has been learned bears primarily on the complaint that a randomized allocation to a new program or to control conditions is illegal.

Consider, then, law and the courts' interpretation of it. Privately sponsored field tests, such as those supported by the Rockefeller Foundation, generally are immaterial to the Fifth and Fourteenth Amendments. The laws bear on government action. In a few cases, other laws may bring a private institution's research to the courts' attention.

For publicly supported experiments, the due process clause is pertinent in requiring that rights established under the law cannot be denied. In some cases, the clause may present a legitimate obstacle to experimentation by entitling individuals to a government program and prohibiting a downward adjustment of program services. Entitlement laws ordinarily specify only a few conditions of denial of benefits. Field tests that require manipulation of benefits within those constraints may then be feasible. The exceptions in entitlement statutes involve laws, such as the demonstration project provisions of the Social Security Act, that permit limited adjustment of program benefits in the interest of improving the programs.

The federal government's administrative authority for randomized experiments stems from the enabling statutes of the various federal agencies. The statutes may be specific, as in the case of the law that directed the

Department of Housing and Urban Development to undertake housing allowance experiments. The laws also may be general. Statutes can provide that an agency head may waive compliance with other statutes for purposes of experimentation or demonstration projects. The waiver authority of the Secretary of the Department of Health and Human Services permits social experimentation within limits, for example.

Some conflicts between research and law require judicial resolution. Despite the administrative authority for conducting comparative tests and Congress's efforts to pass statutes that avoid legal problems and the courts, interpretations of each are important. Federal authority for randomized field tests of social programs, for example, has been challenged in the courts on a few occasions. The courts have interpreted the authority broadly, rejecting the challenges in *Aguoyo v. Richardson* and *California Welfare Rights Organization (CWRO) v. Richardson*. In an earlier decision, *Truax v. Corrigan* (1914), Justice Holmes rendered a dissenting opinion that:

> [T]here is nothing I more deprecate than the use of the Fourteenth Amendment beyond the absolute compulsion of its words to prevent the making of social experiments . . . in the insulated chambers of the several states, even though the experiments may seem futile or even noxious to me and to those whose judgment I most respect.

A similar spirit was reflected by Justice Brandeis in *New York State Ice v. Liebmann* (Federal Judicial Center, 1981).

The use of a "safety-valve category" in randomized tests has been used to ensure that unfairly harsh burdens are not imposed as a consequence of blind randomization in traffic offender experiments. It is a device that can reconcile institutional responsibility to take action on the basis of special needs or conditions of the individual in law, medicine, and elsewhere with the need for fair assessments of innovative practices. See Breger (1983) generally.

SCARCE RESOURCES
AND LOTTERY ALLOCATION

Considering social ethics, Donald Campbell appears to have been the first to enunciate a kind of fundamental ethical rule in deciding whether to randomize (Campbell & Stanley, 1966). The rule, simply put, is that when there is an oversupply of eligible recipients for scarce program services, randomized assignment of candidates for the resource is fair. The Rockefeller Foundation's Minority Female Single Parent Program could not offer training and services to all eligible women at each site. The lottery allocation was acceptable, if not attractive to site administrators on equity grounds.

This rationale accords neatly with ordinary administrative constraints on the introduction of new programs. Despite the aspirations of program advocates, for example, new programs usually cannot be emplaced all at once but must be introduced in stages. Services for some, then, may be delayed on a random basis.

The argument that random assignment accords with good ethical standards when resources are scarce and needs are great is not pertinent when the program manager can simply spread resources more thinly. A manager may do so, for example, by expanding the size of classes dedicated to special instruction in tests of training projects. In the early stages of the Rockefeller Foundation's experiments on the Minority Female Single Parent Program, this option was indeed broached by service providers who opposed the random assignment of women to special services (Boruch, Dennis, & Carter, 1988). Others observe, however, that the option ignores quality control.

TECHNICAL APPROACHES
TO MEETING ETHICAL STANDARDS

The ethical issue just described can at times be addressed through technical means, that is, by altering features of the experiment's design. For example, program managers whose preference is to serve as many individuals as possible may reject an experiment in which only half of an eligible group is assigned randomly to their service. They may, however, accept a design in which two thirds of the groups are so assigned, the remaining third constituting a control group or alternative treatment group. Altering allocation ratios in this way facilitated the Rockefeller Foundation's experiments by meeting the local service providers' standards of ethics. Moreover, using such a ratio did not appreciably affect the quality of the experiment.

There are many other ways to tailor an experiment's design so as to meet ethical concerns. An obvious tactic is to ensure that the number of people exposed to potentially burdensome treatments is kept to a minimum. The minimum sample size necessary for a reasonable level of statistical power can be identified (see Chapter 4). Technology for minimizing the number of questions that must be asked also is available. Testing parts of new programs rather than entire programs often is warranted on ethical grounds. Full-blown tests may not be worthwhile on management or policy grounds in any event. For example, one might conceive of undertaking an experiment to determine whether testing and counseling programs for HIV exposure are effective by randomly assigning target individuals to the programs or to a no-program control group. The experiment would be unethical in the judgment of some, as well as illegal (Turner et al., 1989; Coyle et al., 1991). Doing experiments on different ways to provide counseling, however, arguably would meet ethical standards.

Similarly, variations in program intensity may be compared to one another in a randomized experiment. This tactic may be employed in the interest of meeting an ethical standard that says that a no-program control group is unacceptable. Such experiments inform science and policy regardless of the ethics standard. In the Spouse Assault Replication Program, for example, Sherman et al. (1992) examined the relative effectiveness of arresting purported assailants in domestic violence cases against arresting them and holding them in jail for as long as local law permitted. A "normal" arrest for misdemeanor assault might involve only a few hours of jail time. The "hold" condition would double or treble this and was thought to be more intensive.

Consider, as a last example of technical approaches to resolving ethical problems, a setting in which all eligible individuals, for ethical reasons, must be served at roughly the same level. That is, they cannot be assigned to control conditions or variations on a program. Suppose further that the scientific or policy interest lies in the effect of the new service. One way to handle the matter is to identify a number of settings that are eligible for and willing to deploy the new services and then to randomly allocate those settings to receive resources to provide them or to a control group that does not receive the resources. This tactic can meet a local ethical standard that demands service for all or none. It can meet other standards, of the sort described earlier, that demand that innovative services be tested well. In fact, controlled experiments that involve randomly allocating schools, communities, and other entities have been done. Ethical issues are a part of the implicit rationale for such studies. Other rationales are describe in Chapter 4.

EMPIRICAL APPROACHES TO UNDERSTANDING
FAIRNESS IN RANDOMIZED FIELD TESTS

Programs that are advertised as new or innovative often become popular. An attempt to mount a controlled experiment, in the interest of discovering the new program's effect, will at times be frustrated by claims that such an experiment engenders an ethical dilemma; that is, individuals ought not be deprived of the innovation because it works, or at least appears to work. Randomly assigning individuals to the program and to a control condition in which they avail themselves of an existing service is regarded as not being ethical.

This ethical dilemma may be legitimate insofar as good evidence exists that the new treatment works better than existing ones. Indeed, if such evidence exists, the Federal Judicial Center standards and IRB guidelines imply that another experiment, one that deprives people of a known good, ought not be done.

The ethical dilemma is vacuous, however, insofar as the evidence about effectiveness of the particular innovation is absent or ambiguous. Moreover, random allocation in an experiment might be justified partly on the basis of empirical studies of how often researchers succeed, fail, or discover equally effective alternatives.

If one looks at carefully designed studies of innovative primary and secondary medical therapies, as Gilbert, McPeek, & Mosteller (1977) have, one would find the new treatment very successful about 20% of the time. In about 20% of the cases, the innovation performs worse than the standard treatment. In the remaining cases, the innovation works about as well as the conventional approach. Evidence of similar kinds also has been generated for nonmedical fields. For example, Gordon and Morse (1975) reviewed the published reports of high-quality evaluations of social interventions and found that 35% of new programs succeed notably; slightly more than 20% failed relative to control conditions.

A related stream of relevant empirical work over the last 15 years suggests that nothing improves the chances of apparently successful innovation as much as lack of experimental control. Marked enthusiasm for an innovation is negligible in reports on controlled trials. Declarations that a program is successful are about four times more likely in research based on poor or questionable evaluation designs as in that based on adequate ones. These findings support a more general point made by Rutstein (1969) in his analysis of medical experiments. Badly designed research can yield misleading results and is ethically unacceptable on that account.

More generally, syntheses of multiple experiments in different program areas constitute an empirical base for understanding whether certain experiments are ethically justified. Such meta-analyses have been used productively to generate rates of failure and success for innovations (Lipsey, 1990; Light & Pillemer, 1984). These rates can then be used to illuminate arguments about the ethics of an experiment; they are not yet used often to do so.

4

Population, Power, and Pipeline

As soon as the contract is signed, or the grant is awarded, the size of the target group available for the experiment drops in half.

—Anonymous

Which individuals or entities are the proper target for services? The answer to the question determines, for the study's designer, who or what will be randomly assigned to the treatments that must be compared. In the statistical vernacular, the *experimental units* have to be identified for the study's design, implementation, and analysis of resultant data (Glass & Hopkins, 1984). The units may be individuals or "cases," as in court experiments or police encounters. They might be defined as communities and legal jurisdictions, groups, or organizations such as schools, hospitals, and police departments. These units are members of a larger target population; it too must be specified.

Specifying the unit of randomization and the target population from which they are drawn usually entails the creation of eligibility criteria. That is, individuals or entities are screened to ensure that indeed they merit, need, or are otherwise appropriate for any of the treatments that are randomly assigned to them. These eligibility criteria will affect the number of cases that flow into the study, that is, the pipeline. This in turn influences statistical power. Roughly speaking, statistical power refers to the probability of discerning differences in the effectiveness of treatments despite considerable variability in human behavior.

The field study's designers are responsible for anticipating how many individuals or entities must be allocated to each treatment in order to detect the relative differences among treatments with any confidence. The question of how many units are necessary is not trivial. There is remarkable variety in human and organizational behavior; it can swamp the small but important effects of efforts to improve programs. Understanding how to design the study so that it has sufficient statistical power, taking into account variability, sample size, and other factors, is fundamental to producing useful research.

Understanding how individuals or other target units find their way into a treatment program, progress through it, and eventually exit also is critical. This "pipeline" or "client flow" is an integral part of the social context in which programs and experiments operate. These topics and the issues that they engender are considered in what follows.

UNITS AND
TARGET POPULATION

Options

Choosing a particular unit for random assignment engenders a choice of target population, that is, the totality of individuals (or entities) from which a sample is drawn. Results of the study at hand will then be generalizable to this target population. The choice of a unit of assignment also drives data collection and analysis. That is, when individuals are the unit, observations are made at the individual level and observations on each individual are exploited in the core analysis. When communities are the unit, it is aggregate data on each community—crime rates, for example—that usually are analyzed to assess effectiveness of treatments rather than data on individuals within the unit. Further, the effective sample size depends heavily on the number of communities engaged in the study, not the number of citizens in the communities.

Deciding which unit is appropriate for random assignment is then crucial in designing the study. The decision usually rests on two considerations: the nature of the treatment and the independence of the units. Considering the nature of treatments, programs that are clearly directed at entities invite using the entity as the unit. Incentive programs in schools, for example, generally are applicable on a schoolwide basis, though particular incentives within the school might be relevant to particular individuals. Because the school, and not the individual, is the focus of treatment, the school is the proper unit for random assignment. For example, Bickman's (1985) tests of incentive programs involved random assignment of schools from a large pool of eligible schools to alternative programs in the interest of discerning differences in the effectiveness of the various incentive programs. Similarly, evaluations of programs designed to prevent substance abuse among junior high school students have assigned volunteering schools randomly to different programs to learn, for example, that treatments based on social pressure resistance and normative education were far more effective than alternatives (Hansen, Johnson, Flay, Graham, & Sobel, 1988; Hansen & Graham, 1991).

On the other hand, treatment of the chronically mentally ill who live in the community often involves services provided directly to the person. Consequently, the random assignment of a sample of eligible individuals to alternative treatment strategies to determine their relative effects is sensible (Test & Burke, 1985). The treatment's focus on specific persons, rather than persons considered in the aggregate, has similarly justified the choice of the individual as the unit of assignment in law enforcement and corrections experiments (e.g., Sherman, Schmidt, & Rogan, 1992; Land et al., 1991), tax compliance experiments (Roth et al., 1989), and others identified in this book.

The statistical theory underlying the conduct of experiments and conventional analysis of resultant data assume that the units of assignments are independent of one another. The performance of one school—the unit—in a multischool study of school-based incentives is presumed, for example, not to affect the performance of other schools in the study. The well-being of a mentally ill person living in the community often is assumed to have no influence on the well-being of others in a study of how to enhance the well-being of individuals.

If the units are not independent of one another, conventional statistical approaches to characterizing uncertainty may be misleading (see, e.g., Kruskal, 1980). Determining whether and how they may be inappropriate and how corrections may be made is a complex matter and beyond the scope of this book. For the designer of field tests, the implication is that if units tentatively chosen are not independent, then choosing a unit at some higher level of aggregation may be necessary. Alternatively, considerably greater investment must be made in measurement and analysis to determine whether it is possible to adjust for the nonindependence. For example, it has become clear that children within classrooms are not independent despite their random assignment to alternative education treatments within a classroom. They talk to one another and interact in ways that arguably engender nonindependence. Partly, as a consequence, the classroom, rather than the student, has become the unit of random assignment and analysis in contemporary field experiments. Furthermore, in cases in which classrooms cannot be regarded as independent, schools are chosen as the unit.

A Note on Entities as
the Unit of Randomization

Experiments that engage individuals are frequent and are the primary focus of this book. Field experiments that employ institutions, groups, or communities as the unit are not common. Nevertheless, this kind of experiment has come to be considered often in policy research partly for the reasons suggested above.

Schools, for example, have been the unit in research on how to reduce the negative effects of interschool transfer on high-risk students who must change schools. The Jason, Johnson, Danner, Taylor, and Kuraski (1993) study of the topic involved 20 schools allocated randomly to different programs for handling such children. Schools have also been the unit in schoolwide health promotion efforts and programs to reduce the incidence of substance abuse. See, for example, Aplasca and colleagues (1995) on AIDS prevention in the Philippines; Ellickson and Bell (1992), Rosenbaum et al. (1991), and Dent, Sussman, and Flay (1993) on drug use prevention; and Flay (1986) on smoking prevention in the United States and Canada.

When new communitywide efforts to reduce a community problem must be evaluated, it is natural to consider the community as the unit of assignment (and analysis) in a randomized experiment. The strategy has been encouraged by advisory groups for research on AIDS prevention (Coyle et al., 1991), substance abuse prevention (Kaftarian & Hansen, 1994; Peterson, Hawkins, & Catalano, 1992), crime (Reiss & Roth, 1993), and illness (Murray et al., 1994). Such experiments have indeed been mounted. For example, LaPrelle, Bauman, and Koch (1992) undertook a study of communitywide media campaigns to prevent smoking among adolescents. They screened, matched, and randomly assigned communities from a sample of 10 to treatments or to a control group.

In some experiments, small geographic areas, groups, or organizations are the proper unit for study. See, for example, Bickman's (1985) work using health service sites, the McKay et al. (1978) experiments on cultural enrichment using sectors of Colombian barrios as the units, and Kelling, Pate, Dieckman, and Brown (1974) on the use of police zones in Kansas City tests of patrol strategies. An interesting randomized test of a program to improve mathematics education for women, based on groups of female students who were randomly assigned to different conditions, was reported by Harskamp and Suhre (1995).

BOX 4.1
Eligibility Criteria for Cases in the Charlotte Police Department
Experiment on Handling Misdemeanor Domestic Violence

Legal criteria

There is probable cause evidence for a misdemeanor offense

There has been no felony assault

Police department policy criteria

The victim is female

The offender is male, 18 years of age or older

The relationship is heterosexual and spouselike: married, formerly
married, separated, or cohabiting

There is no threat to officers

The victim does not insist on arrest

There is no imminent danger to the victim

Experiment design criteria

The suspect is present

SOURCE: Adapted from *Charlotte Spouse Assault Replication Project: Final Report*,
Hirschel, Hutchison, Dean, Kelley, and Pesackis.

Eligibility Criteria

The units of assignment to a program and the target population units
usually are specified partly in terms of program eligibility requirements.
The latter are developed by the treatment program staff or service provider,
at times in collaboration with the research design group. Depending on the
particular context, the eligibility criteria may be a function of law, program
objectives and resources, and other factors. The criteria must be specified
prior to the initiation of the experiment and should be regarded as a
component of the treatment program.

Consider, for example, the Spouse Assault Replication Program (SARP).
In each of six sites, cases of domestic violence that resulted in calls for
police assistance were the target for random assignment to alternative
treatments. Not all such calls were judged to be eligible for experiments
on police methods for handling the cases, however. Box 4.1 outlines the

eligibility criteria used in the Charlotte experiment. Hirschel, Hutchison, Dean, Kelley, and Pesackis (1991) classified them as based on local law, police department policy, and the research design. This categorization reflects the interests of various stakeholders in the study.

The criteria exclude offenders under the age of 18, for example, because law demands that these cases be handled differently from the way adult offenders are handled. Local judgments about where the serious problems occur led to focusing on heterosexual rather than homosexual relationships. The fact that a victim insisted on arrest, regardless of whether an arrest was warranted, also was grounds for elimination of a case from the experiment. In this instance, the police procedures required were sufficiently complex to deem such cases as not appropriate for inclusion. Felony assault cases also were eliminated; the treatments to which cases would be randomly assigned included mediation, for example, and felony assaults automatically justify an arrest.

Detailed eligibility criteria similarly are required in randomized controlled field tests in the welfare and employment arenas. Multisite evaluations of the JOBSTART program for unemployed high school dropouts, for example, relied partly on legal criteria, notably proof of residency, age, and economic disadvantage. Further, the target individual had to be a high school dropout in the age range of 17 to 21 and, upon testing, be found to read at below the 8th-grade level. Because the program was voluntary, the individual's willingness to provide informed consent to participate in the experiment also constituted an eligibility criterion (Auspos, Cave, Doolittle, & Hoerz, 1989).

The foregoing illustrations concern what can be regarded nominally as a single target population. At times, the program under investigation will have several distinct targets. Each must be defined explicitly for randomized controlled field test. Each requires the construction of eligibility criteria. Each may constitute a stratum or block in the design of the experiment.

For example, the Supported Work Program involved a 5-year effort to determine effects of a program that involved crew-based training and close supervision over a period of 8 to 12 months. The initial target population, individuals with severe employment problems, was judged too broad to be useful in a policy study. Four target populations, all involving unemployed individuals, appeared to be justified: women receiving Aid to Families With Dependent Children, adult former addicts, adult former offenders, and 17-20-year-old high school dropouts. In effect, the research involved four experiments, one for each target, undertaken in multiple sites (Manpower Demonstration Research Corporation, 1980; Hollister et al., 1984).

The choices of eligibility criteria and units of randomization have technical implications for design of the study. Stringent criteria, for example, usually result in a sample that is less heterogeneous than one would obtain with broad criteria. This homogeneity increases statistical power; that is, differences among the treatments' effects will be easier to discern. On the other hand, very restrictive eligibility criteria could result in a target population that is relatively small and idiosyncratic. Other things being equal, small sample size will impede the detection of differences.

STATISTICAL POWER

Definition

Consider a hypothetical situation in which an adult literacy program actually works to improve reading and writing skills but defensible evidence on effectiveness has not been collected. Suppose that a field experiment is undertaken to estimate the program's effect and that a sample of eligible individuals is drawn and allocated randomly to the program and to a control group, for whom the program is delayed.

One might expect such a study to show the program's effect if it was conducted properly. In fact, however, even a perfectly run study of an effective program will, at times, produce results that show a negligibly small effect, or no effect, or even a negative effect. The likelihood of uncovering the program's effect will be high if the statistical power of the study is sufficient.

The reason for the range of possible outcomes—a finding of no difference, and so forth—is that individuals and other units of analysis vary. As a consequence, the average difference between treatment groups also will vary. For example, any given sample of individuals may be assigned randomly in numerous different combinations to the treatment and control groups. Any given combination will produce a slightly different result from other combinations because of this variability. This is true despite the program being effective on average across all possible combinations of individuals who make up the groups.

The purpose of statistical power analysis is to take this variability into account. More specifically, it is to ensure that the study is sufficiently sensitive so that real differences among treatments will be detected very frequently. Put simply, statistical power in this context refers to the probability of detecting differences among treatments in the sample at hand.

This probability, a calculable number, depends on the supposition that the treatments would indeed differ in their impact had they each been applied to all eligible members of the target population. It depends also on characteristics of the study design, including sample size, that are considered below.

Inadequate Power in Laboratory and Field Studies

Studies of the kind typically reported in scholarly research journals over a period of about 20 years often have been characterized by low statistical power. Reviews of such work have been undertaken by Lipsey (1990), Polit and Sherman (1990), and Cohen (1992), among others. Lipsey (1990), for example, suggested that fewer than 7 out of 10 such studies are sufficiently powerful to detect differences of even moderate size; most such tests are not powerful enough to detect small differences. Cohen (1992), a vigorous proponent of research designs that have adequate power, relied on contemporary evidence to argue that there has been little material improvement in many researchers' attentiveness to issues of statistical power over the last two decades or so.

Controlled field experiments that are the focus of this book have not been exempt from the problem. The small samples used in research on new employment and training projects during the 1970s, for example, involved low power. They were arguably not sufficient to learn about small but important differences in the effectiveness of alternative approaches (Gueron, 1985; Betsey t al., 1985). Similarly, randomized clinical trials of medical interventions have, at times, been characterized by studies that had sample sizes too small to have a good chance of uncovering the more effective approaches (Committee on Evaluating Medical Technologies in Clinical Use, 1985; Meinert, 1986).

To judge from controlled tests in the public policy arena during the late 1980s and 1990s, however, and from earlier exceptional studies cited in this monograph, the interest in statistical power has become more conscientious. This results partly from the realization, among those who design the studies, that it is sensible to expect only modest improvements to come about as a result of efforts to improve. "Big bang" effects are rare. A finding of "no difference," in the sense that no one treatment appears to work better than another, is a real prospect. There are other reasons why contemporary experiments are better designed with respect to their sensitivity. A class of these is discussed next.

Resources for Statistical Power Analysis

In recent years, the task of designing controlled field experiments that are sufficiently powerful on statistical grounds has been simplified. Research journal articles, for example, show how the sample size and other parameters in the study can be chosen so as to ensure power in research in mental health and health services (Arkin & Wachtel, 1990; Rosenbaum, 1987), psychology and education (Cohen, 1992), and other areas. The topic is handled in textbooks by Kraemer and Thiemann (1987) and Cohen (1988). Lipsey's (1990) volume is distinctive in relying heavily on meta-analyses of large groups of studies from a variety of discipline areas to guide the power calculations.

Personal computers ease the task of understanding power. Some of the pertinent computer programs have been reviewed by Goldstein (1989). Ex-Sample (Brent, Mireilli, & Thompson, 1993) for example, is an expert system designed for clinical trials and surveys in medicine. It is no less useful for designing experiments in education, social work, and the behavioral and social sciences. Borenstein and Cohen's (1990) power program is a fine adjunct to contemporary textbooks on statistical power analysis.

The Experiment's Design
and Statistical Power

Put more precisely, statistical power in controlled experiment is defined as

- the probability of rejecting a specified null hypothesis, for example, that two treatment groups do not differ,
- when the null hypothesis is tested against a specific alternative hypothesis, for example that the group difference is of a specific magnitude, and subject to specific variation,
- using a particular statistical test and reference distribution, such as Student's t and significance criterion (such as an alpha level of .01), and
- based on a specific experimental design and sample size.

The following material summarizes the ways to ensure that the study has sufficient statistical power based on these factors.

Effect Size. The size of the true mean difference in how individuals (or organizational units) respond to alternative treatments affects statistical power. To the extent that this difference is large, it is more likely to be detected in an experiment. That is, the statistical power of any formal test of the null hypothesis that treatments do not differ is higher when the actual differences in the effects of the treatments are large. The variability of individuals or of institutions that are assigned to alternative regimens also affects effect size and, therefore, power. For example, to the extent that variance among schools is large, a study that is designed to compare two different school-based strategies for reducing students' health risks might be low in power. The high variability from school to school in the sample of schools reduces the likelihood of detecting real differences among the strategies in formal statistical tests.

In the design of randomized experiments, information about both expected variance and expected differences among the treatments is used in choosing sample sizes for the groups being compared. The information usually is combined to produce a standard index that is related to the particular statistical tests planned for the comparison. For example, a common index for a simple two-group comparison is $(\mu_1 - \mu_2)/\sigma$, where $(\mu_1 - \mu_2)$ is the expected mean difference between groups, σ is the expected variance within groups, and the reference distribution for the statistical test is the Student t.

Contemporary texts on statistical power in the behavioral and social sciences and education denominate this index as effect size (ES). Cohen (1992), for example, presents indices of effect size for a variety of statistical tests and their reference distributions (F, chi-square, and so on). The use of this index, together with other parameters, in selecting sample size for a field study is described below.

In disciplines apart from the social sciences, related indices have been used to the same end. For example, Bowman and Kastenbaum (1975) presented tables for sample-size selection in factorial experiments based on "standardized maximum difference" among means. Work in some of the physical and biomedical sciences uses a less easily interpreted index—the noncentrality parameter—in developing estimates of power based on different study designs and sample sizes (Goldstein, 1989).

Neither the true differences among treatments nor the variance is known in advance of the experiment. They bear on a study that has not yet been done. To ensure adequate statistical power in a study, the differences and variability must be guessed. Several sources of information generally are used to produce a set of magnitude guesses.

First, pilot tests that precede the main study or an independent earlier study often can serve as a basis for enhancing the power of a new experiment. For example, the design of the multisite evaluations of Supported Work Programs, including power calculations, relied on data generated in an earlier test mounted by New York's Vera Institute (Hollister, 1984). Similarly, the sample sizes chosen for studies in each of six sites that engaged in the SARP experiments on police handling of domestic violence depended on an earlier study to inform each new experiment's design (Garner et al., 1995).

A second major source of information about what one can reasonably expect in a controlled experiment is a meta-analysis, that is, a quantitative summary of the results of earlier field tests. For example, Light, Singer, and Willett (1990) summarized a half dozen meta-analyses of research in higher education, in the interest of showing how to design sufficiently powerful evaluations in that arena. Their summary suggests that the mean effect size ranges from about .1, based on testing programs designed to enhance persistence in college, to about .5, based on evaluations of person-alized instruction systems.

Similarly, Cordray and Orwin (1983) consolidated work on psycho-therapy effectiveness studies to develop the results presented in Table 4.1. The designer of an evaluation to test a particular therapeutic approach relative to a control condition would learn from the table that effect sizes of less than 1.00 are very common, occurring about 70% of the time. Indeed, more than half of earlier experiments appear to have resulted in effect sizes of .70 or less. Effect sizes in the range .70-1.00 are considered large. For the pragmatist, expecting a large effect and designing the field test to detect only these effects then would be unwise.

Lipsey's (1990) text on statistical power in experiments extends work of the kinds described above. He provides information on nearly 200 meta-analyses in dozens of program areas, information that can be exploited in an experiment's design. The text also provides a discussion of alternative indicators of effect size.

Type I Errors. Differences among treatment groups will be found at times, despite the fact that treatments are equally effective, simply because of normal variability from one experiment to the next in the groups that are randomly constituted. A Type I error is the finding of a significant difference among treatments in a particular study sample when in fact the difference is a function of chance.

The probability of finding a significant difference in the sample at hand, when treatments do not really differ in their effects, is a real prospect. It can be controlled by the experiment's designer. In particular, the designer specifies a value for the probability of Type I error, the probability of finding a difference when the treatments are equally effective.

TABLE 4.1

Distribution of Effect Sizes in Smith, Glass, and
Miller Meta-Analysis of Psychotherapy Effectiveness Studies (N = 1,766)

Effect Size	Cumulative Proportion	Effect Size	Cumulative Proportion
−.50	.02	1.10	.75
−.40	.03	1.20	.78
−.30	.04	1.30	.81
−.20	.06	1.40	.83
−.10	.08	1.50	.86
0	.11	1.60	.88
.10	.16	1.70	.89
.20	.20	1.80	.90
.30	.25	1.90	.91
.40	.32	2.00	.92
.50	.39	2.10	.93
.60	.46	2.20	.93
.70	.54	2.30	.94
.80	.60	2.40	.96
.90	.66	2.50	.96
1.00	.71		

SOURCE: Adapted from "Improving the Quality of Evidence: Interconnections Among Primary
Evaluation, Secondary Analysis, and Quantitative Synthesis," Cordray and Orwin, © copyright 1983
by Sage Publications, Inc.
NOTE: The table can be read as follows. As an example, the effect size of −.10 shows a cumulative
proportion of .08; in other words 8% of the effect sizes found in this sample of studies were negative
(the program tested had negative effects). As another example, in slightly more than half the studies
(54%), the effect size was .70 or less.

The probability of Type I errors typically is set at .01, .05, or .10 by
designers for formal statistical tests of the null hypothesis that treatments
do not differ in their effectiveness. Other thresholds may be chosen depending on the particular experimental design and the nature of the decisions
that the designer seeks to make. To the extent that the probability of Type
I error is set high, say at .05 or .10, the power of the experiment is greater
than in the case in which the probability is set at .01.

Sample Size and Statistical Power. Statistical power depends heavily
on the number of individuals (or other units) assigned to the treatments
that are under investigation. Roughly speaking, the smaller the samples
within each treatment group, the less likely it is that the experiment will

detect subtle or even moderate differences in the effectiveness of the treatments.

Consider a study designed to determine whether counseling offenders or arresting offenders in misdemeanor domestic violence cases leads to fewer subsequent domestic assaults. Suppose that cases are assigned randomly to one or the other treatment and tracked over time to determine the proportion of individuals in each group that desist from later assaultive behavior. How many cases would be required for each group? The answer, for the study's designer, depends partly on suppositions about the factors that influence power and were described above. To be specific, suppose that a formal statistical test based on a chi-square reference distribution will be undertaken to determine if the recidivism rates differ remarkably. Suppose further that it is understood, from earlier work, that the ambient recidivism rates have been about 60% among arrestees and that it is important to determine whether the counseling results in reducing the recidivism rate to 50%. Finally, suppose that the alpha criterion level is .025.

Table 4.2 summarizes the sample size needed in each of two treatment groups that are of the same size in order to achieve statistical power of .85 and .80 in a formal analysis under these suppositions. For a power level of .85, 444 cases in each group are necessary. If a higher probability of failing to detect a difference is tolerable and power is then fixed at .80, then 387 cases are necessary in each group.

The rates given for recidivism, 60% and 50%, constitute a worst case scenario relative to statistical power standards. When rates of an outcome such as recidivism fall well outside the 40%-60% range, one can achieve high statistical power with much smaller sample sizes. For example, if recidivism rates of 75% and 85% can be expected for the two treatments, then only 250 cases are required for each group to obtain a formal test with statistical power of .80.

Table 4.2 was developed for studies in which the outcome variable of interest is binary, for example, whether an individual commits a crime. In many experiments, measures of continuous variables are obtained, such as for wages, achievement test scores, or severity of illness. Consider a study to evaluate the effect of a new therapy relative to a conventional one, when the response variable of interest is level of depression. The study's designer, in seeking to ensure that the test has sufficient statistical power, may tentatively propose that a small effect size (ES) of .20 is important to discover in an experiment that involves a simple comparison of the mean level of depression of the two treatment groups following treatment. With a significance level set at .01 for a conventional statistical test based on the Student t distribution, the experiment's designer can capitalize on tables

TABLE 4.2

Sample Size Required in Each Group for Comparing
Two Proportions, P_1 and P_2, With Statistical Power
of .85 (upper triangle) and .80 (lower triangle)

P_1					Proportion P_2				
	.95	.90	.85	.80	.75	.70	.65	.60	.55	.50
.95	498	160	86	56	40	30	24	19	16
.90	434	786	228	114	70	49	36	28	22
.85	140	685	1038	286	138	83	56	40	31
.80	75	199	904	1254	336	158	93	62	44
.75	49	99	250	1093	1434	376	174	101	66
.70	35	62	120	293	1249	1578	408	186	106
.65	27	43	72	138	328	1375	1686	430	194
.60	21	31	49	81	152	356	1469	1758	444
.55	17	24	35	54	88	162	375	1532	1794
.50	14	19	27	38	58	93	169	387	1563

SOURCE: Adapted from "How Many Patients Are Necessary to Assess Test Performance?", Arkin and Wachtel, © copyright 1990 by the *Journal of the American Medical Association 263*(2) pp. 275-278. Reprinted by permission.
NOTE: Tabled values are based on the assumption of a one-tailed test at alpha = .05 and a two-tailed test at alpha = .025. Entries in the upper triangle give sample size per group required to detect a difference between p_1 and p_2 with power of .85. Entries in the lower triangle give sample size per group for power of .80. For example, each group in an expeiment that compares two treatment groups must engage 328 individuals if the object is to detect a difference of .65 versus .75 with power of .80 in a given study.

such as those given by Cohen (1992) or the related PC-based programs to make decisions about the necessary sample size. An excerpt from the tables, pertaining to a statistical power of .80, is given in Table 4.3.

The table implies that nearly 600 individuals per group are necessary to be reasonably confident of discerning an effect size of .20, that is, a small difference between treatment outcomes. Larger effects are easier to uncover; for example, only about 40 units in each treatment group are required when the effect size is .80. If the research can tolerate higher levels of Type I errors, indexed by increasing levels of alpha (α), the required sample size decreases. If one expects a large effect (ES = .80) and a 10% rate of falsely declaring that there are effects is tolerable ($\alpha = .10$), then a sample of 20 in each group is sufficient.

Static tables on statistical power, of the sort that must be used in a book, will continue to be useful in a variety of settings. Readers who have access to personal computers will find it productive, however, to rely on software

TABLE 4.3

Statistical Power As a Function of Alpha Level, Effect Size,
and Number of Units in Each of Two Treatment Groups

	$\alpha = .01$			$\alpha = .05$			$\alpha = .10$		
Effect Size =	.20	.50	.80	.20	.50	.80	.20	.50	.80
N =	586	95	38	393	64	26	310	50	20

NOTE: The table is based on the power of a simple t test of the hypothesis of no difference between the means of two independent groups. Effect size is defined, for this test, as (M1 − M2)/σ, and where M1 − M2 is the guessed difference between the mean outcomes of two treatments and σ is the variance within each treatment group. N is the number of units assigned to each of two treatment groups. The α level represents the probability of a Type I error.

programs of the sort described earlier. The major benefit of these programs lies in their dynamic character. One can, in a little time, command the program to tell the reader what sample size is sufficient in a variety of scenarios.

Relevance, Reliability, and Validity of Observations. Statistical power is increased to the extent that measures of the outcome variables in an experiment are relevant, valid, and reliable. Random errors in measurement, for example, reduce reliability in a conventional psychometric sense and degrade one's ability to detect differences among treatments. Low validity in tests of academic achievement, inventories of social adjustment, or other outcome measures will result in data that do not accurately reflect what the participants in an experiment understand or do. This also reduces statistical power. Finally, the measures of outcomes that one might choose may be irrelevant to treatments or at least have a dubious relation to the treatment's objectives.

Chapter 7, on observation and measurement, considers the matter of how to reduce and describe the measurement error. Here, the focus is on two brief illustrations that show how random fallibility in data affects the statistical power of the study. The first, based on Rosenbaum (1987), involves count data. The second, based on Light et al. (1990), is in an educational context and involves measures on a continuous scale of academic achievement. Rossi and Freeman (1989) provided related illustrations in the broad context of program evaluation.

Consider first a simple comparison of the outcome proportions observed for two treatment groups. Suppose that measures of recidivism in a criminal justice experiment are imperfect and that misclassification of recidivism may occur in two ways. First, individuals who have committed an offense

TABLE 4.4

The Effect of Random Misclassification on the Sample Size Required
to Detect a Difference Between 30% Response on the Control Treatment
(Mediation) and 60 Response on the New Treatment (Arrest)

Probability That a Nonassault Will Be Misclassified As an Assault	Probability That an Assault Will Be Misclassified As Nonassault		
	0%	10%	20%
0%	49	58	70
10%	60	75	95
20%	74	97	131

SOURCE: Adapted from "A Nontechnical Introduction to Statistical Power and the Control of Bias," Rosenbaum, © copyright 1987 by National Institute of Mental Health. Used by permission. Random misclassification is assumed to occur at the same rate in two treatment groups. Entries in the table are sample sizes required in each group to achieve power of .80 in testing the null hypothesis of no difference between groups using a two-tailed test at the .05 level. For example, when the misclassification in each group is 10%, samples of about 75 individuals per group are required in a given study to be confident of detecting 30% versus 60% true difference in the treatment effects.

may go undetected or their offense may go unreported. For example, the individual who is arrested in a controlled experiment following an assault may later engage in an assault, but the assault is misclassified. That is, the offender is recorded as not having made an assault. The probability of the misclassification over all assailants may vary. Table 4.4 assumes rates of 0%, 10%, and 20%. Similarly, individuals who were initially arrested and who did not engage in an assault later may be improperly classified as having done so. The victim's memory of an incident, for example, may be such that the victim erroneously recalls an assault outside the time frame to which the interviewer directs attention. The table posits values of false positive claims of 0%, 10%, and 20%; for example, 20% of nonassailants may be mistakenly classified as assailants.

Table 4.4 assumes that there is a large true difference between recidivism of the counseled (30%) and that of the arrested (60%). Suppose this difference would appear if the entire population were studied and measurement was perfect, and that the conventional statistical test is two-tailed at the .05 level, for the sample and experiment at hand. The entries in the table are sample sizes needed to reject the null hypothesis of no difference between the groups with power of .80 for the formal statistical test. With no misclas-

TABLE 4.5
How Many Individuals Are Needed When
Measurement Is Not Perfectly Reliable?

	Anticipated Effect Size (ES)								
	ES = .20 Reliability =			ES = .50 Reliability =			ES = .80 Reliability =		
Statistical Power	.60	.80	1.00	.60	.80	1.00	.60	.80	1.00
.90	1,754	1,316	1,052	282	212	170	112	84	68
.80	1,312	984	786	212	160	128	84	64	52
.70	1,032	774	620	166	126	100	66	50	40

SOURCE: Adapted by permission of the publisher from *By Design: Planning Research on Higher Education* by R. J. Light, J. D. Singer, & J. B. Willett, Cambridge, Mass: Harvard University Press, copyright © 1990 by the President and Fellows of Harvard College.
The table is based on calculations for a two-tailed *t* test of differences between two independent groups at a significance level of .05. Effect size (ES) is a standardized index of expected difference between groups; it is defined in the text. As an example of the meaning of the table values, when the expected difference between treatments is small (ES = .20) and reliability of measurement is perfect (1.00), a sample of 1,052 individuals is needed to achieve a power level of .90. Almost twice as many individuals are needed in the sample (1,754) when the reliability is .60.

sification, 49 cases per group are required. With a high probability of misclassification in both groups, 20%, the required sample size almost triples to 131 per group. Even "low" false positive and false negative rates of 10% increase the required sample size by a factor of 1.5, to 75.

Consider as a second illustration Table 4.5. The table shows the total sample size that is required in both treatment groups to achieve a specified level of power in testing a formal hypothesis that there is no difference in mean achievement of college students engaged in a special program and those involved in ordinary college experience. The significance level is fixed at .05 for a simple two-tailed Student's *t* test. Embodied in the table are different levels of reliability in measuring the response variable of interest, achievement as measured by some standardized test. The reliability levels range from a low of .60 to a high of 1.00.

When the effect of the program is "small" (.20) but measurement reliability is at the high level (1.00), nearly 400 individuals are required in each group to attain a statistical power level of .80. That is, the minimum total sample size is 786. More students would be needed for the study if higher power is required. More than 500 students per group would be engaged if the experiment's designer wished to ensure that the chance of detecting the difference is 9 out of 10. If reliability of measurement is low (.60), the sample size needed to achieve power of .80 increases notably; a sample size of more than 600 is required in each group.

The effect of random measurement error on the likelihood of discerning differences is also appreciable if the true difference between two treatments is moderate (.50). When measurement quality is very high (1.00), slightly more than 60 students are needed in each group if the experimenter wishes to be reasonably confident of detecting a difference, that is, the power level is .80. When measurement reliability falls to .60, more than 100 students must be engaged in each group to reach the same confidence with a moderate treatment difference.

PIPELINE STUDY

Definition

A pipeline study directs attention to how, why, and when individuals may be included in the experiment or excluded, and to the number of individuals who may enter or exit the study at any given point. In planning the controlled studies that were part of the Spouse Assault Replication Program, for example, the principal investigators tried to understand how domestic calls came to the attention of police and could be screened for eligibility for the experiment, and how the case flow varied over time and conditions.

In the most basic form of a pipeline study, one might scout a site prior to planning an experiment. The information so acquired may be sufficient to abandon the idea of mounting a controlled field study in the site on account of the small case flow. Indeed, such an effort led to the rejection of some sites and to the adoption of Milwaukee as the preferred site by one scholar involved in the Spouse Assault Replication Program (Sherman et al., 1992). There are many uses for a full-blown pipeline study beyond ensuring statistical power, however, and they are considered next.

Rationale

In the Spouse Assault Replication Program, understanding how and how many cases of domestic violence came to the attention of police was important to justifying community or research interest in the topic. For example, knowing how many telephone calls were made to a police department and eventually were classified as domestic calls was important to obtaining an estimate of the incidence of domestic violence. It was important to learn about the various ways that a call will be classified as "domestic" by the police communications personnel. Similarly, understanding how many calls, initially described as "domestic," were later found to involve no violence helped to avoid naive political argument that the problem was more severe than it in fact was.

A second rationale for a pipeline study is implied by the aphorism given at the beginning of this chapter. In particular, a common finding in field tests of programs is that the target population is smaller or more difficult to reach than was anticipated. A common result is that the experiment takes more time to complete than was planned. The type of information is important in developing statistical power calculations and in other aspects of the experiment's design. For example, when police departments in six sites initiated randomized tests of different ways to handle domestic violence in the SARP, only two sites produced the number of cases needed in the time frame that was planned. The experiments in other sites had to be extended over time to ensure adequate sample sizes.

A third rationale for a pre-experiment pipeline study is good management of the experiment. Certain supervisors or officers in a police district, for example, might take a stronger interest than others in providing cases for a field experiment, or the department's communications center may not be well enough trained to identify relevant domestic cases accurately. To the extent that such upstream factors can be identified, then the management of the flow of cases into the field experiment can be improved.

Producing a good statistical description of how individuals come to participate in the programs that are compared in an experiment is essential to communicating the study's results. This description also facilitates efforts by independent investigators to replicate the experiment; the careful definition of flow rates and influences on them can be exploited and perhaps controlled in similar ways in other settings. For scholars with an interest in replicating earlier experiments, and in understanding why replication is imperfect or misguided, such description is important. The Garner et al. (1995) critique of the multisite SARP experiments could not, for example, take the pipeline studies into account partly because the studies were insufficiently uniform.

Finally, pipeline studies also can be expected to facilitate the analysis of multisite experiments. That is, remarkably different pipeline processes in different sites may lead to different results in otherwise identical experiments. For example, pipeline studies would help to explain the extent to which various kinds of eligibility requirements (e.g., spouse only versus couples living together) restrict flow rate and limit the generalizability of a given experiment's findings. These local limits do not affect the internal

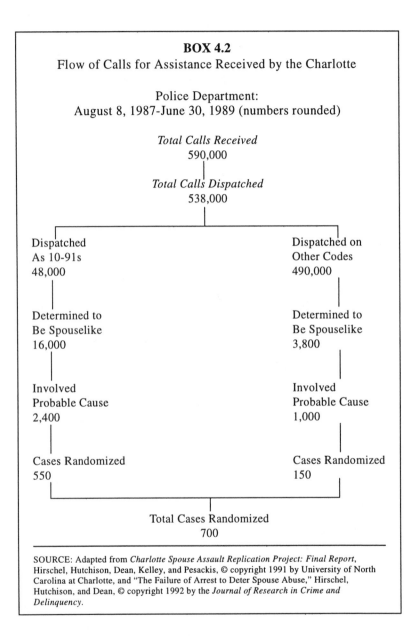

BOX 4.2

Flow of Calls for Assistance Received by the Charlotte

Police Department:
August 8, 1987-June 30, 1989 (numbers rounded)

Total Calls Received
590,000

Total Calls Dispatched
538,000

Dispatched
As 10-91s
48,000

Dispatched on
Other Codes
490,000

Determined to
Be Spouselike
16,000

Determined to
Be Spouselike
3,800

Involved
Probable Cause
2,400

Involved
Probable Cause
1,000

Cases Randomized
550

Cases Randomized
150

Total Cases Randomized
700

SOURCE: Adapted from *Charlotte Spouse Assault Replication Project: Final Report*, Hirschel, Hutchison, Dean, Kelley, and Pesackis, © copyright 1991 by University of North Carolina at Charlotte, and "The Failure of Arrest to Deter Spouse Abuse," Hirschel, Hutchison, and Dean, © copyright 1992 by the *Journal of Research in Crime and Delinquency*.

validity of the local experiment. Comparisons will be fair if members of the selected sample are randomly allocated to alternative treatments.

An Illustrative Pipeline Study

The "ideal" pipeline study, in a study of police approaches to handling assault cases, would begin with all assaults, reported tolice and other - wise, and trace the process of how and when reports are made, of how cases are diverted or discovered to be ineligible at various times, and of how eligible cases enter the criminal justice system at various times.

The illustration given in Box 4.2 is based on the experience of the Charlotte Police Department over a 2-year period (Hirschel et al., 1991; Hirschel, Hutchison, & Dean, 1992). It is less than ideal but is instructive. The box invites the experiment's designer to attend to

- total calls received,
- total calls for which police were dispatched to the scene, given that a call was received,
- calls dispatched as domestic violence cases (10-91s), given that they were dispatched,
- calls found to be of a domestic violence case, given that they were dispatched as domestic violence,
- domestic violence cases found to involve "probable cause evidence" to believe the law had been violated, and
- cases actually randomized, given all the above.

Good pipeline studies usually incorporate qualitative observations. In principle, at least, learning about how and why some people behave can help to inform the design of treatments and the interpretation of the experiment. The benefit is likely to be in avoiding the premature narrowing of the focus of either (Fetterman, 1989).

Other Examples and Variations

Partial pipeline studies appear, at times, in the research reports on clinical trials of new medical devices, procedures, and drugs. Variations also appear in reports on social experiments.

Most medical experiments involve identifying a target group, determining the eligibility of individuals in the group, and eliciting their cooperation. Data on these three features are relevant to any pipeline study. Research reports on these clinical trials frequently have reported such information. The Canadian National Breast Screening Study (Barnes, 1984), for example, tried to identify target populations of professional women and to elicit their cooperation in a variety of ways. Letters to all the women who were thought to be eligible resulted in more than 120 letters being sent on average for each appointment that was actually made by a woman for breast screening, a "hit rate" of less than 1%. Follow-up studies of women who declined to be screened for cancer were undertaken to determine why they had refused. As one might expect, reasons vary considerably from "regular checkup already" (30%) to "too busy, uninterested" (17%); some women were found ineligible (11%).

The reasons for refusal to participate in an experiment, or to be incorporated in the pipeline that feeds into an experiment, may also lie with service providers. A clinical trial for breast cancer (Taylor, Margolese, & Soskolne, 1984), for example, investigated some of the reasons why 35% of physicians refused to refer patients to the trial. Those refusing to do so reported concerns about patient/doctor relations in a clinical trial (73%), trouble with informed consent (38%), and dislike of open discussion about uncertainty (23%). Other medical examples are not hard to find.

The Seattle and Denver Income Maintenance Experiment was designed to understand how various levels of income support affect work effort and other activities of the recipients. The pipeline data given in Table 4.6 from the Seattle research are detailed, covering the stage from the initial search for eligible households through the stage of enrolling individuals in the program (Murarka & Spiegleman, 1978; Christopherson, 1983).

Pipeline, Power, and
Insufficient Sample Size

Experiments fail to be implemented well, at times, because the experiment's designer made incorrect presumptions about the number of individuals in need of treatment or who were eligible for treatments and available. The problem has occurred in randomized tests of employment and training programs over two decades (Rossi, 1969; Betsey et al., 1985). The presumption that there are many who are in need and know it also has been unfounded in medical screening experiments designed to detect and reduce the incidence of breast cancer (Barnes, 1984). Because the number of domestic violence cases reported to police is large, local experiments to evaluate different approaches to handling such cases have assumed that the flow of cases is large when, in fact, it is moderate or even small, depending on the local context.

The pipeline study outlined in Box 4.2 illustrates one form of the problem in an experiment on approaches to police handling domestic violence cases in SARP. The study in Charlotte was initiated partly because the number of such cases was thought to be large. One would be led to

TABLE 4.6

Sample Selection in the Seattle and
Denver Income Maintenance Experiments

	Initial Listing	Supplementary Listing	Total
Housing units attempted	24,168	11,856	36,024
Vacant	2,383	1,129	3,512
Occupied units	21,785	10,727	32,512
Refused	3,076	2,276	5,352
Uncompleted	2,042	1,560	3,602
Terminated	8,224	5,208	13,432
Completed interviews	8,443	1,683	10,126
Ineligible	3,145	0	3,145
Eligible	5,298	1,683	6,981
Selected for pre-enrollment interviewing	5,298	1,683	6,981
Moved	521	0	521
Refused	443	0	443
Ineligible	789	0	789
Not completed	413	0	413
Completed interviews	3,132	1,683	4,815
Assigned to enrollment			2,452
Moved			244
Refused			125
Ineligible			84
Not completed			46
Total enrolled			1,953

SOURCE: Reconstructed from tables in "Sample selection in the Seattle and Denver Income Maintenance Experiment," Murarka and Spiegleman, © copyright 1978 by SRI International.

believe from police records that numerous cases would be available in an experiment because the number of calls denominated as "domestic" is large (48,000 each month). The number of cases that were discovered on site to involve spouselike relations can also be regarded as large (16,000 each month). Both the pilot stage research and the pipeline study in the experiment helped to better anticipate the actual available sample size, to uncover influences on the flow of offenders into the system, and to ensure adequate statistical power.

The reasons why some experiments do not engage sufficiently large samples may lie with failure to undertake scouting research, pilot stage work, or a pipeline study. They also may lie in a failure to recognize that a roughly defined target in any given experiment usually will be, on account of eligibility criteria, smaller than the actual target population. That is, many individuals in a roughly defined population may not meet legal, policy, or design requirements. Box 4.2, for example, suggests that of 16,000 domestic disputes each month, only 2,400 were eligible for the SARP experiments because "probable cause" evidence to believe that a misdemeanor crime had been committed was absent.

Mistaken assumptions about the size of a group that is purported to be in need of treatment and available for a study are based at times on public exaggeration of the need for services. Inflated claims about the number of domestic assaults, about the number of women in need of nutritional assistance, about the number of homeless persons, and so forth may increase the likelihood of support for relevant programs. They also may be misleading indicators of what happens in the field, to judge from Rossi and Freeman (1989), among others. They may also mislead the design of an experiment.

Despite a pipeline study prior to an experiment, the flow of target individuals for the randomized controlled field test may be constricted. This is especially likely in settings that are unstable. Local support for an experiment that compares different programs, for example, might change with changing political administrations. Regardless of what causes a con-striction in the case flow to an experiment, common approaches to ensuring an adequate sample are

- extending the time frame for the experiment,
- intensifying outreach to identify and engage target group members, and
- altering some eligibility requirements.

Extending the study's time frame is a tactic that was used in the SARP experiments, in the Rockefeller Foundation's tests of training programs for minority female single parents, and others. It is often reasonable. Resources available to do so, including the patience of the organizations responsible for delivering services, are likely to be limited, however, and the study sponsor's need for information in time for such things as legislative decisions may be critical. These factors put bounds on the time available for any extension and must then be taken into account as the experiment proceeds.

Intensifying outreach efforts to engage target group members in the experiment is not an uncommon tactic. It is one that has been used in most studies that encountered difficulty in attaining necessary sample size, such as the Rockefeller experiments on programs for minority female parents (Cottingham, 1991) and the SARP experiments on police handling of domestic violence (Garner et al., 1995), among others. Resources must be diverted to the task, of course. This diversion may incur reduced resources for service delivery, quality control, analysis, or some other feature of the study. Balancing the need to invest in enrolling individuals into an experiment against other needs can be difficult. How to do this well remains unclear because there is little written about the matter.

Altering eligibility requirements solely in the interest of increasing sample size in an experiment can create complex problems. If the new eligibles are, for example, the type of individuals who would not benefit from the treatments being compared, then nothing is gained. If they can benefit but the average treatment effects for them are different from "old" eligibles, then the study design and analysis become more complex, and it is possible that statistical power for assessing major group differences still will be insufficient. Finally, the treatments themselves may have to be altered to handle those who are engaged under new eligibility rules. The tactic must then be used cautiously, if at all.

Terminating a controlled study rarely is a palatable choice for the study's sponsors, the experiment's designers, and other stakeholders. Nevertheless, it might be sensible when the necessary sample size cannot be attained. The resources that then become available can be used to investigate and explain why the difficulties were insurmountable and to understand how a less ambitious (but more feasible) study might be designed. There is no substantial body of literature on the orderly termination of experiments.

5

Randomization Plans and Processes

> *The problem (of youthful violence) is one for which public remedies are most likely to be found by choosing the most obvious issues and tackling them experimentally . . . [T]he commissions of study are likely to be more productive if they can study the effects of practical experimentation.*
>
> —Walter Lippmann, *The Young Criminals* (1963)

This chapter considers randomization procedures in field experiments, addressing questions about when to randomize and how, what entity should be responsible for implementing the procedure, and how to assess its quality. Because random assignment can be and has been subverted, this topic also is discussed.

THE RANDOMIZATION
PROCEDURE AND SEQUENCE

Generally speaking, random assignment must be such that the selection of any individual or entity for a treatment is independent of all other selections, not predictable from earlier ones or later ones, and free of systematic influences that might produce a difference between the groups that are constructed. Operationally, the randomization is done as one step in a sequence of steps.

The sequence begins with the entry of prospective research subjects into the study, continues with their screening and certification of eligibility, and ends with their eventual random assignment to treatments. This process is a natural extension of the pipeline study of client flow discussed in the preceding chapter.

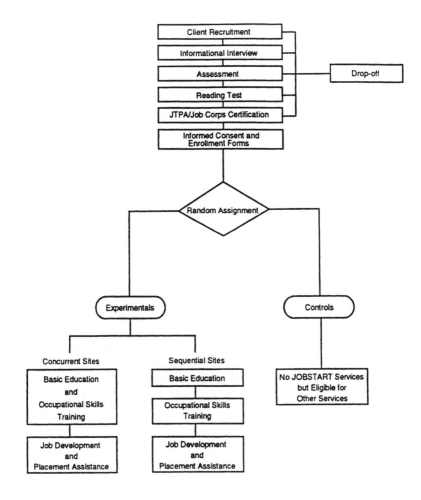

Figure 5.1. The JOBSTART Evaluation Design and Sample Flow

SOURCE: Adapted from *Implementing JOBSTART*, Auspos et al., © copyright 1989 by Manpower Demonstration Research Corporation. Reprinted by permission.
NOTE: Support services such as child care and transportation were offered at both concurrent and sequential sites.

A random assignment plan of the kind illustrated in Figure 5.1 is not uncommon. It was used in a comparative test of JOBSTART, a system for providing occupational skills, basic education, and other services to better the economic well-being of high school dropouts (Auspos et al., 1989). The procedure began with identifying dropouts, informing them about services that are potentially available, and trying to engage them in the research. Preliminary interviews were undertaken with those who sought further information. Their eligibility for the program was determined partly by their meeting government requirements, such as having dropped out of school and being of specific age and income level. Prospective participants in the study then were "certified" as eligible. There was an assessment of their earlier training and reading ability so as to place them properly in training programs. Prior to their random assignment, the prospective trainees were told orally and in writing about the program and the fact that their selection into the program was done by lottery. Their written consent was then sought. Those who chose to provide it were then enrolled in the study.

In the JOBSTART experiment, dropouts were allocated randomly to one of two new treatments under investigation and to a control group having access to conventional community services. The first of the special treatment programs involved an integrated approach to basic education and occupational skill training; the second involved a sequence of basic education followed by training. Determining which approach worked best relative to the control condition was the main object of the study.

A plan of the sort given in Figure 5.1 is the product, of course, of a good deal of effort. It leaves out the tasks that must be performed to actualize it. Box 5.1 summarizes some of these tasks, ones that normally are a part of operations planning and negotiation and the technical design of the study. These tasks include pre-experiment negotiations to determine if indeed random assignment is appropriate and feasible. Decisions must be made about who is responsible for the random allocation of individuals (or entities) to treatments, about the algorithms for generating random assignments, and about the timing of the assignment. Pilot tests or run-in periods may be undertaken to assay the feasibility of the plan. The random assignment procedure, once activated, must be monitored for integrity. Contingency plans may be developed for failures. Finally, plans usually must be developed for termination of the process.

Each task in this series is related to others. For example, determining who will be responsible for doing the random assignment is linked to the need to ensure integrity of the randomization. To motivate attention to these topics, the next section of this chapter discusses examples of the ways in which assignment procedures have been undermined.

BOX 5.1
Sequence in Developing and
Implementation of Randomization

Negotiation on random assignment
Planning/decisions on randomization procedures, timing, and so on
Pilot tests, run-in tests
Activation of randomization procedures
Quality control
Contingency activity
Termination

SUBVERSION OF
RANDOM ASSIGNMENT

The randomization procedure in an experiment can be subverted, just as any other element of an experiment might be undermined. For a high-quality study, it is critical that the procedure's integrity be ensured and that flaws be detectable.

Subversion may occur for a variety of reasons, including "good intentions." For example, in clinical trials on enriched oxygen environments for premature infants, nurses periodically removed infants who had been assigned to the control condition and provided them with the enriched oxygen treatment under the belief that the latter treatment would help infants. Later experiments disclosed, among other problems, that the oxygen treatments caused blindness in many of the children exposed to the high dosage (Silverman, 1977).

Field tests undertaken by Test and Burke (1985) encountered analogous difficulties in evaluating a community approach to caring for the severely mentally ill. The randomization procedure required that hospital admissions staff use sequentially numbered sealed envelopes containing the assignments for each patient. Some staff members evidently departed from the protocol after discovering that a patient whom they judged to be highly symptomatic had been assigned randomly to the community-based service instead of to conventional hospital services. These departures occurred despite the fact that the patients did meet eligibility criteria that had been the subject of earlier negotiation and agreement with staff. The subversion was discoverable partly because envelopes were selected out of numerical order.

In some experiments, the departure from a randomization plan cannot be verified. Rather, evidence on the problem is informal or indirect. In the Minneapolis Domestic Violence Experiment, for example, the randomization procedure involved the officers using a booklet of randomly arranged colored pages, each color indicating the assigned treatment. Red might indicate that the offender was to be arrested, green indicated conventional treatment, and so on. This procedure permitted the officers to anticipate the next offender's assignment. Informal conversations with police officers suggested that they did indeed choose pages out of order to implement the assignment they wanted for the particular offender being handled. The magnitude of this problem appeared to be small but could not be determined precisely (Berk, Smyth, & Sherman, 1988).

Indirect statistical evidence on whether the randomization has been degraded can be generated, at times. For example, Puma and his colleagues (1991) mounted small-scale feasibility tests of a particular assignment procedure to determine how to run a study of a new program for enhancing the nutrition and health status of women, infants, and children. The random allocation was based, in part, on the mothers' social security numbers. Its procedure was designed to produce treatment and control groups of equal size. The local use of the allocation algorithm by program staff during a pilot period resulted in far more women being assigned to the new program group than to the control condition. Perhaps the algorithm was not one that would produce a 50-50 selection rate. More plausibly, the intake workers made mistakes in recording or interpreting the social security numbers; the mistakes were such that the workers were able to channel certain women to the new program. The researchers recommended alternative procedures that were less susceptible to compromise. In particular, a unit independent of the local program was authorized to execute the procedure, based on computer-generated random assignments.

INTEGRITY IN THE RANDOM
ASSIGNMENT PROCEDURE

To judge from the preceding examples and from the history of controlled field experiments it is essential to employ methods to ensure the integrity of the randomization. Integrity depends on the institutional independence of the assignment process, centralized procedures, the timing of eligibility determination and randomization, and a quality control system that includes the registry of departures from random assignment.

Institutional Independence

The random assignment procedure must be independent of the individuals or entities responsible for the delivery of treatments or the analysis of the field experiment's results. The independence is justified simply because integrity of randomization is suspect if the procedure can be compromised. Independence here means satisfying several criteria.

- The service provider or other principals in the field test must not be able to manipulate the generation of the random assignment.
- The service provider or other principals must not be able to anticipate the treatment actually assigned.
- The service provider or other principals must not be able to alter the random assignment.

As a practical matter, these criteria imply that the following methods are not generally acceptable.

- Books or listings of the random assignments that will be used for prospective participants and that are accessible to service providers
- The use of quasi-public numbers, such as social security numbers, that may be known to service providers or others and that invite alteration, tabulation, or anticipation of assignment
- The use of randomization algorithms that permit easy anticipation, such as random assignment of treatment A always being followed by an individual's assignment to treatment B.

The use of coin flips, selection of a card from a stack of playing cards, and similar gaming devices also are inappropriate because of their subvertibility. It takes little skill to manipulate the devices. An equally important reason for rejecting them is that they are known to generate assignments that in practice often do not appear random. For example, the assignments generated by selection of a card from a deck of shuffled cards often are clustered or exhibit patterns more frequently than one would expect by chance alone. The imperfections in coin flipping and other such methods constitute a major reason for depending on computer-based algorithms to generate the random assignments.

In contemporary policy experiments, it has become common to employ institutions that are independent of service delivery to accomplish the randomization. New York City's Career Magnet Schools, for example, accepted some students who were randomly assigned to them and some who were not, the rules governing students' application and acceptance being well documented. The random assignment was done by the Educational Testing Service, an organization that was independent of both Magnet Schools and of the research group employed to estimate the effects of Career Magnet Schools on students (Crain et al., 1992). The randomization algorithm used by the Educational Testing Service was complex in that it took the preferences of the student applicants into account. Nevertheless, it met the standards discussed above in that neither the service providers, the Magnet Schools, nor the researchers could manipulate which students would be assigned to the particular school versus other schools, could not anticipate the assignment, and could not alter it. For similar reasons, independent groups have been given responsibility for the random assignment in tests of methods for police handling of domestic violence (Reiss & Boruch, 1991), transitional employment for the mentally retarded (Bangser, 1985), strategies for reducing crime (Dennis, 1988), and others.

Centralized Assignment and Control

As a practical matter, the responsibility for random assignment usually is centralized, although responsibility for screening prospective research participants and other activities in the assignment sequence may be dispersed. At each site involved in the Spouse Assault Replication Program, for example, police officers telephoned a special unit at their headquarters to announce their encounter of an eligible case and to receive the random assignment of a case to (say) arrest or restoration of order immediately prior to taking further action. The assignment itself was generated by a computer-based algorithm known to produce numbers with random properties.

That the central unit rather than the individual police officer at the scene generated the assignment enhanced integrity. The procedure provided an opportunity for closely monitoring the assignment process and checking on its quality. The approach also reduced the need to train officers in the use of random assignment procedures, a task that would have demanded resources.

The justification for vesting responsibility for random assignment with a single unit lies partly in experience. An important lesson of Conner's (1977) review of field experiments is that controlling the randomization process counted heavily in the success of experiments done in the 1970s. Control has been no less important in medical randomized trials. Nordle and Brantmark (1977), for example, took pains to discuss how plans for randomization in drug effectiveness experiments can be too easily undermined by clinicians involved in the trials. The lack of control over randomization accounts at least partly for failures of television experiments in El Salvador, the Roos, Roos, and McKinley (1977) trials in health services, and the Bickman (1985) tests of nutrition programs for the elderly, among others.

Centralized control has been used in multisite experiments on employment and training programs (Gueron, 1985), statewide studies of the effect of class size on achievement (Finn & Achilles, 1990), corrections program evaluations (Petersilia, 1989), and, as suggested earlier, the evaluations of New York's Career Magnet Schools (Crain et al., 1992). In most such cases, the assignment is made through a telephone or other linkage to the entity responsible for assignments.

Exercising control over random assignment also implies limits on control. The physician's influence over treatment of a patient is displaced, partially and in a sense, when the patient cooperates in a clinical trial. Tension concerning what is perceived to be the service provider's diminished authority has been evident in negotiations over randomized field tests in civil and criminal justice and elsewhere (e.g., Sherman & Berk, 1985). This in turn implies that it is crucial to construct exclusionary rules, defining who is legitimately eligible for treatment and who is not. It is to this topic that we proceed next.

Eligibility Determination and Random Assignment

Whether individuals or other entities are eligible for the treatments in an experiment must be determined prior to their random assignment to the treatments. The main justification for this requirement is that when eligibility is determined after random assignment, the assignment procedure is more vulnerable to subversion. If undetected, this subversion will result in groups that differ systematically; this in turn will result in biased estimates of the treatments' effectiveness.

In the Spouse Assault Replication Program, for example, a purported offender was ineligible for the experiment on alternative police methods of handling domestic disputes if the offender was found to be the subject of a warrant for arrest. The offender on whom a warrant had been issued was arrested immediately.

In one jurisdiction, it was difficult for police to determine, while at the crime scene, whether there was an outstanding warrant. If discovery of a warrant could not be made until after random assignment, then the treatment employed could influence such discovery; that is, the treatment could affect eligibility for the experiment. For example, offenders who were randomly assigned to the arrest condition arguably were more likely to be discovered after arrest to be the subject of a warrant simply because police checks, including a search for warrants, are more thorough when the individual is in the custody of police. The result would be that the group randomly assigned to the arrest condition would differ systematically from the group assigned to a second treatment, restoration of order. That is, the arrest group, after eliminating ineligible offenders, would include more law-abiding citizens than the restoration of order group. Even if both treatments were equal in their effectiveness in reducing recidivism, arrest would then appear to be more effective in reducing crime.

The need to determine the individual's or entity's eligibility for treatments, prior to random assignment, is in the interest of producing a fair test of the effects of different treatments. Its importance has been emphasized in descriptions of tests of programs for individuals with chronic mental illness by Test and Burke (1985), experiments on work and welfare initiatives for welfare-dependent families by Gueron (1985), evaluations of innovative education incentive systems by Bickman (1985), and others.

Timing of the Random Assignment

In most experiments, two time points are critical to the randomization procedure. The first is the point at which determinations are made about which individuals or entities are eligible for each treatment. As suggested above, the individual's eligibility for all treatments should be established prior to random assignment.

The second critical point is just prior to the individual's receipt of a treatment. Good practice suggests that the random assignment be made just before the actual delivery of the treatment that is assigned. There are two reasons for this tactic. First, a long time period between the individuals' random assignment and the treatment's delivery can increase the likelihood of loss of contact with eligible cases. This results in decreased sample size and statistical power. Second, a long time period between random assignment and engagement of treatment provides an opportunity for departures from random assignment; that is, the treatment assigned will not be the one that is delivered. Such departures may be initiated by the prospective participant, the target of assignment, who for example may decide that rather than wait to enter a training program to which he or she has been assigned, he or she will initiate another activity. The departure also may be influenced by the service provider. A police officer who knows that his next misdemeanor violence case has been randomly assigned to arrest will look differently at the offender, and perhaps determine eligibility differently, than if the assignment and delivery are close in time. The officer may "game" the system deliberately or merely be influenced unconsciously by the advance knowledge.

Eligibility determinations, random assignments, and engagement in treatments must, at times, occur in rapid sequence. Such was the case in the Spouse Assault Replication Program: Officers had to establish whether evidence and conditions met criteria and to call for their assignments while at the scene of the crime. The time constraint may be influenced by other burdens of the treatment provider. In a multisite evaluation of intensive supervision for probationers, for example, one site found 25% of the cases to be ineligible on deeper examination. The problem appears to have been attributable to the workload carried by probation case officers who were responsible for screening and for providing service (Petersilia, 1989).

To the extent that the intake into the experiment must be brisk, randomization plans must take this into account. The timeliness of the assignment may be enhanced, for example, by simplifying eligibility determinations, transferring the burden of eligibility determinations to independent staff, or finding ways to expand the time available for the process.

Departure From Assigned Treatments

The treatments that are randomly assigned to individuals or to entities in an experiment will not always be delivered. As a consequence, accurate records on discrepancies are important to understanding how well the experiment has been conducted, how the employment of treatments may be altered under normal (nonexperiment) conditions, how to interpret the experimental results, and how to design better experiments in the future. The evidence on discrepancies usually is statistical. The plausible explanations of discrepancies or their purported causes often are based on qualitative or process-oriented work. Consider some examples.

The police departments that undertook randomized tests of various methods for handling domestic violence under the Spouse Assault Replication Program were conscientious in registering the treatment assigned and the treatment actually delivered. Treatments entailed arrest, restoration of order, citation, or other approaches. More than 85% of the treatments that were randomly assigned in each site were actually applied by police (Dunford, Huizinga, & Elliott, 1990; Hirschel et al., 1991; Sherman et al., 1992). A 10% or 15% rate of discrepancy between treatments assigned and those delivered is high enough to warrant investigation. The difference between assigned and delivered treatments in the Spouse Assault Replication Program was attributable, in some measure, to the offender's violent behavior following the random assignment to certain treatments. For example, an offender who had been randomly assigned to a mediation condition (police restoration of order and departure from the household) might subsequently assault a police officer or further threaten the victim. In such cases, the officers departed from the randomly assigned treatment of "restoration of order." Instead, they arrested the individual.

When the object is to understand whether a mandatory action works to reduce a social problem, such as domestic violence, it is a police officer or an officer of the court who bears responsibility for imposing the treatment. In many field tests, this responsibility is mixed, partly because of the voluntary dimension of a study, and may be borne by the recipient of a service. The individuals scheduled to receive treatment, rather than those responsible for treatment delivery, also influence the departure from random assignment. For example, the Puma et al. (1991) exploratory research on programs for women, infants, and children focused partly on adherence to treatment protocols. The researchers found that women who were assigned initially to one treatment program sometimes found their way into other similar programs that were thought earlier to have been serving clients up to their capacity. The crossover rate was sufficiently high to warrant rethinking the study's design. In particular, the experiment's sponsor and the research team reframed the objectives of the field test. Instead of comparing the existing program to services that may or may not be available in the community, the program was compared to a considerably enhanced version of the program.

PILOT TESTS, RUN-IN STAGES, AND PRECEDENT

Pilot studies often are undertaken prior to a full-blown randomized field experiment when the site characteristics, resources, appropriateness of randomization procedures, and other factors are unclear at the design stage of the experiment. The pilot study may be designed as a stand-alone project with results used in the later decision to mount a larger experiment. The pilot study also may constitute the first stage of a large experiment to which a definite commitment has been made. Pilot tests of the stand-alone kind are infrequent on account of their cost. They nevertheless have been recommended (Riecken et al., 1974). Corsi and Hurley (1979), for example, conducted tests in one city, Denver, to decide that multicity experiments, mounted later in New Mexico, were indeed feasible in assessing telephone-based approaches to administrative hearings on disputes about unemployment and social security payments. As a practical scientific matter, earlier experiments always can be regarded as pilots for a later one, and they are. Rossi and colleagues (1980), for example, mounted field experiments in Texas and Georgia to produce evidence on whether post-prison subsidies for released prisoners actually reduced crime or increased employment. They depended heavily on results of an earlier experiment in Baltimore in designing their studies.

Similarly, a large-scale evaluation of programs to assist disabled individuals in returning to productive employment, sponsored by the U.S. Social Security Administration during the 1990's, was preceded by two smaller-scale studies (Rupp et al., 1994). Both of these latter experiments focused on related target populations and program goals. Each helped to inform randomization procedures for the 1990's experiment, even though they had been completed during the 1980's (Thornton & Decker, 1989; Kerachsky et al., 1985).

Developing a pilot stage prior to the main experiment is sensible if a stand-alone test or the opportunity for serious reconnaissance is absent. In engineering vernacular, this is a "run-in" period for the main test. For example, in the Spouse Assault Replication Program, all sites engaged in some form of run-in testing. A number of problems were uncovered and resolved during the 3-month pilot test, and cases accumulated during the period were discarded for core analyses (Hirschel et al., 1991; Hirschel et al., 1992). In one site, Milwaukee, the pilot period was sufficiently trouble free, in the principal investigator's judgment, that the cases accumulated during this period were included in the final core analyses (Sherman et al., 1992). Similarly, large-scale tests of alternative treatments for handling severely depressed patients were preceded by a pilot/training stage (Collins & Elkin, 1985). It was designed to familiarize the hospital staff with the randomization procedure as well as to provide a period of training to those responsible for treatment. The pilot-stage data were not used in core analysis.

RANDOM NUMBERS AND
RANDOMIZATION ALGORITHMS

Tables of Random Numbers
and Permutations

A variety of textbooks in statistical methods and handbooks for statistics contain tables of random numbers that can be employed in small- to medium-scale field experiments. The textbooks that include tables and instructions on how to use them include Snedecor and Cochran (1989), Winer, Brown, and Michaels (1991), and Rosenthal and Rosnow (1991). Handbooks of statistical tables and formulae include Beyer's (1988) general handbook and Schuster's (1990) tables on design of clinical trials in medicine. Ordinary tables of random numbers repeat integers. This repetition, in some experiments, is awkward. Consequently, Fleiss (1986), among others, has developed tables of random permutations of sets of numbers.

To employ such tables, consider a simple experiment in which two program variations are compared, each variation being provided to roughly the same number, N, of individuals. A simple approach to random allocation is to list the eligible individuals and then turn to a table of random numbers. Moving down an arbitrary column in such a table, assign the first individual to one treatment if the random number is odd and to the other if it is even (counting the random digit 0 as even). The process continues until the last individual is allocated. For three groups, one might follow a similar procedure, assigning each allocation unit as it appears to the first treatment if, in moving down the column, the random digit ends in a 1, to the second if the digit is a 2, and to the third if the digit is a 3, ignoring other numbers. More efficient algorithms are possible and routinely are invented for larger-scale studies.

In field experiments, the numbering of individuals who are assigned to treatment is part of normal accounting. This creates an audit trail to ensure that individuals are indeed identified and randomly assigned. Normally, the random number assigned to any given individual would not be disclosed until the assignment was required. The use of opaque sealed envelopes containing the random number and stamped with a sequential case number is not uncommon.

Machine-Based Algorithms

Machine-based generation of random assignment lists is common and feasible with available software. A spreadsheet program such as Excel 5.0

supports not only statistical analysis of data from controlled tests but also random number generation. Excel 5.0, Quattro Pro, and SPSS, for example, include algorithms for generating random outcomes from a number of independent Bernoulli trials, facilitating random assignment of individuals to treatment or control conditions. The SAS/Stat *User's Guide* (SAS/STAT, 1990) gives command instructions for using random assignment algorithms with simple randomized experiments, involving a two-treatment comparison, and more complex designs (split plot, hierarchical, and incomplete blocks).

Time-Based Algorithms

Certain environments invite the automatic generation of random assignments that are linked to time. For example, eligible cases of domestic violence in police experiments occur episodically over time, and the specific time point can be the basis for randomization. Eligible cases for experiments on new procedures for handling cases in emergency medical settings, in hot line telephone settings, and in school disruption, for example, are characterized by a trickle flow of cases that is marked by the time of their occurrence.

In the Charlotte experiments on police handling of domestic violence, for example, each call made to the police department was entered by the department operator into a computer. The computer automatically registered the time of the call in hours, minutes, and seconds counted from midnight. The seconds digits, regarded as random, were treated mathematically as modulo 3 to generate the random number. That is, the two-digit number was divided by 3. The arithmetic remainder from this division, a 0, 1, or 2, was regarded as random and served as the basis for assigning individual cases to one or another of three treatments employed in the Charlotte experiment. This approach protected the integrity of the random assignment because the time registration is made automatically and prior to the police learning about the specific reason for the call (Hirschel et al., 1992).

Quasi-Public, Quasi-Random Numbers

At times, the ending digits of social security numbers have been used to generate random assignments. The applications that appear best justified are those in which manipulation is not possible and in which the applications can be audited easily. For example, the U.S. Internal Revenue Service has used such numbers in assigning individual taxpayers to alternative administrative treatments to learn about the efficiency of such treatments in handling taxpayer returns (Perng, 1985).

When manipulation in reporting such numbers is possible, or when their ownership is ambiguous, the use of social security numbers is unwise. Economically deprived individuals who are eligible for income support experiments, for example, may have no numbers, or they may have multiple numbers. If there are benefits to altering numbers, they may be altered.

Quality Assurance

Good practice requires that the randomization procedure be monitored for quality. This entails formal statistical analyses of the algorithm used to generate the random assignment. The quality assurance may also involve an oversight group that visits sites to review randomization procedures in each site involved in an experiment. In the Spouse Assault Replication Program, for example, members of the program review team encountered an easily accessible random assignment book in one site that permitted police officers to anticipate assignments. The team discovered a procedure in another site that resulted in a string of random numbers being duplicated each time the police department's computer "went down" and the random number generator was restarted. Both problems were identified early enough to avoid seriously compromising the experiment.

Finally, understanding how well the randomization procedure works normally involves looking at data on the treatment groups that are generated on the basis of the procedures. To put the matter crudely, the groups that are randomly constituted should be similar. It has become common to publish data on baseline characteristics of the groups, in the interest of establishing that they do not differ appreciably prior to treatment. Such data routinely are laid out in reports of experiments on employment and training programs, such as Rupp et al. (1994) and Hollister et al. (1984); in medical clinical trials (e.g., Meinert, 1986); in criminal justice programs in intensive supervision (Petersilia & Turner, 1990) and domestic violence (Sherman et al., 1992; Hirschel et al., 1991); and in other settings.

ARRANGEMENTS FOR
RANDOM ALLOCATION

Individuals or entities may be assigned to treatments singly, or they may be assigned by "blocks," for example five at a time to five treatments, their assignment being at random. The units may be stratified prior to random assignment according to gender or other factors. The possible arrangements vary and depend on how prospective participants appear for treatment, on the particular experimental design, and on nontechnical factors that may constrain the assignment process.

Simple Allocation

Eligible individuals or entities may be assigned randomly to alternative treatments as they appear in a sequence. This approach, a common one, is designated as simple allocation.

The random assignment may be arranged so that the sample size allocated to each treatment is equal. For an experiment involving two treatments, then, the uniform allocation ratio is 1:1. This allocation ratio yields estimates of the mean response to treatments that are equally precise. It is on account of this equal precision that a uniform allocation arrangement generally is recommended.

More generally, the allocation ratio may be fixed such that some treatments are assigned a larger number of participants than others. In experiments that compared an integrated training program against ordinary community services in the Minority Female Single Parent Program, for example, original arrangements called for 2:1 or 3:1 allocation arrangements depending on the program site.

Allocation ratios other than 1:1 are justified on several grounds. One treatment may be considerably more expensive than another, suggesting that when the overall budget is fixed, the less expensive treatment might be employed more frequently. The treatment provider's capacity and interest in efficiency may also be pertinent. For example, some of the community-based organizations responsible for new training approaches in the Minority Female Single Parent Program believed initially that they could provide new intensive service to two-thirds of those who were eligible for the training at any given point in time. This invited a fixed allocation ratio of 2:1 for the new program and the ordinary services respectively. During the course of the experiment, this allocation ratio was revised to 1:1. This was in reaction to unexpected difficulties in identifying and engaging prospective trainees and to a realization that more training was needed than was anticipated.

Blocked Allocation

In a field test that employs a simple random allocation procedure, the number of individuals assigned to each treatment group will differ, on account of chance, over the course of the study. A test involving a target sample of 200 individuals per treatment group might, during the first month, engage 30 people in one group and 20 in the second because the list of random assignments produced this result. The second month's operation might produce a string of assignments such that the imbalance is reversed, for example 60 in the first treatment and 80 in the second.

Imbalances in sample size across treatment groups will disappear over time and become negligible for large samples, but the magnitude of temporary imbalances in a lengthy experiment will be such that making plans to provide treatment services is difficult. For example, a training facility to which individuals have been assigned randomly might at one point in time have too few clients and at a second point have too many.

A procedure usually employed to handle the matter is blocked random allocation. Put briefly, the arrangement requires that individuals first be blocked into groups of two or more, for subsequent random allocation to two or more treatments. The random assignment within a block is such that the same number of individuals is assigned to each treatment.

In a two-treatment test, for example, the eligible individuals could be grouped into blocks of two. The members of each pair are then allocated to treatment 1 or to treatment 2, as a 1-2 combination or a 2-1 combination based on a random selection.

With four treatments, four individuals may constitute a block. Their assignment to treatments is made on the basis of random selection from all possible permutations in assignments, that is, from 24 allocation patterns of the form

1 2 3 4	. . .	4 3 2 1
2 3 4 1		3 2 1 4
3 4 1 2		2 1 4 3
4 1 2 3		1 4 3 2

Equivalently, the selection may be made from a table of random permutations of the sequence 1 2 3 4 generated by contemporary statistical packages or available in published sources such as Cochran and Cox (1950).

Stratified Allocation

Blocked randomization conventionally refers to and prevents imbalances in allocation across all treatments over time, regardless of the characteristics of individuals being assigned (Friedman et al., 1985). Imbalances in the baseline characteristics of individuals will at times be important for operational reasons.

In the Minority Female Single Parent Program tests, for example, eligible women in one site included Hispanics, African Americans, and Caucasians. Periodically, one group or another would be overrepresented in a treatment group. For example, no Hispanics were assigned to the intensive program during a 2-week period; all had been assigned randomly to the control condition, receiving services ordinarily available in the community. Most African American women, on the other hand, had been randomly allocated to the new training program, an enterprise that was regarded as more attractive, although its effectiveness relative to the services provided to the control group was entirely unknown.

One tactic for avoiding imbalances of this kind is denominated as stratified random allocation in the medical trials arena (Friedman et al., 1985; Meinert, 1986). In such a procedure, individuals are first classified as to their membership in a stratum—African American, Hispanic, and so forth. For each stratum, a randomization plan is developed. Individuals are then randomly allocated to the alternative treatments. A 1:1 allocation arrangement within a stratum, for example, would then ensure that the same number of Hispanics would enter the control and treatment groups. A similar random allocation is made within each of the other strata.

In the preceding illustration, the stratified assignment was motivated by a political condition in the field. Random assignment of individuals from a particular ethnic or racial group to one treatment, even over a short time period, generated skepticism about the fairness of the randomization. More generally, stratification is driven by the need to enhance statistical precision. That is, a stratified group of, say, males is more homogeneous than a large group that includes a mixture of males and females. Stratification can increase the statistical power of the analysis.

Incorporating strata into the randomization procedure usually is possible for only a small number of stratification variables, such as ethnic group or gender. This is partly because screening and random assignment in the field must be accomplished briskly. Moreover, when the purpose of stratification is precision, the relevant variables often can be taken into account at the analysis stage, rather than at the design and implementation stage of the study. As long as the data on strata are available and are unchanged by treatment, they can be exploited in a conventional covariance analysis, for example.

**The Special Problem of
a Small Number of Units**

Consider an experiment in which the number of units that are to be assigned to treatments is small. A few high schools willing to engage in special dropout prevention efforts, for example, might be compared to a few other equally willing high schools. Ten high schools might, in such an experiment, be randomly assigned to the special program or to a control group in a 1:1 allocation plan. One may find, following randomization, that all five schools that were assigned to the prevention program contain high concentrations of children from impoverished families, and that those schools assigned to the control condition do not. Such an arrangement can occur as a matter of chance.

This random arrangement, however, is "unsuitable" on its face. That is, the groups differ in an obvious way before the imposition of treatments. They differ in a way that arguably would influence outcomes, making straightforward estimates of the effectiveness of a dropout prevention program difficult or impossible. Inasmuch as using institutions as the unit in experiments is desirable at times, the implications of such arrangements have to be confronted.

Cox (1958) offered three approaches to the problem. One, covered earlier, involves forming the different types of schools into blocks. Each block may constitute pairs of schools matched (say) on poverty level; they are then assigned randomly in a blocked randomization scheme. When such pairs can be constructed beforehand, the matter is straightforward. When only two matched pairs can be constructed with a remaining mismatch, or when the randomization cannot be blocked, the matter is more complicated.

The second approach to an unsuitable randomized arrangement is to rerandomize. Cox (1958) argued that as long as the ineligible configurations are specified beforehand, rerandomization is legitimate. With a small number of units in an experiment, it is possible to enumerate all possible random configurations and, with collateral information, to specify which are unsuitable. The general criteria for rejecting certain configurations, without enumerating all, also might be specified; for example, no given treatment will contain fewer than two high-poverty schools. The basis for elimination must be made clear in the interest of replication and interpretation. The subjectively chosen criteria for choosing unsuitable configurations is a feature that is unattractive to some experts.

A third approach, restricted randomization, is one that is rarely exploited but was regarded by Cox as promising. The basic idea is to construct a set of all possible configurations of random assignments and to exclude configurations that are grossly imbalanced. A configuration is then randomly selected from the ones in the eligible set. Mosteller's (1978) handling of the matter is plainer than Cox's but more instructive. As valuable as randomization is, he cautions, chance can strike the investigator stunning blows. Restricted randomization requires specialized statistical advice, a reason for its infrequent use. Nevertheless, instructive examples exist. Ellickson and Bell (1992), for example, basically linked "unlike" schools from districts into pairs and then randomly assigned pairs to intensive programs for preventing substance abuse and to control conditions.

6

Identifying, Engaging, and Maintaining Contact With Target Individuals

The individual who has choice also has trouble.

Dutch proverb

A randomized field test requires that the eligible members of the target population be identified and engaged in the randomization, the treatments, and observation process. People's willingness to participate in a randomized field study depends on a variety of factors that must be taken into account in the study's design. In a study that asks for cooperation over a long time period, for example, the burden of providing information has to be recognized. Methods for reducing the burden and ensuring that individuals can be located periodically need to be invented and employed. Individual rights must be protected, and responsibilities must be made plain.

This chapter focuses on settings in which individuals, rather than institutions, are assigned randomly to alternative treatments in the interest of determining which program works better, and for whom. The incentives and burdens for individuals are stressed.

IDENTIFICATION

Individual Versus Cohort Identification

Individuals may present themselves or be encountered one at a time as prospective subjects in an experiment. An individual also may appear as a member of a cohort, each of whose members may be eligible for the study.

Processes in which individuals appear singly are typical of medical clinical trials and therapeutic field tests in the mental health arena, where, for example, patients periodically are referred to a facility for treatment. The gradual identification of people who may need or want service is also common in field tests in civil and criminal justice. Particular kinds of cases, such as domestic violence in police, court, or other contexts, emerge over time rather than all at once. Incremental flow is also a feature of some tests in the human resources training arena, in which training slots, open for some periods, are filled continuously over a time period.

In such cases, individuals usually are informed about the experiment as they appear, are screened, and are asked about their willingness to participate (see Chapter 3). They are assigned randomly in serial order of appearance unless other experimental design factors take precedence (Chapter 5). For example, small blocks of two or more individuals would be formed, then randomly assigned to treatments as suggested in the preceding chapter, to ensure that each treatment is allocated to at least one individual. When the process for screening eligibility is brisk, individuals may be stratified into, say, racial or gender groups and then assigned.

At the other extreme, some field experiments begin with a complete list of individuals who are eligible for treatments and later will be randomly assigned to alternatives. This scenario typifies education experiments in which a specified sample of students, schools, or classrooms is assigned randomly to different treatments all at once. It is characteristic of some experiments on new approaches to tax administration in which a complete listing of delinquent taxpayers, for example, is the basis for the study.

Surveillance and Outreach

In some testing environments, accruing the study sample depends on the spontaneous appearance of individuals. The experimenter's task is to ensure that the individuals who appear over time are considered as prospective study participants. In other environments, the appearance and identification of participants may be a function of strenuous outreach efforts.

Detecting individuals who appear spontaneously in the pipeline for a field test requires good surveillance and conscientious management. For example, all eligible cases in the Spouse Assault Replication Program experiments were not identified as eligible, because police officers in some sites were motivated insufficiently to identify them as such (Garner et al., 1995). That is, some officers were uninterested in the experiment, despite their department's agreement to test ways of handling misdemeanor assaults. Increased motivation came from the executive level, through directives and encouragement from middle-level supervisors, and as a consequence of special incentives created by the research staff.

When individuals who may be eligible for services must be sought actively, an outreach system must be designed. The term "outreach" is somewhat vague. One might exploit a variation on a definition suggested by Leviton and Schuh (1991). They defined an outreach project element as establishing contact with members of the target population; maintaining contact until the individual's eligibility is determined, assignment to treatment groups has been made, and the individual engages in the treatment regimen; and maintaining contact, when appropriate, until the treatments are completed.

In the Rockefeller Foundation's multisite field tests of integrated training programs, for example, each site tried to learn how to identify potentially eligible individuals: minority female single parents. In some sites, staff members were hired specifically to do this. Several sites doubled the rate at which clients were identified by employing women who were familiar with local communities, inventive about ways to inform single parents about the programs, and gently persistent in encouraging and facilitating participation (Boruch et al., 1988). The tactics that local community-based organizations used to inform potentially eligible mothers that they might participate in the study included

- public notices, notably radio announcements on the most pertinent channels, local news coverage, pamphlets, and so forth;
- networks, notably neighborhood groups, housing groups, community-based organizations, and kinship and friend networks,
- presentations at churches, meetings of community-based and neighborhood organizations, public housing projects, and tenants' meetings, and
- attending conscientiously to service providers or relevant government offices, such as employment agencies, that made referrals to the program.

Randomized field tests of intensive support services for dislocated workers in Texas similarly relied on referrals from offices of the Texas Employment Commission, notably of dislocated workers receiving unemployment checks. This supplemented outreach efforts in corporations that had initiated substantial layoffs of employees and public notices in the cities affected by the corporations' actions (Bloom, 1990).

These and similar tactics have been used in research on more volatile topics, such as AIDS. For example, Valdiserri and colleagues (1989) targeted outreach efforts to male prostitutes as well as to homosexual men through television and radio as well as through social and community organizations to recruit participants for experiments on more effective ways to teach risk reduction skills.

The problem of engaging individuals in a test of different programs is difficult when the prospective participants are dispersed over a substantial geographic area, their access to information is variable, and they are distracted by economic or other factors that demand their attention. The problem is sufficiently complex to warrant research on the outreach component of programs apart from the service components in an experiment. Investigations by Brooks-Gunn et al. (1989) and McCormick (1989), among others, suggest that labor-intensive case finders or outreach workers may not always be effective. Leviton and Schuh's (1991) review and the experiments described earlier, however, provide evidence for the contention that vigorous outreach is necessary for identification and continuous engagement of participants in many, if not all, such studies.

It is worth noting that outreach methods employed for initial identification of prospective participants in a study also are used, at times, to locate participants long after their initial engagement. For example, simple public notices about the need to locate former participants have been used in follow-up studies of participants in preschool experiments over a 25-year period (Schweinhart, Barnes, & Weikart, 1993; Oden, 1993). The notices helped to legitimize and set the stage for more intensive location efforts of the sort described later in this chapter.

MANDATORY ENGAGEMENT
IN THE EXPERIMENT

In some settings, institutions have the authority to require that individuals (or entities) be randomly assigned to treatments that are thought to be appropriate and effective. Individuals who are eligible for treatment then, and who are assigned randomly, have no choice in the matter.

For example, the Spouse Assault Replication Program involved randomly selecting alleged assailants for different treatments. Police in the relevant jurisdictions had the authority to arrest an offender on a misdemeanor assault charge or to handle the case in other ways. In the social welfare arena, California's GAIN legislation required mandatory participation of welfare recipients in randomized tests of new welfare-to-work services, education, and employment programs (Ricchio & Friedlander, 1992). Some field experiments on tax administration or compliance involve the mandatory participation of taxpayers (Roth et al., 1989).

To the extent that the individual's participation in an experiment is mandatory, the study's designers need not be concerned about creating incentives to enhance engagement, as they would if participation were voluntary. Nevertheless, two matters have to be addressed. First, the participant's rights must be protected. This protection ordinarily comes about through scrutiny of the ethics of the study by an institutional review board. See Chapter 3 on ethics and Sieber (1992) more generally.

The second important matter concerns the act that even when a person is required to become involved in a particular treatment program, certain aspects of the individual's participation may be voluntary. A sample of offenders who were arrested in the Milwaukee Spouse Assault Experiment on police handling of domestic violence, for example, later were asked to provide information voluntarily to the research group (Sherman et al., 1992). Their participation in the experiment and treatments—arrest being one treatment—was mandatory, authorized under the law. Having been arrested, their provision of information to a research team interviewer while in jail was voluntary, and some offenders declined to provide information. From individuals who agreed to answer questions, researchers learned that at least some assailants were "surprised" at their arrest for assault. The point is that, in this case and others, mandatory participation does not preclude voluntary provision of information. To the extent that this information is useful, it is necessary to develop incentives or reduce disincentives for the participant.

VOLUNTARY ENGAGEMENT
IN THE EXPERIMENT

Most of the experiments undertaken in the United States to compare ameliorative programs involve volunteers. For the experiment's designer, a number of issues have to be addressed in setting up an engagement process. They include

- Deciding who should explain the experiment and how
- Determining and laying out conditions for participating in the study
- Making decisions about what is explained, and
- Developing incentives and ways to reduce or remove disincentives

Who Explains the Experiment, and How?

The individuals responsible for explaining the study to prospective subjects must have some stature among members of the communities to which information is directed, and those individuals must be well-informed. An explainer without credibility will achieve little and may cause damage.

At San Jose's Center for Employment and Training and the Atlanta Urban League, for example, seasoned staffers and executives, women who understood how to explain and what to explain, had responsibility for part of this task in experiments on programs for minority female single parents. The women were familiar with local cultures, vernacular, and values in subcommunities of Latinos, African Americans, and others. At their best, they were knowledgeable—on account of training—about the purposes of randomization and about the political and economic need for evidence about what works better. Partly because visual evidence on their performance could be useful in these other experiments, the Rockefeller Foundation supported videotape productions on the topic (Cottingham, 1991; Rockefeller Foundation, 1988).

In the Spouse Assault Replication Program, several vehicles for explanation were developed. The principal investigators had to explain the experiment to those in a position to identify cases: police officers. They shared this responsibility with sergeants, lieutenants, and captains who were able to communicate well with streetwise officers. The task of explaining the need for information to victims of assault fell to interviewers. The latter were selected because of their familiarity with the community and their ability to track down victims and gain their cooperation.

By way of illustrating what not to do, Kershaw and Fair (1976) criticized the early use of graduate students in economics to enroll poor families in the New Jersey Negative Income Tax Experiment. They failed to enroll families at a high rate. This led to hiring staff who, unlike the students, "thoroughly understood the attitudes and problems of welfare recipients" (p. 27).

What Is Explained?

In field experiments that are characterized by voluntary participation, the information given to prospective participants usually must accord with standards for ethical conduct of research. This means that, at a minimum, individuals must be told about the treatments and random allocation, the foreseeable costs and benefits of participation, and so on. Chapter 3, on ethics and law, outlines the topics that must be handled in an experiment. Sieber (1992) discusses the requirements of informed consent in the broader context of social research.

What Are the Conditions of Participation?

Beyond meeting minimum requirements, it is good practice to identify what might be viewed as incentives and disincentives by prospective participants. Developing trust between the research group and those who might agree to become engaged in an experiment arguably is important. This trust, and other factors, can be regarded as an incentive or as a prerequisite for cooperation. Enhancing incentives and decreasing disincentives are considered next.

INCENTIVES AND DISINCENTIVES

Treatment Alternatives

In randomized field tests, different treatments are compared because their relative effectiveness is uncertain. For the individuals who are the targets of treatments, however, the alternative treatment programs may differ in their attractiveness for reasons other than their scientifically determined efficacy. Individuals may therefore decline to cooperate in randomized tests because of their view of certain treatments as unattractive. At one site in the Minority Female Single Parent experiments, for example, some women appear to have been put off by the training, notably in electromechanical elevator repair, despite its potential economic benefits. The work did not accord with their image of a job that is suitable for women (Boruch et al., 1988).

It is important to anticipate how individuals might view participation in an experiment. Building a knowledge base on the topic seems sensible. Collins and Elkin (1985), for example, added to the knowledge base in their reports on experiments to test the efficacy of treatments for more than 600 severely depressed individuals. As part of the study, 56 eligible participants who declined to participate were asked about their reasons for declining. In this experiment, the inclusion of a drug treatment as one of four treatments emerged as the primary reason for failure to agree to participate (see Table 6.1). This factor was mentioned by a majority of the decliners. The use of a placebo as an alternative and a psychotherapy treatment, or both, was given as a reason by nine people, some of whom may have also been put off by the drug treatment.

The attractiveness of treatment alternatives as perceived by prospective study participants has not been well explored. Partly as a consequence,

TABLE 6.1

Patients' Reasons for Refusing to Consent
to Participate in a Randomized Experimentation:
Four Therapeutic Approaches to Treating Severe Depression

Reasons Given for Refusal	Totals	Number of Patients Giving the Reason
Inclusion of drug treatment condition		29
Inclusion of placebo treatment condition		9
Inclusion of psychotherapy treatment condition		3
Random assignment to treatments		14
Assessment procedures (measurements)		2
Audiotape recordings		8
Other (miscellaneous reasons)		17
Total number of patients who did not sign the consent form	56	
Total number of patients who were eligible to sign informed consent	590	

SOURCE: From "Randomization in the NIMH Treatment of Depression Collaborative Research Program", Collins and Elkin, *New Direction for Program Evaluation*, 28. © copyright 1985 by Jossey-Bass.
NOTE: The table includes all reasons given by patients, not only primary reasons. For example, any one of the 56 patients who did not agree to participate in the experiment may have given several reasons for declining participation. Most patients who were eligible did agree to be subjects in this experiment to assess four treatments.

there are no ground rules and there is little literature. The matter nevertheless deserves attention when the object is to enhance cooperation in a field experiment.

Random assignment can be and is, at times, reported as a reason for noncooperation in experiments. The cognitive processes and values that bear on such a decision are not clear. For example, of 56 patients who chose not to participate in the tests of treatments for severe depression described above, 14 said that their choice, wholly or in part, was based on the random assignment (Table 6.1). Pilot studies that are undertaken prior to the main field test can help to identify and reduce such problems. The incentives, for example, may hinge on the odds of an individual being assigned to one or another regimen. The matter deserves attention in a side study when the odds can be altered, within limits, to satisfy both standards of statistical power and the views of prospective subjects that affect their willingness to cooperate.

Financial Compensation

Participants in experiments often answer questions during interviews that may last from 15 minutes to 2 hours or more. In health-related studies, such as those regarding AIDS prevention, participants may be asked for blood, urine, or hair samples. Long-term studies may ask that the individual be attentive to recontact by the researchers over a 3-year period following treatment (as in employment and training experiments), and in at least a few cases, such as High/Scope, over a 20-year period. All this imposes some burden on participants, a burden that at times warrants remuneration or some other incentive.

Treatments that are regarded by participants as very attractive, on the other hand, raise a question about whether compensation is necessary. Receipt of the treatment may be sufficient to ensure continued cooperation in the research. Similarly, if participants view the provision of substantial information as a duty or as part of the treatment even when treatment ends, then compensation arguably is unwarranted. These scenarios appear uncommon.

More common are scenarios in which treatments have an uncertain attraction, many of the participants are economically vulnerable, and providing substantial information following treatment is not a cultural or civic norm among the participants. In these scenarios, one might view payments partly as compensation for the time and expense of providing information. The participants might also view stipends or the prospect of future stipends as an incentive for sustained engagement. Evidence on the matter, presented next, is a bit fragmentary.

Methodological research on enhancing cooperation rates in passive surveys has at least an indirect bearing on this topic. In particular, understanding whether payment enhances cooperation in a survey can be viewed as analogous to the problem of learning whether payments help in experiments on social programs and in enhancing cooperation rate of individuals assigned to control conditions.

Consider two illustrations. The National Adult Literacy Survey was preceded by field tests designed to determine whether no stipends, $20 stipends, or $30 stipends worked to increase people's willingness to participate in such a survey. Controlled tests on the stipends suggest that a $20 stipend did improve cooperation; the $30 stipend did not improve cooperation remarkably beyond this (Berlin et al., 1992). The National Survey of Family Growth undertook similar research prior to the main survey of women aged 14-44. Again, stipends had an appreciable effect on response rates, especially on women who were economically vulnerable. Payments

TABLE 6.2

Reasons for Nonparticipation in Most Recent Survey

	Mail	Personal Telephone	Visit
Total mentions/surveys not participated in	218	154	47
Lack of interest, or inconvenience	165	80	27
Topic uninteresting or inappropriate	43	20	4
General lack of interest, did not want to bother	62	23	11
Oversight	31	0	0
Too busy	21	23	9
Inconvenient time	0	12	0
Other	8	2	3
Objection to approach or consent	36	65	16
Topic objectionable	14	11	7
Questions poor	6	1	0
Method objectionable	1	23	1
Distrust			
In research	2	3	2
Of interviewer	0	26	0
Of sponsor	5	0	1
Dislike of interviewer	0	0	2
Purpose objectionable	8	1	3
Miscellaneous, including no answer and don't know	17	9	4

SOURCE: From "What Subjects of Survey Research Believe About Confidentiality," Turner ©
copyright 1982 by Springer-Verlag.

had far less effect on individuals whose income was higher (Duffer, Lessler, Weeks, & Mosher, 1994).

More generally, to judge from Table 6.2, being "too busy" to respond to a survey is a reason for nonparticipation in 5%-10% of cases. Financial remuneration arguably alters the individual's view of how to spend his or her time in an experiment, as in other settings. Similarly, a general lack of interest accounts for at least 15% of reasons given for nonparticipation. Again, one would expect remuneration to generate interest among some people who would otherwise be disinclined to provide information.

It has become customary, irrespective of such methodological research, to pay individuals for their participation in controlled experiments. Many, if not all, of the studies cited in this volume, for example, have done so, including High/Scope, the Social Security Administration's tests of employment programs for the disabled, and Florida's Project Independence. When payment is customary or necessary, there is some justification for providing stipends to all treatment groups, not only to control group members. The groups are supposed to be treated identically apart from treatment, and different stipends mean that they are not. In any case, differential distribution of stipends may be unwarranted to the extent that some members of each treatment group are not pleased with the treatments they receive.

Reducing the Burden of Response

Reducing the number and length of interviews, inventories, and questionnaires is a natural approach to easing the participant's burden. This approach is mandatory in comparative experiments conducted under contract with the federal government. In particular, the U.S. Office of Management and Budget (OMB) has responsibility under the law to ensure that respondent burdens are minimized in federal surveys, experiments, and administrative reporting more generally.

Field tests that are supported by grants, rather than by contracts, are free of the legal obligation to clear questionnaires and other inventories with the OMB. Minimizing the burden in such research nevertheless is desirable if only out of respect for the participants. As a consequence, it often is an explicit part of data collection policy in field experiments to "collect only data that are central to the analysis" (Bloom, 1990, p. 45).

Intrusiveness of Questions

To judge from common experience and methodological research, the intrusiveness of an inquiry plays a role in individuals' resistance to answering questions, apart from the time required to address the inquiry (Boruch & Cecil, 1979). Minimizing intrusiveness often will be warranted on ethical grounds in the view of an institutional review board that reviews plans for experiments. In contract-supported experiments, the sensitivity of questions posed to study participants also is reviewed by organizations such as the OMB.

Intrusiveness is partly a function of the circumstances of the question's presentation. The Spouse Assault Replication Program, for example, involved interviews with women who had been assaulted. Interviews had to be scheduled by the research team so as to ensure that the woman's partner was not present, was ignorant of the interview, or at least was out of earshot. This approach was taken partly to ensure the woman's privacy and reduce the risks associated with lack of privacy. See, for example, Sherman et al. (1992).

The method of interview may be as important as the intrusiveness of the questions. Among the reasons given for not participating in experiments on depression therapy (Table 6.1), tape recordings were objectionable to 8 of the 56 patients who declined. Table 6.2 shows that when a telephone is used for an interview in surveys, about 15% of those who decline to be interviewed will refuse on account of the use of the telephone by the interviewer.

Trust, Personalization, and Persistence

Depersonalization in the process of eliciting data can affect cooperation. The remedies for depersonalization include vigorous attention to the respondents' well-being and their perception of research staff and treatment providers. Long-term longitudinal studies that take the matter seriously have employed a variety of proactive measures, including birthday cards and similar recognition, personalized reminders and inquiries delivered by telephone and mail, and the construction of interview protocols that are sensitive to local culture and values.

Depersonalization also is a function of the use of scientific vernacular. For example, a study that refers to individuals who choose to cooperate in a field test as "subjects" is, at best, unappetizing. Despite the frequent use of the word "subjects" in the research literature, it does not belong in the language of comparative field tests in the public policy arena.

Individuals who are enrolled in a study, voluntarily or otherwise, and who are randomly selected for alternative treatments may have little or no basis for trusting the study's staff. Assault victims in tests of police handling of domestic violence, for example, will not necessarily trust the treatment providers, the police officers or the counselors to whom they are referred. Insofar as people have no experience as participants in a legitimate research project, they have little reason to trust interviewers who elicit information from them. Distrust or skepticism developed over the course of a study will affect their willingness to be located and to provide accurate information.

At least three approaches to enhancing trust have been used to good effect. First, the burdens of participation can be reduced, beyond reducing demands on the participant's time. The individual's privacy, for example, will on occasion be a critical issue. The legal assurances of privacy, discussed in Chapter 3, can help to allay suspicions. Participants, when appropriate, can be assured that any information provided will not be used to make decisions about them as people.

A second approach to enhancing trust depends on advisory boards. To the extent that a group appointed is to ensure that the participants' interests are met, bases for mistrust can be reduced, if not eliminated. Participants must be informed about the group; the various members of the group are responsible for informing study participants at times. At a minimum and as a matter of law, studies that involve federal support must be reviewed periodically by an institutional review board that oversees the ethical propriety of the work. That is, the board attends to the rights of the individuals engaged in the field test.

Expert counsel beyond ethics usually is necessary. Advisory groups must then be created to focus on how the experiment can best recognize cultural, ethnic, or local customs so as to enhance participants' confidence in the study team and the treatment providers. For example, the national evaluation of TRIO programs, such as Upward Bound, was influenced by an advisory group whose members had considerable experience in operating or participating in such programs (U.S. Department of Education, Planning and Evaluation Service, 1991a). Their counsel and assistance was helpful in developing good working relationships in 70 field experiments on the programs. In the Spouse Assault Replication Program, the study teams at each site were advised by local representatives of victim advocacy groups and police departments. This was partly in the interest of developing at least tentative trust among those with an influence on the conduct of the experiments.

A third important approach to building trust is based heavily on mutual education and respect. Philadelphia's Play Buddy project, for example, involved testing ways to increase the resilience of children at risk of unseemly aggressiveness. It engaged vulnerable children who have reasons to distrust both adults and their playmates. It involved the children's parents, who themselves are economically and politically vulnerable. In the Play Buddy project, Fantuzzo and Stevenson (1993) and their colleagues took mutual education and respect, among the researchers, parents, graduate students, and children, as prerequisites for developing an effective Play Buddy program.

The trust theme pertains to interviewers and other research team members in long-term studies as well as to the program staff. Stouthamer-Loeber and Van Kammen (1995), for example, stressed the importance of the participants' initial contact with interviewers in ensuring subsequent contact. Experiments that involve testing programs directed toward vulnerable populations, such as dislocated workers (Vinokur et al., 1995) or the homeless people who are beset with mental illness or alcohol problems (Wright, Allen, & Devine, 1995), also put a premium on rapport.

Depending on Administrative Records

By capitalizing on existing administrative records, the individual's burden of providing information to an interviewer or research group can be reduced. Evaluations of the effectiveness of employment and training programs, for example, usually rely on reports of unemployment stipends from relevant government offices, or of pay statements provided by businesses to tax or employment agencies. Randomized field tests on dislocated workers programs in Texas and Delaware took this approach (Bloom, 1990). The approach has the benefit of reducing the errors associated with individuals' self-reports of income (see Chapter 7 on observation and measurement).

In the criminal justice arena, where an offender may be unable or unwilling to answer questions, the researcher may rely on police records of the offender's criminal history. The RAND Corporation's evaluation of intensive supervision of probationers in California, for example, relied heavily on this source of data to estimate the effect of the program on probationers' recidivism (Petersilia & Turner, 1990). Each of the sites in the Spouse Assault Replication Program relied on criminal justice records rather than on assailants, whose willingness to cooperate was dubious at best, to produce evidence about whether arresting an assailant led to better outcomes than did other strategies (e.g., Sherman, et al., 1992).

Relying on administrative records reduces substantially the demands on individuals who participate in an experiment. Provisions must be made, however, for record retrieval. That is, the information must be searched for, acquired, and consolidated in a form that is useful for analysis. Further, the quality of the record—the accuracy of its contents—needs to be assessed. These tasks may entail additional burdens for those providing the treatments, for the study's staff, or others. Usually, the compensation for this burden is monetary. Research funds, for example, may be provided to medical records personnel in a randomized clinical trial or to a school's information officer in an educational experiment as recompense for the burden of their participation in the study.

BOX 6.1
Summary: Disincentives and Incentives for
Participating in a Randomized Field Study

Disincentives	Incentives and Reduced Disincentives
Unattractiveness of the treatment alternatives	Enhancing attractiveness of treatment alternatives
Time-related burdens of responding to questionnaires, interviews, and travel to interview and treatment sites	Minimizing respondent time and travel burden
	Financial compensation
	Enhancing convenience
Intrusiveness or sensitivity of inquiry	Privacy guarantees
	Reducing sensitivity of queries
Disinterest and depersonalization	Personal attention
	Material compensation
	Persistence
Distrust	Credible representation
	Legal and procedural assurances
	Personal attention
	Responsiveness and explanation
	Mutual education
Random assignment	Explanations
	Appeals
	Processes

Summary: Disincentives and Incentives

Identifying the incentives and ways to reduce disincentives that affect the prospective participants in an experiment are important. They are summarized in Box 6.1.

Box 6.1 and the foregoing discussion simplify a considerable body of research on eliciting cooperation in surveys. Deeper summaries of the topic are given in textbooks by Groves (1989) and by Stouthamer-Loeber and Van Kammen (1995). They cover cooperation among others and measurement error as a function of the mode of inquiry, characteristics of the respondents and the inquirer, costs, and other matters. Reports on relevant methodological research appear frequently in the *Proceedings of the American Statistical Association: Section on Survey Research Methods*. The methodological advances are reported in a wide range of research journals, nearly 50 of them, to judge by the papers cited in Groves (1989) and in other state of the art books such as Kasprzyk, Duncan, Kalton, and Singh (1989).

MAINTAINING CONTACT

A basic condition for sustaining the engagement of individuals who have agreed to participate in a field experiment, or at least determining their interest in further cooperation, is knowing their whereabouts. People may be lost to contact in a variety of ways and for numerous reasons. Individuals are mobile in a variety of senses. It is then sensible to develop methods for ensuring that contact is possible and to plan for an inevitable loss of contact.

Retention Rates in Surveys

To appreciate the order of magnitude of the problem of sustaining engagement or reestablishing contacts that are lost, consider Tables 6.3 and 6.4. Table 6.3 summarizes the field experience in following up dislocated workers in three Texas sites, workers who had agreed to cooperate in randomized tests of services that might lead to placement in good jobs. The completion rate for the final telephone interview, done 1 year after individuals' initial engagement in the test, was in the 70-79% range. Up to eight attempts were made to contact each worker. A remarkable fraction, 15-24%, were not located. Bloom (1990), the principal investigator for the study, took pains to make such data available and to understand whether the fact that some individuals were neither located nor contacted would affect the results of the test.

Table 6.4 illustrates the variety in cooperation rates for randomized experiments. In the table, the "retention" rate is defined as the fraction of individuals initially enrolled in a treatment who then cooperated in a later survey. The Sherman and Berk (1984) study of police handling of domestic violence was the first randomized test in the arena. It generated retention rates in the 55-80% range. The study was sufficiently important but

TABLE 6.3

Follow-Up Survey Experience in a Randomized Field Test
of a Program for Dislocated Workers (percentages of cases)

	Interviews Completed	Interviews Refused	Located but Not Contacted	Not Located
Site A				
Treatments	75	3	7	15
Treatment I/II	75	4	5	16
Control	72	5	6	17
Site B				
Treatment I/II	70	< 1	9	20
Control	72	0	4	24
Site C				
Treatment I/II	79	< 1	5	16
Control	78	0	6	16

SOURCE: From *Back to Work: Testing Reemployment Services for Displaced Workers*, Bloom, ©
copyright 1990 by W. E. Upjohn Institute for Employment Research.

vulnerable, on this account and others. Berk et al. (1988) initiated further
studies and new experiments were undertaken by the National Institute of
Justice (Reiss & Boruch, 1991). The National Health Insurance Experiment
yielded a remarkably high rate of sustained engagement (Newhouse, Marquis,
& Morris, 1979).

The mobility of participants in an experiment usually is one reason for
disconnection between a participant in the experiment and the research
group. Table 6.3 helps to make the point more emphatically: The rate of
failure to locate is in the 15-24% range. The thoughtful observer might
reckon that the subjects of the table, dislocated workers, may be inclined
to move more frequently than other groups, making the location task very
difficult.

More generally, mobility rates are sufficiently high in the United States
to warrant substantial investment in forward and backward tracing. Table
6.5 is taken from Cantor's (1989) examination of the National Crime
Survey, a national study of victimization. The rates at which individuals in
the population move over a 1-year period is in the 15-40% range. As one
might expect, older Americans move less frequently than the young. The
high movement rate among young people (18-33%) influences follow-up

TABLE 6.4

Cooperation Rates in Five Illustrative Randomized Field Tests

Study	Total N	Years From Baseline to Last Measure	Treatment Group	Control Group
Klein et al. (dental care)	10,000	4	39%	56%
Berrueta-Clement et al. (preschool education)	120	8	> 95	> 95
Kane et al. (hospital care)	250	2	93	95
Sherman and Berk (police action)	330	1	> 60	> 60
Brook et al. (health insurance)	4,000	3-5	> 85	> 85

SOURCE: The table is summarized from data published in *Evaluation studies review annual 10*, Aiken and Kehrer (Eds.), © copyright 1985 by Sage Publications.
NOTE: Entries are rounded.

rates in randomized tests of programs for preventing high school dropouts, teenage pregnancy, substance abuse, auto accidents, and violence. The mobility rate among young adults in the 20-24-year-old bracket affects rates in studies of those at risk of substance abuse, AIDS and other sexually transmitted diseases, and other problems.

Mobility data at the county and state, rather than national, level are more pertinent to experiments that are mounted locally. For example, reports on 25-year follow-ups on the High/Scope Perry Preschool Project benchmarked the mobility rates for relevant counties by using data from the large-scale Panel Study of Income Dynamics (PSID). The project participants remained within the state, Michigan, at a rate somewhat higher, 86%, than one would expect from the PSID rate of 76% (Schweinhart et al., 1993).

The main implication is that considerable resources need to be invested in gathering information that will help to sustain contact, in capitalizing on institutional sources of the kind described earlier, and in developing incentives for enhancing participants' willingness to remain in contact. Without such resources, the problem of handling missing observations, under a variety of assumptions about why contact could not be sustained, can be exceedingly complex. See, for example, Orwin, Sonnefeld, Garrison-Mogren, & Smith (1995) on tracking homeless alcoholics, an ambitious multisite experiment.

Locating Individuals

Loss of contact with a study's participants decreases the statistical power of tests and, more important, can introduce serious biases in estimating differences in the relative effectiveness of treatments. In police experiments on domestic violence, for example, the loss of contact with some victims reduced sample sizes that were available for victim-based comparisons. This in turn reduced the ability to detect small differences among the treatments tested. Furthermore, a difference in contact rate, say between women whose spouses were randomly arrested versus women whose cases were randomly mediated, raises the possibility that a difference found in outcomes of the treatments is attributable to differences among women lost in the two groups rather than to the influence of treatments.

It is then essential that field experiments obtain sufficient information to sustain contact between the study participants and the research team. Information that is elicited early in the experiment, during a screening for example, forms the basis for *forward tracing*. Similar information may be sought later and, more important, other methods may be brought to bear in *backward tracing*.

Forward-tracing information is of the kind that makes recontact easier, at modest cost. Contemporary longitudinal experiments usually elicit such information during the screening stage or shortly after randomly assigning eligible participants to treatments. This information conventionally includes a participant's name, address, and telephone number. More important for recontact, it includes locator information on a friend or relative who is likely to be aware of the participant's whereabouts in the future, the participant's current employer, and the names of civic, professional, or religious organizations to which the individual belongs.

When it is expected that individuals will be difficult to relocate, more strenuous and imaginative methods can be employed. Wright et al. (1995), for example, obtained photographs and recontact permission statements from respondents in their homeless study to enable the research team to follow up on individuals' unstable addresses. More generally, a principle enumerated by Stouthamer-Loeber and Van Kammen (1995) seems wise: "[C]ollect identifying information as much and as often as possible" (p. 77). This advice is applicable especially to studies in which target families are unstable units and name changes are not uncommon, as in longitudinal studies in delinquency, homelessness, and criminal justice. It also seems sensible in less volatile contexts, given population mobility and continuously changing family structures.

TABLE 6.5

Mobility of Respondents (one interview to the next, 1 year span)
in a National Probability Sample Engaged in the National Crime Survey

Age	Percentage Moved
12-15	18.0
16-19	33.0
20-24	38.6
25-34	25.3
35-49	17.1
50-64	14.7
65+	15.2

SOURCE: Adapted from "Substantive Implications of Selected Operational Longitudinal Design Features: The National Crime Survey As a Case Study," Cantor, © copyright 1989 by John Wiley and Sons. Used by permission.

Consider a specific example of backward tracing. The High/Scope Foundation undertook to locate individuals who, 18 years earlier, had participated in High/Scope-based preschool programs and in ordinary Head Start programs. Attention was directed to two sites, Fort Walton/Pensacola (Florida) and Greeley (Colorado). This follow-up study's purpose was to estimate long-term differences between individuals in each group, and it was motivated by an earlier randomized experiment that showed remarkable effects of High/Scope preschool programs on outcomes such as crime rates (Schweinhart et al., 1993).

The backward-tracing techniques used by the foundation are summarized in Box 6.2. They have been used in other surveys and experiments. As the foundation acknowledged, there is a considerable body of work on such tracing methods, for example, Ross, Begab, Dondis, Giampiccolo, and Meyers (1985), Lally, Mangione, and Honig (1988), Guenzel, Berckmans, and Cannell (1983), and Oden (1993).

The High/Scope locators put considerable emphasis on a community resource network, consisting of current and former teachers, directors, and former students and their parents, among others. These sources provided location information on the former students at times. Furthermore, the locations of former teachers and others could be identified; questioning them often provided location data on some former students.

Local schools, at times, could be used to provide addresses of parents of former students at the points of entry and exit from the schools over the

---

BOX 6.2

Backward Tracing Methods
Used By High/Scope Foundation

Community resource networks, including current and former staff, directors, students, parents, and community leaders
School records, yearbooks, and directories
Public records, including driver's licenses; marriage, birth, and death certificates; and voter registration records
Institutional resources, including prisons, churches, employers, and mental hospitals
Mail, including post office forwarding, forwarding address requests, and forwarding by intermediaries such as parents
Telephone directories, including standard directories, address/telephone directories, and operator tracing
Neighborhood canvassing

---

first 8-12 years of the follow-up term. Yearbooks and related directories appear to have been of some assistance.

Public records were used in this study and commonly are used in other longitudinal research. The sources include state departments for licensing drivers, which provide addresses; birth, death, and marriage certificate bureaus; and voter registration agencies. Institutional membership of other kinds also was used to locate former participants. Name lists also were checked against local church and prison lists.

Mail was used here, as in other studies, in several ways. The post office will forward mail if requested and able to do so. Parents or other intermediaries were used when necessary to forward letters to the participants that elicited cooperation in the follow-up study. Telephone directories of the conventional sort are an obvious locator device and were used by High/Scope. Street address/telephone directories also were used when necessary.

High/Scope also used neighborhood canvassing by locators—members of the community resource network and others—when information from other sources was insufficient. In the New Jersey Negative Income Tax Experiment, among others, similar devices were used: storekeepers, bartenders, and other such community members assisted and were, at times, remunerated for their assistance in the location task (Kershaw & Fair, 1976).

It is not common in randomized field studies to depend on ethnographers to track study participants and to persuade individuals to provide information. Nevertheless, ethnographic methods that involve, for example, engaging a member of the community as an intermediary to introduce an interviewer are not uncommon. This approach is put forward by Groves (1989) as worth exploring, in the context of survey research.

7

Observation and Measurement

*If you want to find out what's going on,
you have to go look at what's going on.*

—Yogi Berra (attributed)

*If he trusts . . . information in its plain
transmitted form . . . he often cannot avoid
stumbling and slipping and deviating
from the path of truth.*

—Ibn Khaldun (1377/1978)

Deciding what to observe about people's response to a treatment and how to do so obviously is important to designing a good experiment. Learning about whether treatments are deployed is also crucial despite our willingness to assume, at times, that treatment programs are emplaced. Baseline data, collected prior to treatment, are used to increase the statistical power of comparisons among the treatments. They also are used to characterize target samples and to check on the integrity of the random assignment process.

The experiment's context influences the characteristics of the target sample and the relative effectiveness of treatments; its measurement is then important. Costs entailed by treatments and other aspects of the study are basic to analyses of cost-effectiveness. Finally, missing data can reduce the statistical power of the study and induce biases in estimates of treatment differences; making observations about missingness can enhance interpretation of the study's results.

Contemporary experiments usually generate numerical data on each of these topics. The best of these studies also involve collecting qualitative, process-oriented, or ethnographic information on each. Narrative descriptions of treatment processes, for example, can enhance understanding of the statistical outcomes. They often are used to illustrate the activities that underlie the treatments to program sponsors, service providers, and policymakers. In what follows, the focus is on both numerical and narrative information.

Technical aspects of reliability and validity of measurement are ably discussed in textbooks on social surveys (e.g., Bohrnstedt, 1983) and psychology (e.g., Rosenthal & Rosnow, 1985), as well as in specialized tracts by Bejar (1983) and Feldt and Brennan (1993), among others. Volumes such as these, however, usually do not explain measurement in the context of randomized field experiments. Similarly, textbooks on the design of randomized experiments, as a rule, do not consider deeply the quality or the choice of measures. This chapter's purpose is to reiterate fundamental ideas about observation and to link them to the design and execution of experiments. It focuses on the quality of measures and on methods of observation in the special environment of randomized field experiments for planning and evaluation.

THE ROLE OF THEORY

Theory concerning how the programs being studied are supposed to work is fundamental to the design of measurement and observation systems in experiments. In the ideal case, such theory specifies what response variables ought to be observed and when, what treatment and context variables are relevant, and so on. See, for example, Bickman (1990) and Chen and Rossi (1980).

Consider, as an illustration, contemporary experiments to assess the effectiveness of school-based health programs. The socio-cognitive theories that drive the design of the programs emphasize treatment variables that are deployed at the school level. That is, the object is to build an institutional culture and a cohort of students who are oriented toward reducing high-risk behaviors. The theoretically justified units of analysis in experiments in this arena are schools or communities (Killen & Robinson, 1988). Measures of treatment implementation, then, are made at the institutional or group level, as well as at the individual level.

Further, socio-cognitive theories are often specific as to the short-term, intermediate, and long-term outcomes that are expected to be influenced by the program. For example, some theory suggests that children need to learn how to resist the influence of peers who might encourage drug use, as well as why such resistance is warranted. This implies that children's knowledge of resistance tactics ought to be measured. It also implies that their attitudes, including those bearing on incentives and disincentives for using such tactics, such as peer pressure, ought to be understood. That is, they ought to be measured. Such theory further suggests that behavior will change as a consequence of the program, but that this change depends on earlier or collateral changes in (say) knowledge and attitudes. Insofar as the theory specifies high-risk behaviors as important, experiments on school-based health promotion programs then must try to measure the behaviors. Questions about the onset of tobacco use and the frequency of its use, for example, are routinely asked in experiments on theory-driven health-promotion programs because the theory usually includes behavior in its ambit, not only attitudes or beliefs.

Rudimentary theory also has guided experiments on return-to-work programs sponsored by the Social Security Administration. For example, it was reasonable to expect that being disabled would affect productivity and therefore wages, time preferences for leisure versus work, and the time available for accommodating the disability. Theory further suggested that the longer an individual received disability payments, the less likely he or she would be trained to be employed. These variables became targets of measurement in a large-scale experiment, Project NetWork, to determine whether a specialized return-to-work program might work (Rupp et al., 1994).

In some evaluations, theory must be invented to provide a framework for assessing programs. Bickman et al. (1994), for example, were confronted with the problem of estimating the effects and cost of a modified health system on a military base. To clarify what ought to be measured, the system's operations were hypothesized to depend on intake processes, diagnostic assessment procedures, and treatment. Within each of these factors, theory was developed to characterize microlevel processes. At the intake side, the new system of care was supposed to enhance access to services, a proximal outcome, and this in turn was supposed to lead to intermediate outcomes such as increased numbers of clients, increased client satisfaction, and decreased cycle time. All these variables eventually were measured in the study.

RESPONSE VARIABLES

Response variables are the characteristics of individuals or entities that are supposed to be affected by the treatments under investigation. The response variables that actually are measured need to be in accord with this supposition. The method of their measurement must yield observations that are valid and reliable. These topics and the timing of measurement are discussed in what follows.

Relevance of the Response Variables

The treatments employed in the Spouse Assault Replication Program (SARP) experiment, notably arrest versus restoration of order without arrest, were each expected to have an effect on assailants. Arrest was viewed theoretically as a specific deterrent to criminal activity. Whether arrest is indeed a deterrent should be reflected in subsequent criminal behavior of the arrested group as contrasted with that of the mediated group. As a consequence, considerable effort was made to measure assaultive behavior following the treatments, using police records and victim interviews.

Contrariwise, a variety of potential response variables were not observed in the SARP because they were insufficiently related to the treatment's purpose. The offenders' commission of crimes apart from assault—burglary, for example—was not recorded, partly because this was not expected, on theoretical grounds, to be influenced by the police handling of domestic violence. Each victim was asked to report on the partner's assaults on other members of the family following the treatment because there was a theoretical rationale for expecting that later violence would be displaced to another family member.

There are no well-explicated technical standards for establishing the "relevance" of a response variable to treatments in the behavioral and social sciences or in educational research. Nor are there generally agreed upon procedures for making a choice in the context of field experiments. As a matter of good practice, however, such determinations have been a function of review of prior research, examination of theory, and the judgment of self-critical experts.

For example, each of the research teams in the five SARP experiments undertook literature reviews to determine whether "assault" and other variables had been used productively as outcomes in earlier research. Each relied on a rudimentary theory of "specific deterrence" to guide their thinking. That is, arrest for a violent offense would have a deterrent effect on the individual, leading to fewer such offenses by the same individual. Each team also relied on experts, including local advisory groups. Such groups included police officers, who were disposed to use police arrest records as a measure of assault, and victim advocates, who argued for depending on victims' reports. Each research team was also a party to negotiation in this multisite effort to agree on what to measure and how to measure it (Reiss & Boruch, 1991).

Making the decision that a particular response variable is relevant to the treatments can be difficult on account of exaggerated claims about what treatments will accomplish. The congressional testimony leading to federal support of adult literacy programs in the United States, for example, included claims that the programs would increase employment and wage rates, the health and well-being of participants, education levels, and literacy. Neither extant research nor theory was sufficient in the early 1990s to reach easy agreement. Consequently, the U.S. Department of Education undertook workshops to discuss which outcomes should be measured in controlled field tests of literacy programs. Workshop participants included experts in adult literacy who averred that even if primary response variables, such as "literacy" or "enhanced literacy," could be identified, they were difficult or impossible to measure. Others maintained that, with a bit more work and research, it would be feasible to agree on the selection of the main outcome variables. Some experts put themselves at a distance from claims made in legislative hearings that literacy programs would produce measurable increases in wage rates and other outcome variables. Others maintained that such variables should be measured.

The sponsors of the program and of the experiment also play a key role in discussions about which response variables ought to be measured. The role is reflected partly in the convening of workshops of the sort just described. It is reflected in the financial support of research on new ways to measure outcomes. Consider, for example, the Request for Proposals (RFP) issued by the U.S. Department of Agriculture's Food and Nutrition Service (1992) on tests of the WIC program. The RFP recognized that nutritional supplements would be "associated with" changes in the anthropometric status of children, but because severe malnutrition in the United States is rare, the document recognized that one could not expect, as a consequence of additional supplements, remarkable change in the children's measured height, weight, or other growth measures. The RFP identified a variety of other response variables warranting attention. It discussed the relevance of each variable to program goals and the concerns or problems that the experimenter may encounter in attempting to measure and use each in an evaluation of the program.

The theoretical relevance of any particular response variable may be clear. Low quality in measurement in the field degrades relevance, however. This topic is discussed next.

Reliability

Reliability in this context refers to the reproducibility of a measurement and describes the extent to which a particular method of measurement will yield the same result repeatedly on a trait presumed to be stable. One expects, for example, that measures of intelligence, when made twice on the same person over a short interval, will remain at about the same level. Departures from the level are regarded as random variation.

For the specialist, reliability of a measure usually is defined as the ratio of true score variance to total observed variance on a stable trait. The presumption is that observations that are reproducible, apart from random differences across observers or random perturbations over time, are trustworthy within limits. Feldt and Brennan (1993) give more precise and technical definitions and attend briefly to the way reliability affects estimates of group differences.

Definitions of reliability that are pertinent to narrative or case study observations are broader than but related to statistical definitions. At least some experts define the reliability of case study observations in terms of reproducibility (Yin, 1989). The idea is that the procedures used in generating the case study are such that independent investigators would produce the same observations.

In randomized controlled field experiments, random error produces no systematic bias in estimating the relative effectiveness of treatments. Such error, however, does degrade statistical power. The true differences among treatments will be harder to discern from the sample at hand. The random error will also result in larger confidence intervals that are constructed to characterize such differences. (See the illustrations given in Chapter 4 and the references therein.)

Validity

Validity refers to the degree to which the measurements actually reflect the true variation in the outcome of interest. If children are given a test of their knowledge of history in a language with which they are unfamiliar, for example, estimates of their mean level of achievement will be systematically biased. That is, the results will not reflect their understanding of history. Studies of validity usually involve looking at the pattern of agreement between the results produced by one method of measurement and the results generated by other measures that produce results known to be valid or invalid in different respects. For example, an employment experiment that relies heavily on self-reported income of participants might use actual income tax reports in a side study of the validity of self-reports. Messick (1993) provides an instructive summary of the topic in simple and complex settings.

The definition of validity for case study or process-oriented observations does not differ appreciably from this at the abstract level. Multiple sources of evidence are used to determine and ensure the validity of the case material (Yin, 1989).

To the extent that validity is low in measures across all treatment groups in an experiment, statistical power will be reduced. The relevance of the measures to the treatment goals and operations also will be low. To the extent that validity is uniformly high across treatment groups, the effects of treatments on the response variable will be easier to detect.

The measures used in the Spouse Assault Replication Program are illustrative. The main outcome variable of interest was assaultive behavior of an offender. Continuous monitoring, using videotape or other recording equipment, or daily interviews with victims, family members, and so forth, arguably would produce the most valid measures of the behavior. Intensive monitoring of this sort was not feasible. Instead, both police records and victim interviews were used to generate data on the response variable, that is, assaultive behavior.

Police records of an offender's arrest following treatment could be regarded as a reasonably valid measure of the fact of arrest. Such evidence was sufficient for police to judge that the individual had engaged in an assault that warranted arrest. Police records, of course, will not include assaults that are not reported to the police. In this sense, they are a measure of assault but one of imperfect validity.

Victim reports arguably can produce valid information about the frequency of assaultive behavior. Because these reports usually are retrospective, and because memory decay even over a short period can be substantial, the measures are imperfect. The absolute level of their validity is unknown.

Obviously, if measures of outcome for one treatment group are less valid than measures made on a second treatment group, then estimates of treatment effectiveness will be compromised. In the Spouse Assault Replication Program, victims were surveyed periodically after the event. The victims' self-reports of assaults, one can argue, would be quite accurate for victims whose partners were arrested because, one supposes, the arrest increases saliency of assault. Victims whose partners were not arrested, one can argue, would be less accurate because nothing special occurred to heighten the ability to remember assaults. Data on the relative differences in validity of self-reporting were not collected in the SARP experiments. The assumption was made that validity of measures was the same across treatment groups.

The issue is not confined to experiments designed to reduce the incidence of volatile events. Consider, for example, education experiments. The main outcome variable of interest is the academic achievement level of students. Students involved in treatments in which test-taking is practiced may produce data on their achievement that is more valid, relative to what they know, than data generated by students who did not engage in the practice. The more valid measure may inflate the apparent effect of one of the treatments. That is, the quality of the measurements may have improved, not the students' actual achievement level.

The potential problem of differential validity of measurement across treatments is pertinent to experiments in a wide variety of arenas. Individuals who are assigned randomly to special nutrition programs, for example, may increase awareness of their eating habits and report more accurately than control group members. Participants in human resource training programs may, following graduation, produce more accurate estimates of wages or wage rates than individuals who did not participate. Health care professionals may be more careful in measuring characteristics of clients involved (randomly) in one program rather than another.

It is partly on account of concerns about validity of self-reports, including differential validity across treatment groups, that controlled experiments often employ measures that are less vulnerable to the problem. The Project NetWork experiment on the return-to-work program for the disabled, for example, relied heavily on Social Security Administration records on the types of disability payments that individuals received, the time of onset or termination of payments, amounts of disability payments, and earnings from employment (Rupp et al., 1994). The administrative reporting system had been in place and integrated with quality ensurance systems. Beyond this, self-reports on such variables arguably would have been of lower quality than the SSA system data.

The need to depend on administrative record systems is especially critical when an experiment involves long-term follow-up of participants. In the High/Scope Perry Preschool Study, for example, individuals who had been engaged in specialized preschool and control conditions at the age of 3 or 4 years have been followed up periodically since the 1960s. The follow-up through age 27 relied on police and court records to get at juvenile and adult arrests and convictions. It depended on social service agency records on welfare assistance and the use of other social services, as well as school records on suspensions, special services, grades, and so on to generate valid data on outcomes and process (Schweinhart et al., 1993).

Timing the Observations

Deciding when and how often observations are made in an experiment depends heavily on one's expectation about how people will respond to the treatments. This expectation may be based on prior longitudinal surveys such as event histories in criminal justice research, growth curves in human development research, employment or wage rate changes in panel studies of income dynamics, and so on.

Decisions about when to measure might also be based on earlier field experiments. The experiments mounted in the Spouse Assault Replication Program, for example, involved measuring assaultive behavior up to 6 months following an offender's initial contact with police. The decision was based on results of an earlier field experiment that showed that most recidivism would occur within this period.

When little is understood about when individuals will respond to treatment or how response to treatment changes over time, pilot research is justified. This work may constitute the initial stage of a formal experiment, one designed to assay the quality of measures as well as to inform one's choice of when observations should be made.

In the absence of prior information on how a treatment may affect the target individuals and without theory about the matter, the decisions about timing of measurements are difficult. Consider Figure 7.1, illustrating alternative scenarios for how the effect of treatment may appear over time. The difference between the two treatment groups may involve a step function, illustrated in the first figure. Individuals involved in a special training and income support program, for example, may take some time to look for better jobs and go to work only at the end of some period. Measures of income taken only during the period prior to the step may show no discernible effect of treatment relative to a control condition.

The response may be such that, on average, individual status changes gradually rather than abruptly, and reaches a high plateau relative to a control condition. For example, measures on a chronically ill group in an innovative program designed to enhance self-sufficiency may show such a pattern of incremental change. This scenario, illustrated in the second panel of Figure 7.1, implies that measures must be taken late rather than early to establish maximum impact and must be taken frequently if the rate of the change is important.

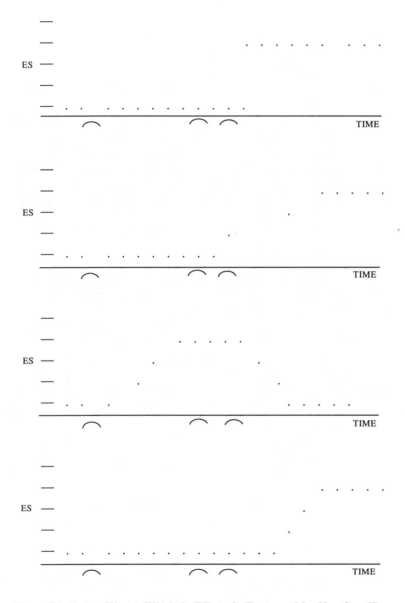

Figure 7.1. Various Ways in Which the Effect of a Treatment May Vary Over Time

SOURCE: Adapted from *Design Sensitivity: Statistical Power for Experimental Design*, Lipsey, © copyright 1990 by Sage Publications.
NOTE: Response is measured along the vertical axis (ES); time is on the horizontal axis. Observations made only at the tick marks are common but can be entirely misleading. See the text for details.

Alternatively, the effect of treatment may be very rapid and be followed by a decay in the effect size. For example, certain preschool programs for children have shown a notable and relatively rapid effect, but the effect decays over a year or two following entry to primary school. The implication of this process, illustrated in the third panel of Figure 7.1, is that measures ought to be taken soon after exiting the preschool program if the immediate effects of the program are important to discern. Later measures ought to be taken periodically if the decay is important.

Similar decays in the immediate effect of an intervention have been documented in randomized field tests of Summer Training and Education Programs (STEP). STEP provided intensive academic and job related activities to 14- and 15-year-old youth who had had considerable difficulty in school in the preceding year. The program produced remarkable changes in achievement test scores (a half grade higher relative to controls) early in the study. Three years after exiting STEP, however, there were no discernible differences between youths in the STEP group and the control group. Across five sites, 15% were neither working nor in school; a fifth of the women had children, and most of these were receiving public assistance (Walker & Vilella-Velez, 1992).

The treatment may have a delayed effect of the sort illustrated in the fourth panel of Figure 7.1. That is, there is a long delay between treatment and the discernible changes in individuals who have had the treatment. The effect may be induced by local conditions; well-trained individuals, for example, may not be employed during a recession period. The effect of special health care programs for children may not be apparent until the children reach adolescence and are at risk of diseases that do not impinge on children. Although delayed effects are plausible at times, empirical evidence on the phenomenon is sparse.

TREATMENT VARIABLES:
PROGRAMS, PROJECTS, OR PRACTICES

The treatment in randomized field tests at times has been conceived of as a simple variable that is either present or absent. Arrest occurs or it does not, for example, in a controlled test of the effect of arresting an offender in a police experiment. Engaging in Job Corps, it is supposed, occurs or it does not in a study of the effect of Job Corps participation on subsequent employment.

For a core statistical analysis of an experiment's results, this conception is adequate. Deeper observation was recommended more than 20 years ago, however, in the interest of understanding the "treatments" as all the interventions to which individuals (or entities) are exposed, including the control conditions (Riecken et al., 1974). Contemporary field tests do not view the treatments simplistically. They confront hard decisions about which aspects of program and control conditions ought to be measured.

Choices About What to Observe

Deciding what to observe about the treatments being compared in an experiment depends on the function of information and the "client" for the information. That is, thuses of the data should drive the design of data collection on treatment variables. The information users generally include the experiment's designer, analysts, and the sponsor of the program that is under examination. They include the program's staff or management. At times, they include other stakeholders. Consider some illustrations.

All Those With an Interest in the Experiment. It makes little sense to "test" a program unless one understands the program and the control condition against which it is compared. In the Spouse Assault Replication Program, for example, neither the experiment's designers nor the police knew exactly what arrest meant beyond the obvious. Advocacy groups that argued for the arrest of domestic violence offenders did not know much about what is entailed in an arrest. It was a revelation to some that "arrest" involved no more than 4 hours in jail and no substantial follow-up by the victim.

The Experiment's Designers and Analysts. For the evaluation team, knowledge of the program being tested requires more than understanding the sets of activities being compared. To design the experiment well, one also needs to understand specific program stages that inform decisions about exactly when to allocate individuals to alternative regimens randomly, whether and when to measure characteristics of program participants beyond those captured by a program's internal information system, and what types of analysis to perform.

For example, in designing the evaluation of Job Corps, the evaluation team had to decide when to randomly allocate individuals to the treatment (Job Corps) and to control conditions, that is, any other community services that were available. The candidates for Job Corps emerge from different referral sources. The individuals who are accepted may or may not actually make a commitment at the eligibility screening stage or the stage of actually going to a Job Corps center to work.

The experiment's designers decided to randomly allocate individuals to Job Corps and the alternatives after initial screening for the candidates' eligibility. Although all eligible candidates do not turn up for Job Corps training, this point of random allocation seemed sensible. The choice was based on an understanding of the programmatic stages of screening and entry into Job Corps.

Sponsors of the Experiment or of the Program. If the sponsors of the experiment and the program are one and the same, measurement of the program is essential to the experiment's credibility. For example, the Job Corps program and its evaluation in a controlled test were both sponsored by the U.S. Department of Labor (DOL). The DOL's claims, prior to the experiment, about what happens in the Job Corps may be accurate.

Insofar as Congress must distrust claims, or at least invite verification of claims, validity of observation is an important standard. The experimenter must then take responsibility for independently generating relevant information. In the Job Corps experiment, the evaluation team, in consultation with the program's sponsors, made a deliberate attempt to generate data on program activity beyond the data generated in the DOL's information system. Others, such as the U.S. General Accounting Office, may have focused on an audit of program records of activity.

The Program Staff and Sponsors. If the program is new, the experiment team will, at times, assist in designing a management information system for the program. This system, or part of it, will help program staff and experimenters to understand the treatments.

Even when the program is not new and there is no real need to invent a system, the measures that the experiment team takes apart from the products of an existing information system can be important. This is partly for the credibility engendered by independent examiners, as suggested earlier. It is partly in the interest of refreshing the way one views existing systems and perhaps improves them.

Once decisions have been made about whether treatments ought to be observed, other choices remain. One may make observations at the study level, the level of the treatment provider, or the service recipient. Box 7.1 outlines these levels.

BOX 7.1
Observations on Treatments

Experiment level
  Treatment assigned
  Treatment delivered
Provider level
  Number of providers
  Duration and frequency of engagement, contact hours
  Engagement composition and dynamics
Target individual (or entity) level
  Number assigned/received
  Frequency, duration of engagement
  Dimensions/dynamics of engagement
Target affiliate level
  Same
Multisite level
  Treatment goals
  Providers
  Operations
  Resources

Study Level Observation

Three kinds of observations on treatments are important at the study level. First, the treatment that is randomly assigned to a unit, whether delivered or not, must be recognized and recorded. Second, the treatment that is actually delivered, regardless of what treatment was randomly assigned, must be similarly recognized. Third, the reasons why the treatments delivered are at times not the same as those randomly assigned must be understood.

Understanding which treatments are randomly assigned to whom (or what) is essential to a legitimate analysis of the statistical data generated in a study. The core statistical analysis hinges on comparing the randomly constituted groups (see Chapter 9 on analysis). It is to these groups that formal statistical characterizations, about certainty in the test results, pertain. The "observation" of which treatment was randomly assigned is often an integral part of the assignment process. A computer-based system for randomization, for example, normally can be programmed to ensure that the particular assignment is recorded along with the identity of the person or entity so assigned.

Observations on the treatment that is actually delivered, in contrast to the treatment assigned, help to establish the integrity of the study's execution and to interpret outcomes. If, for example, none of the treatments that were assigned to schools in a study of how to reduce school disorders was actually employed by the schools, the statistical analyst must recognize the fact. Unless observations are made on what treatment was actually employed, the analyst cannot produce a comparison that is fair and well-informed.

Departures from random assignment are not uncommon. They have occurred at low rates in tests of nutrition and health programs for women, infants, and children (Puma et al., 1991), experiments on police handling of domestic violence (e.g., Hirschel et al., 1991), evaluation of medical regimens (Friedman et al., 1985), and elsewhere. In field tests that are badly run, no information on such departures is available. In field tests that are well run in stable environments, the rate departures are in the 0-10% range. Studies that are undertaken in volatile environments or under conditions in which adherence to the treatment assigned receives scant attention usually are characterized by higher departure rates.

The imperfect correspondence between the treatments that are randomly assigned and the treatments that actually are provided needs to be observed for several reasons. By way of illustration, consider the Spouse Assault Replication Program, in which misdemeanor assailants were assigned randomly to either a mediation treatment, in which police officers restored order and left the premises, or an arrest treatment, in which the offender was booked and formally charged with a misdemeanor crime. At least some offenders who were randomly selected into the mediation group were sufficiently obstreperous or threatening to justify the police officers' arresting the individual. The offender was randomly assigned to one treatment but given another.

The reasons for the imperfect correspondence between treatments assigned and delivered in this case, as in others, must be sought. The relevant evidence may be based on ethnographic or qualitative observations made on the scene or on retrospective reports from participants at the scene. In the Spouse Assault Replication Program, for example, researchers relied on both their own observations, made during ride-along with police officers, and retrospective reports from police officers to understand that departures from the treatment assigned often depended heavily on the immediate offensive behavior of the assailant.

Narrative and statistical information on the matter is important to understanding how treatments can at times be tailored to suit local conditions. It is also important to analyzing statistical data on outcomes. For example, if the departures from the treatment assigned in the field test are similar to those that would occur if the treatment was mandatory, then the field test results can be relied on to inform policy decisions about the desirability of the treatments under investigation.

Provider-Level Observation

Although a "yes" or "no" characterization of which treatment is assigned is essential to the statistical analysis of outcomes, deeper observation on treatments often is warranted. High-quality description of the treatments and the procedures, activities, time, and resources that they entail enrich one's understanding of them. "Arrest" as a treatment, for example, is merely a label until one learns whether the individual who is arrested is handcuffed, how much time the arrest and booking takes, whether jail time is involved, and whether and how release occurs.

Similarly, activities called "bilingual education" have been discussed often in the education media. The term may have political meaning. Its substance is ambiguous unless one understands whether the bilingual program actually involves education in two language contexts, how much of either language is used, and when either is employed (National Academy of Sciences, 1992). Field studies of how bilingual education affects the performance of schoolchildren whose native language is not English are meaningless at worst and difficult to interpret at best unless description of the actual activity is thorough.

The second reason for intensive observation and reporting of how treatments in a controlled test are delivered has its origins in ethics. It is not conscionable, relative to some standards of good ethics, to undertake field experiments unless the results of the study are likely to be used (see Chapter 3 on ethics). Be that as it may, a treatment found effective in a field test cannot be employed in other settings unless the activities entailed by the treatment are described well. Without information that is sufficient to re-create the treatment elsewhere, the study arguably is useless.

Third, it is well understood that the delivery of any specified treatment in the social arena may vary in scope, duration, or intensity, or in other ways, across all individuals who are designated to receive the treatment. Delivery may also vary across site in multisite tests. Not all assault cases assigned to a "counseling" treatment in a police experiment are handled the same way by police officers, counselors, or other participants. Not all teachers responsible for "bilingual education" or an improved mathematics curriculum will teach uniformly well or in accord with good professional guidelines. Reliable, valid information about the variation can be helpful to service providers in making decisions about enhancing quality in delivery, allocating resources to accommodate variability, and exploring why such variations occur.

A decline in effect size over time may come about because of changes in the character of the new treatment under investigation. Recent experiments on intensive protective supervision for juveniles, for example, resulted in remarkable effects over the first 18 months of the project. By the end of the 36-month period of the experiment, however, the treatment was found to have a negligible effect. The authors attribute the phenomenon to burnout of service providers, among other factors, over the course of the effort (Land, McCall, & Williams, 1990; Land et al., 1991).

Intensive observation on the implementation of treatment need not be complex. Table 7.1 illustrates how simple count data can be used to characterize the way police officers generated eligible cases for multisite studies on different approaches to handling domestic violence. Table 7.1, one of several kinds of information developed by researchers and the Charlotte Police Department on the topic, summarizes how many officers were the source of how many cases for the test. Nearly half of the department's 600 uniformed police officers generated eligible cases. Most officers encountered or recognized only a few cases. Less than half of the officers generated more than two cases over a 2-year period. Such a table helps to summarize the resources used for treatment delivery. It can inform discussions about future resource allocation and decisions about whether to adopt one or another method of handling cases. Outliers—such as the single police officer who generated the greatest number of cases—and the skewed distribution in officer production of cases invite further study.

BASELINE MEASURES

Observations made on individuals or entities prior to their assignment to treatments in a field test are designated as baseline data. The choice of what to observe depends on the possible functions of the baseline data, outlined in Box 7.2 and discussed in what follows.

TABLE 7.1

Number of Eligible Cases by Officers, Charlotte Experiment

Number of Referrals	Number of Contributing Officers	Percentage of Contributing Officers	Total Number of Referrals	Percentage of Referrals
1	116	46.0	116	16.9
2	48	19.0	96	14.0
3	21	8.3	63	9.2
4	21	8.3	84	12.2
5	18	7.1	90	13.1
6	12	4.8	72	10.5
7	5	2.0	35	5.1
8	2	.8	16	2.3
9	2	.8	18	2.6
10	2	.8	20	2.9
11	2	.8	22	3.2
12	1	.4	12	1.7
16	1	.4	16	2.3
26	1	.4	26	3.8
Total	252	99.9	686	99.8

SOURCE: From *Charlotte Spouse Assault Replication Project: Final Report*, Hirschel, Hutchison, Dean, Kelley, and Pesackis, © copyright 1991 by University of North Carolina at Charlotte.
NOTE: Percentages do not add to 100 because of rounding.

Functions

The baseline data are instrumental in determining that the experiment has been implemented in accord with the study's design. This includes checking on adherence to eligibility requirements. In the Spouse Assault Replication Program, for example, principal investigators were able to use baseline police records and victim reports to establish that cases declared as eligible did indeed meet the experiment's eligibility requirements. That is, the cases involved spouselike relationships, the offenders were over the age of 17, and so on.

Baseline data on eligibility and other variables also facilitate checks on the similarity of groups that are randomly constituted. These groups should not differ systematically. Any differences that do occur should be calculable, that is, within levels of what could happen by chance. These checks

---

BOX 7.2
Functions of Baseline Data

Verifying that eligibility requirements have been met
Verifying that random assignment produced similar groups
Characterizing the type of individuals assigned to treatment
Supporting description of the pipeline
Informing the management of treatments
Enhancing the statistical power of core analysis
Enriching the exploratory analyses
Informing decisions to replicate the experiment
Informing analysis of the generalizability of the experiment

---

are routinely reported; see, for example, any of the final reports on randomized field tests cited in this volume.

Baseline data help to characterize the individuals or entities who become engaged in treatments and the individuals who do not, apart from eligibility characteristics. In the Spouse Assault Replication Program, for example, it was found that offenders who reach the attention of police for a misdemeanor assault are, on average, mature (30-32 years old); that victims are a bit younger; that most have not graduated from high school; and that half appear to be under the influence of alcohol.

In field tests for which pipeline studies are not done, such baseline data are often the only source of information on the types of clients flowing into the treatment system. When pilot studies are done, the baseline data usually provide a more thorough picture of who gets into treatment and, often, how.

The statistical power of core analysis of outcomes sometimes can be enhanced by using baseline data. In particular, power is increased when the analyses take into account the pretreatment characteristics that predict or are correlated with the outcome variables under normal conditions. Offenders' criminal or corrections experience, for example, is often correlated with current criminal activity. The correlation can be taken into account, and in doing so the power of analysis is increased, by using covariance analysis.

Beyond their use in a core analysis that estimates differences in treatment effectiveness, the baseline data generally enrich exploratory analyses. Some theorists, for example, may argue that the use of certain drugs is negatively correlated with assaultive behavior in domestic disputes. To the extent that baseline measures include alcohol level and include urine testing, the argument may be illuminated and the results used in designing other research.

Baseline data, like pipeline data, can be used to characterize and assay the generalizability of results and to inform the design of replication studies. The restriction of treatments in the domestic violence experiments to cases involving spouselike relationships implies that generalizing to other relationships—involving siblings, for example—is unwise. Future studies may then include siblings and other relationships as part of the target if the matter is deemed important by various stakeholders in the domestic violence arena.

Choice

The standards for deciding how to measure baseline variables are no different in principle from those used in choosing measures of outcome or treatment implementation: relevance, reliability, and validity. A further standard pertaining to analysis is that any baseline observations used in analysis of treatment effects are known to be unaffected by treatment. This is guaranteed if the observations are made prior to treatment; that is, the treatments cannot influence measures made before the treatment is imposed. Baseline measures made during treatment (or worse, afterward) are suspect because there usually is no guarantee that the observations are unaffected by treatment. Individuals who are assigned randomly to an arrest treatment, for example, may make claims about their employment status that are different from claims they would have made if they had been assigned to a mediation condition.

OBSERVATIONS ON THE CONTEXT OF THE STUDY

The contextual information may be statistical in character, in which case it might be incorporated into a core analysis that compares the effectiveness of one treatment to another. The information also may be narrative. In either case, developing an understanding about context generally focuses on variables that could influence the implementation of treatments and the analysis of relative differences in their effectiveness.

Social Context

In an economic experiment designed to test the effectiveness of alternative job placement programs, the local market conditions may be such that the demand for labor is low over the course of the study. In the extreme, it may be impossible to produce good evidence that one treatment, a special job placement method for example, is better than another simply because there are *no* jobs available. The relevant contextual data may be drawn from local surveys of employers, counts of jobs that are publicly advertised, administrative data from public employment offices, and so on. See Dynarski (1993) for an interesting related illustration.

Similarly, a school-based program for dropout prevention arguably will be influenced by local labor market conditions. A local and temporarily high demand for labor may swamp any dropout prevention effort. A low demand may or may not put a ceiling on the number of students who drop out. If the ambient number of dropouts in a site is very low, regardless of local conditions, the statistical power of any field test that is designed to compare alternative prevention efforts is unlikely to produce useful information about which approach works better.

Administrative Context

The administrative context will, at times, be important to understanding the field test's operation, treatment delivery, and test results. For example, in the Spouse Assault Replication Program, one site in this multisite trial experienced the death of one principal investigator. Another was affected by the firing of a police chief responsible for the experiment and a subsequent court battle for his reinstatement, along with a variety of other local perturbations that affected field test operations, pipeline, and treatment delivery. The environment changed dramatically in one site, for a time, when considerable police officer attention was directed toward the drug trade and weapons market and away from domestic assault. This shift led, as one might expect, to a decreased flow of assailants into the study.

Local administrative history as well as changes in the administrative environment form part of the context. Indeed, the choice of sites for field tests of innovations often is made on the basis of such history and the prospect that the site will be conducive to good research. Recent experiments on community-based treatment for chronic schizophrenia, for example, were initiated partly because the administrative vehicle for the experiments, the Veterans Administrative Hospital System, had a history of participation in high-quality field tests of treatment regimens. (See

Chapter 8 on operations for more information on scouting sites for experiments.)

Choice and Resources

The choice of which context variables to observe usually is based on the same standards used to choose measures of response variables, treatment variables, and baseline conditions: relevance, validity, and reliability. It is common to rely on existing administrative or statistical information to understand context, partly in the interest of economy. For example, locally available data bearing on the local economy, crime rates, health, and so on are accessible through census data at the tract level and zip code level. Information bearing on local school districts is available from the National Center for Education Statistics. Organizations such as the Bureau of Justice Statistics and National Center for Health Statistics at times can provide contextual information on crime rates and health, respectively, for major metropolitan areas and regions.

COSTS

The effect of treatments on specific response variables has been the focus of most randomized field tests. Student achievement receives attention in studies of effective school programs. Recidivism is of substantial interest in tests of law enforcement and corrections strategies. The differences in effectiveness of treatments, as measured by these variables, is not the only ingredient in making decisions, of course. Costs of treatments are important. In some areas, costs are at least as important as the outcome variables. Costs often have not been measured well, if at all, in randomized tests in education, criminal and civil justice, and health services.

Conscientious efforts to assay costs of treatments have been made at times in randomized studies, most frequently in employment and training studies and some human services research. Illustrations are given in what follows. Furthermore, the state of the art in measuring costs and incorporating them into defensible cost-effectiveness analyses has become accessible to noneconomists in recent years, partly on account of published examples and textbooks. Textbooks such as Schalock and Thornton's (1988), which is designed for program administrators; Rossi and Freeman's (1989), which is directed toward social researchers; and Yates's (1996), which focuses on human services, provide thorough guidance and numerous examples.

When to Measure Costs

Costs of implementing the treatments in a field test vary over time. Start-up efforts may demand resources, for example, in renovating buildings, hiring and training staff, developing information systems, and so on. The treatments may involve costs that continue over the course of their employment: Staff must be paid, equipment must be maintained, and so on. The programs may also demand extra resources at the termination of the test.

It is arguably most productive to measure costs during the period in which the programs under investigation have stabilized. The argument is based on the idea that benefit-effectiveness analyses that inform decisions should focus on the relatively steady state that a program, once adopted as policy, would achieve. The stabilized treatments in the field test are supposed to represent that steady state.

Measuring costs over a stable period is a common practice in research on the effects of programs in the training, employment, and welfare arenas. Pertinent examples include Handwerger and Thornton's (1988) description of expenditures during multisite tests of the Minority Female Single Parent Programs; the Robins, Spiegelman, Weiner, and Bell (1980) characterization of costs of a guaranteed annual income for the poor, based on the Seattle and Denver Income Maintenance Experiments; and benefit-cost analyses given in Hollister et al. (1984) on the National Supported Work Demonstration experiments.

Sources of Data on Costs

Typically, cost estimates are based on several sources of information. The expenditures registered in accounting systems for each of the treatments delivered in a field test, for example, are fundamental. Because accounting practices differ across sites and delivery systems, on-site visits with service providers are essential to understanding local costs.

The management information system employed by the service provider or created by the research staff normally is a source of information. Data on the number of individuals assigned to alternative treatments, the kinds of services provided, and so forth can be integrated with expenditures data to produce a description of average costs for major services, cost per person or per family served, and so on.

In multisite experiments or other cases in which treatments are provided by different organizations in various locations, the structure and contents of accounting information systems may differ appreciably from one organization to the next. This scenario requires considerable resources to understand each system and to construct and apply uniform definitions in the interest of ensuring that cost measurements are comparable. The differences may be sufficiently great to permit only broad estimates of costs rather than finely detailed ones, as in the case of multisite tests in which different community-based organizations implement treatments (e.g., Handwerger & Thornton, 1988) and different hospitals collaborate in randomized clinical trials on new surgical techniques (Bunker, Barnes, & Mosteller, 1977).

Cost Measurement

Which costs are measured depends on why costs are regarded as important in the first instance. In controlled field tests, comparisons of cost across sites and across treatment regimens within each site usually are of primary interest.

Attention is directed most often to operations cost, or the direct costs to the sponsor, service provider, or other entities of delivering the treatments. The stress on operations costs is in contrast to two other ways of enumerating costs, the first focusing on costs to society and the second on clients or service recipients. Generally speaking, the costs incurred in operations are of primary interest because although they are at times ambiguous, they usually require fewer assumptions and rely more on conventional standards (of accounting, for example) than costs based on other perspectives.

Operations costs may be blocked out in terms of broad services categories. For example, the Minority Female Single Parent Programs undertaken by the Rockefeller Foundation were designed to integrate training and education for women, child care, and support services such as counseling. Beyond the cost of these services, administrative and indirect costs had to be taken into account. Table 7.2 illustrates the presentation of costs across sites for the program's operation. The relatively high expenditures for child care and support services relative to other costs evidently were not expected.

The costs given in Table 7.2 were constructed from data on outlays for personnel for each service category, materials and supplies (including training materials, for example,), and financial subsidies that were provided to trainees. The estimates included "off-budget" adjustments such as the value of volunteer labor and child care subsidies from public agencies.

TABLE 7.2

Costs of Service Categories in Tests of the Minority
Female Single Parent Program (rounded in thousands of dollars)

Site	Training	Child Care	Support	Administration	Indirect	Total
AUL	184	77	157	157	84	659
CET	339	303	287	99	105	1,132
OIC	212	168	147	177	118	822
WOW	223	68	171	197	179	838

SOURCE: From *The Minority Female Single Parent Program Demonstration: Program Costs*, Handwerger and Thornton, © copyright 1988 The Rockefeller Foundation. Reprinted by permission.
NOTE: Figures are based on accounting records, financial reports, and interviews at the Atlanta Urban League (AUL), the Center for Employment and Training (CET), the Opportunities for Industrialization Center (OIC), and Wider Opportunities for Women (WOW).

These items, in enumerating costs from other perspectives, would be designated as societal.

MISSING DATA REGISTRY

It is a truism that the best way to handle missing data in experiments is to have none. Despite one's industry in ensuring the cooperation of participants, deploying incentives, employing tracing procedures, training interviewers, designing questionnaires, and so forth, some information will fail to be produced. Respondents, at times, will be unable or unwilling to answer questions. Administrative records will be incomplete. Interviewers and respondents will err in skipping questions in an inventory, especially when the inventory is complex. The missingness will be elevated when the experiment involves volatile activity, as in domestic violence.

Constructing a registry of which data are missing and the plausible or verifiable reasons for missingness is sensible for a variety of reasons. In medical experiments, for example, a registry's import is obvious. One ought to know that the absence of information on a patient being followed over time is attributable to the patient having died rather than having changed residence, for example. In social experiments, formal registries are not yet customary, perhaps because resources are limited. One then suffers the discomfort of knowing that an item of information is absent and not knowing much about the reasons for its absence.

Insofar as missingness is plausibly related to the outcomes of treatments, the scientific justification for a thorough registry is strong. For example, individuals who have been arrested at least once may, for a variety of reasons, be more difficult to locate than individuals who have not. A longitudinal study in which criminal behavior or arrest is an outcome variable then may find a relatively low crime rate only because the criminals are harder to locate. That is, one might presume that an arrest treatment worked in the sense of reducing crime rate, when in fact it did not. Instead, the treatment merely invited the offenders to be less accessible, leaving disproportionately more nonoffenders in the sample.

A registry containing the "what" and the "why" thus permits more thoughtful analysis. It may also help one to better exploit technology for imputing missing data at the person level and item level. Little and Rubin (1987) describe developments in this arena; the *Proceedings of the American Statistical Association* routinely covers advances. Beyond this, a registry can serve as the basis for improving the future experiments. The reasons for missingness might be suppressed or their influence reduced if one has an orderly way of characterizing them. A registry is an instrument for doing so.

8

Operations

What we understand about the management of high quality
applied social research is more akin to the oral history of
primitive societies than one characterized by a written language.

—Wolf (an alias)

In the behavioral and social sciences and educational research, published reports on the operational conduct of controlled experiments are
not common. Indeed, it is sometimes difficult even to learn how the field
test employed randomization. There is good reason nevertheless to take
operations seriously. No trustworthy experiment takes place in the
absence of good management.

Early Examples:
Reporting on Operations

This chapter capitalizes on the precedent set by the Social Science
Research Council's Committee on Social Experimentation in attending to
the management of comparative field tests (Riecken et al., 1974). It builds
on fine early examples of reporting on management. The New Jersey
Negative Income Tax Study, for example, begun in 1968 and costing about
$8 million, arguably was the first large-scale controlled social experiment.
Designed to evaluate special forms of income supplements for the poor, it
resulted in a series of published reports, including one on the experiment's
operations (Kershaw & Fair, 1976). The Seattle-Denver Income Maintenance Experiment was undertaken with similar objectives on a larger scale.
Covering an 11-year period, this too resulted in, among other products, an
administrative history of the operations (Christopherson, 1983).

More Recent Examples

More recent reporting on operations has been encouraged by a few federal agencies and private foundations. The National Institute of Justice, for example, required that information on operations be described in the final report submitted by each principal investigator in the multisite Spouse Assault Replication Program experiments.

The academic research community at times has contributed to understanding in this arena through books and professional journals. Turpin and Sinacore's (1991) edited volume for *New Directions for Program Evaluation*, for example, covered operational issues in multisite tests in mental health, health care, civil and criminal justice, and human resources training. Special issues of the same journal have focused on randomization in controlled experiments (Boruch & Wothke, 1985; Conrad, 1994).

This chapter exploits these resources and others in covering operations. It attends to the role of the sponsor and to the responsibilities of other entities and individuals are involved in randomized field tests. Considerable attention is paid to engaging the cooperation of organizations in the experiment. Scouting and selecting sites—both within site and involving cross coordination—and training are part of most operational plans. They also are discussed.

ELEMENTS OF OPERATIONS

Tasks

Certain tasks are common to all randomized field tests. These drive the organization and management of the endeavor. Box 8.1 outlines the tasks roughly in chronological order. Some elements identified in Box 8.1 can occur often, even continuously, in the course of the experiment. Reviews of the research literature, for example, are undertaken in early stages to identify potential treatments, guide the design of pipeline study, help specify eligibility criteria for treatment recipients, and influence the choice and quality control of measurement methods. Later in the course of the field test, a review of more recent research might illuminate new approaches to analysis of the data.

Similarly, early negotiation is essential, for example to ensure that there is agreement about the objectives of the treatments and that the field test is tailored to the setting. The technical features of a field test's design, sample size determination, and so forth must fit with a local program's

---

BOX 8.1

Tasks in a Randomized Field Test

Reviewing research
Scouting and selecting sites
Negotiating agreements
Pipeline study execution
Pilot testing
Coordinating activity
Determining eligibility
Baseline data collection
Ensuring quality control
Implementing random assignment
Delivering and monitoring treatment and control
Collecting and coding data
Analyzing data
Reporting
Producing data for secondary analysis
Terminating the project

---

intake processes, eligibility determination, and other conditions. Clients must be identified for service and services must be delivered, tasks that will entail periodic negotiation over the course of the work. Data must be collected on the state of clients in treatment and groups, on the level or intensity of treatments, and often on the social context in which the field test operates. The data collection stage may involve negotiations over administrative record production by the service provider, coordination of the survey research staff with intake or outreach specialists, and data sharing.

No design for a randomized field test can anticipate all the issues or obstacles that may emerge in its execution. Consequently, pilot testing the experiment's components is desirable. Systems for the early detection of problems, notably oversight and advisory groups, quality control systems for data management, and so forth usually must be exploited regularly. Operations may change, for example, if it becomes clear that the number of clients flowing into the experiment is far lower than expected. The early detection of the problem and the construction of options for its resolution require both negotiation and a team that is capable of adopting methods quickly.

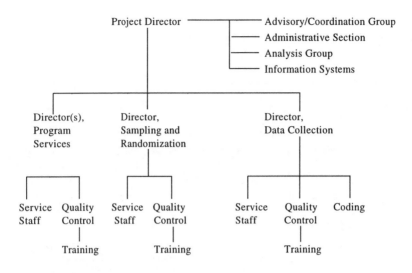

Figure 8.1. Organizational Chart for a Multisite Randomized Field Test

Responsibilities

Good management plans involve identifying such elements and the individuals who take on operational responsibilities. The responsibilities usually are outlined in an organizational chart of the sort given in Figure 8.1. A project director usually is responsible for guidance and execution of the overall experiment. This is usually the principal investigator in foundation-sponsored or contracted efforts. An on-site coordinator usually is essential for managing liaison between the service provider agency (i.e., the organization responsible for treatment delivery) and the experiment's staff; and monitoring the implementation of the experiment, including randomization procedures, measurement, and so forth. A director of program services generally must be identified to direct overall delivery of services following randomization. The responsibility may also include retention and tracking of treatment recipients.

Responsibilities beyond these may take a variety of forms and often require detailed specification. For example, many field tests involve repeated surveys of clients following the random assignment to treatment. Tracking respondents, maintaining contact with them, and eliciting reliable information weekly, monthly, or semiannually often is not easy. The duties may be performed by a small local group, under the direction of a survey director, or they may be met by a separate entity under a contractual agreement with the project director's organization. Similarly, the treatments may entail the need to specify responsibilities at several levels in the treatment process. In the Metro-Dade Spouse Assault Replication Program, for example, a police official had overall responsibility for ensuring that arrests were made properly. Responsibility at middle management levels (regional and district commanders), at supervisory levels (sergeants), and at point of contact (patrol officers) had to be specified.

There are no textbooks that focus on operational tasks, responsibilities, and resources in a social experiment. Fine reports are produced at times, however, for particular evaluations. See, for example, Sherman et al. (1992) on managing the Spouse Assault Replication Program in Milwaukee and Dolittle and Traeger (1990) on the Job Training Partnership Act Experiment. For a broad handling of the topic of resources in evaluation, see Hedrick, Bickman, and Rog's (1993) discussion of data, time, personnel, and money.

THE SPONSOR'S ROLE

Box 8.2 outlines the possible duties of the sponsor of a field experiment. The duty begins with identifying the problem arena. In 1991, for example, the U.S. Department of Education took seriously the sparse understanding of adult illiteracy and sponsored surveys to define the severity and scope of the problem. The department also subsidized research to uncover purported solutions, notably documenting the character of adult literacy programs in the United States. In 1992, the department sponsored workshops to discuss alternative evaluation designs for a national multisite testing effort, including the use of randomized field experiments. The results were then used to decide how to construct field tests of promising programs.

Meetings with similar intent have been undertaken prior to government commitments to experiment in other arenas. They include demonstration projects for the homeless (Orwin, Cordray, & Huebner, 1994; Conrad, 1994) and disabled social security recipients (Rupp et al., 1992). Published descriptions of the character and outcomes of such meetings are rare.

The sponsor's duties usually encompass making choices about the specific administrative mechanism for planning and conducting the experiment and for monitoring and oversight. Monitoring, for example, may

---

BOX 8.2
The Sponsor:
Common Responsibilities

1. Identifying the problem
2. Selecting administrative, fiscal, monitoring, and oversight mechanisms
3. Learning about possible treatments and response variables
4. Deciding whether an experiment is an option for estimating effectiveness
5. Specifying broad experiment objectives
6. Making decisions about adaptive changes and side studies
7. Providing resources
8. Specifying deliverables

---

involve relying only on internal staff of the sponsor or on staff acting in concert with an external advisory group. This latter option is more likely if the sponsor's interest lies in an evaluation that is independent of the sponsor and if the field test requires, as it usually does, specialized skills in survey research, measurement, and local negotiation. The financial vehicle for the external work, notably grants, contracts, or negotiated agreements, must also be chosen by the sponsor, along with criteria for selecting among candidates to undertake the experiment. Oversight mechanisms, discussed in the next section, also must be devised. Making decisions about the broad structure of the enterprise, notably the use of a randomized field test, its objectives, and the expected products, also falls in the ambit of the sponsor's responsibilities.

Three illustrations of these processes are discussed briefly in what follows. They cover experiments sponsored by a federal contracting agency, a grant-making agency, and a private foundation.

Consider first the staged approach taken by the U.S. Department of Agriculture's Food and Nutrition Service (1992) in mounting experiments on the department's Program for Women, Infants, and Children (WIC). The approach involved developing sequential requests for proposals (RFPs) for contracted evaluative work, each RFP being dependent on the products that issued from the preceding one. The first RFP required the independent contractor to review earlier research, undertake policy analyses, and develop design plans to evaluate aspects of the WIC nutrition and health education programs. The contract for this design work was awarded to a union of university and private sector entities that then proposed a comparative field test. Another contract, to do feasibility field tests of the resultant design plan, was awarded later to a different organization; this activity was based on a second RFP that capitalized on the earlier work. A third RFP was issued to elicit proposals for implementing live field tests at four to eight sites. This document included a literature review and a description of the earlier evaluative products, and it made clear the difficulties that could be expected in field tests designed to estimate the effects of nutrition and nutrition education programs on children and their mothers.

In contrast, a grant-making agency, such as the National Institute of Justice (NIJ), generally issues broader invitations to independent scholars in the form of a "program announcement." The NIJ's array of experimental tests in the domestic violence arena, for example, was a consequence of such an approach. The Spouse Assault Replication Program announcement built on an earlier experiment, conducted at a single site, and a literature review. Nearly 20 police departments and scholars responded to the invitation to conduct experiments supported by the federal government.

The private foundations that sponsor controlled tests need not abide by rules that govern public agencies. They achieve their ends differently and capitalize on their particular assets, institutional flexibility for example, in doing so. The Rockefeller Foundation, for example, sponsored randomized controlled field tests of its training program for female single parents partly as a consequence of learning, over a 2-year period, that evidence generated by nonrandomized tests would not be persuasive or defensible in national public forums. The restructuring of the evaluation in four sites entailed renegotiation with community-based organizations that had been responsible for service provision. The sites were asked to cooperate in an experiment involving random assignment. The foundation increased resources to cover the community-based organization's increased responsibilities.

To stabilize financial resources at sites, the foundation took a flexible approach to increasing budgets for program activity when shortfalls threatened the programs being tested and (consequently) the field test. The foundation also was responsible for taking action to change the evaluation design when flaws were uncovered, for developing incentives and resources for sites to intensify efforts to recruit clients when the client flow dwindled, for initiating side studies on the fairness of the randomization procedures, and for production of innovative videotape training materials for the experiment (Cottingham, 1991).

The level of engagement of sponsor staff or management has varied across field experiments. In recent years, the engagement has intensified, at least at the agencies whose staff are themselves well educated about the object and conduct of field tests. The Rockefeller Foundation's project officers, for example, included individuals with advanced degrees in economics and sociology, along with a cadre of advisors who augmented the foundation's capacity to influence the design, execution, and modification of the study.

The Spouse Assault Replication Program, supported by the National Institute of Justice, was characterized by substantial involvement of the government's project monitor. This individual, a Ph.D.-level political scientist, created a role that included coordination of the efforts of six independent investigators and monitoring the experiment on the taxpayers' behalf. The monitor's contribution to discussion of technical issues was such that it often could not be distinguished from contributions of the principal investigators. Indeed, a remarkable synthesis emerged from this engagement (Garner et al., 1995).

At the other extreme, the role of the government or foundation representative may be confined to ensuring that contractual obligations are met. This is common in small field tests, in cases where the research team has expertise that clearly exceeds that of the sponsor's representative, in situations where the representative's other responsibilities simply do not permit deep involvement, and in experiments in which the need for independence of the experimenter argues against direct sponsor involvement.

Regardless of the level of the sponsor's engagement, the sponsor's role and that of the sponsor's representative must be specified, early and at least tentatively, in any controlled field test. The role may change, of course. The initial specification can help to avoid problems of role conflict during the course of the work and to enhance the quality of the effort.

ENGAGING ORGANIZATIONS

No controlled field study of a program, project, or practice takes place without the cooperation of organizations. Their principals, administrators, line staff, and other stakeholders influence the organization's initial agreement to participate in the study. The study's completion depends on their continued willingness to adhere to the study's design, to identify problems, and to cooperate with the experiment team in developing solutions.

This section considers the engagement of organizations whose cooperation is necessary in experiments. It directs special attention to

- who or what is engaged,
- the information necessary for engagement,
- incentives and the reduction of disincentives,
- credibility, and
- tailoring the study design.

Implicit in all that follows is the idea of partnerships among individuals
who are responsible for the design and execution of the study and principals
to whose organizations the experiment is adjoined.

Engaging Whom?

Conducting controlled experiments of new programs is not an idea with
which most public agencies are familiar. Moreover, the experiment's team
may not be entirely certain whose cooperation must be enlisted to get the
experiment off the ground. Questions of whom to engage and how to
engage them therefore are important.

The answers to these questions depends on the specific study. In multistate experiments in the welfare arena, for example, the permission and
counsel of state commissioners of welfare was sought in order to elicit
states' cooperation in tests of work/welfare programs (Gueron, 1985).
Statewide tests of the effect of financial incentives to improve school
performance in Tennessee involved securing agreements at the policy level
from the governor and state superintendent of education (Bickman, 1985).
Initial agreements in this study were followed by meetings between the
Commission of Education and school superintendents across the state in
order to elicit cooperation from the 100 (and more) schools whose engagement was necessary for this multisite effort. A more recent detailed description of engagement strategies for multischool experiments is given in
Ellickson (1994).

Smaller-scale studies also may entail securing agreements at high administrative levels, under the assumption, usually warranted, that such
support is essential to the study's successful execution. For example,
negotiations on the Minneapolis domestic violence experiment began with
the city's police chief, Anthony Bouza (Sherman & Berk, 1985). The
cultivation of interest continued through preexperiment discussions with
managers (e.g., lieutenants, sergeants) and line staff (i.e., police officers).

Similarly, Stevens (1994) argued strongly for a team-based approach that focuses on both program directors and line staff to avoid problems in experiments on residential drug treatment programs for women with children, short-term substance abuse treatments for homeless adults, and HIV risk-reduction efforts.

Advocacy groups are pertinent to the extent that they can impede or facilitate the experiment. Local bar associations, for example, have an interest in some court experiments and, as a consequence, their counsel and support has been sought in studying the effectiveness of pretrial hearings (e.g., Lind, 1985). Victim assistance groups have a formal interest in the way police handle domestic violence, and such groups have been engaged in local oversight of controlled tests of new police approaches to the problem in Minneapolis (Sherman & Berk, 1985), Omaha (Dunford et al., 1990), and elsewhere. Heller and Fantuzzo (1993) and Fantuzzo, Davis, and Ginsburg (1995) conducted controlled tests of methods for reducing the vulnerability of children at risk of violence. These latter tests depended heavily on securing the interest, if not the cooperation, of groups ranging from Head Start mothers to the Black Psychologists Association.

Referral sources must be engaged in field tests that are characterized by a client flow whose volume is not controlled centrally by a treatment provider, but instead is determined by a disparate array of organizations. The Rockefeller Foundation's tests of integrated programs for minority female single parents, for example, depended on community-based organizations to provide training and support services. Prospective clients were directed to the organizations by welfare groups, employment assistance services, and churches, among other referral sources (Cottingham, 1991). In studies of new ways to provide residential therapeutic community services to drug-addicted mothers and homeless adults, referral agencies originally were deemed to be primary sources of clients (Stevens, 1994). In each of these cases, staff at the agencies had to be informed about the experiment and persuaded to continue to make referrals or even increase their number. The process of doing so has required considerable time, and to the extent that agency staff change, the effort must be continuous. When referrals are insufficient, the experiment or program team has been augmented to ensure a reasonable flow of participants into the experiment (Stevens, 1994; Orwin, Cordray, & Huebner, 1994; Boruch et al., 1988).

Information

Accurate information about the study is a condition for an organization's engagement. To understand a small part of the information that must be provided, consider material generated by the U.S. Department of Education and a research group, Mathematica Policy Research, to facilitate experiments on Upward Bound Programs for disadvantaged youth. Initial discussions were undertaken with Upward Bound management, staff, and interest groups to learn about their concerns and possible areas of confusion or conflict. A formal letter on "Concerns and Responses" was developed to address the matter. (The letter is contained in the appendix to this chapter.) The letter's general content does not differ appreciably from materials provided to police officers in criminal justice experiments or that given to stakeholders in studies of programs for homeless substance abusers (e.g., Devine, Wright, & Joyner, 1994), employment programs (Dolittle & Traeger, 1990), and others.

Random assignment in a field experiment is unfamiliar in many organizational contexts despite the commonness of the method in medical clinical trials and some welfare program evaluations. The idea and its purpose and operation often need to be explained. Misconceptions relative to a scientific standard, for example, are common. The language of the law, as one example of a source of misconceptions, usually identifies "random" as being synonymous with capricious or arbitrary, engendering potential problems in explaining the matter to lawyers (e.g., Petersilia, 1989). Regardless of the particular setting and its local vernacular, information that creates a common understanding and language is essential to initial agreement, to tailoring the study design to the particular setting, and to solving problems that inevitably will occur in the test. To the extent that turnover in organizational staff or referral sources in a field experiment is high, as it was in Petersilia's (1989) study of intensive supervision of probationers, there will be a continuing need to educate in the interest of informed engagement.

The *ethical propriety* of random assignment often is a source of concern. It is often reassuring that the individuals assigned to a control condition will be wait-listed for a treatment; that is, they will not be denied program services, but the services will be delayed. This often is made plain in formal communications of the sort exemplified by the "concerns and responses" statement in the appendix. A concern about an increased project burden of recruitment often is addressed by maintaining that only programs with a real surplus of applicants will be engaged in the experiment. Program concerns that certain types of students should be selected have been addressed through design of the randomization process so that once "types" are identified, at least one of each pair are assigned to the program. Because eligible candidates should be informed about the randomization feature, the letter given in the appendix makes the plan plain to parents and students.

Upward Bound project directors worried about the burden and difficulty of explaining the evaluation to their own staffs and other concerned parties. The matter was addressed by making seasoned external professionals available.

Incentives

What attracts or could attract an organization to engage in a controlled field test? The matter depends on incentives and disincentives. They are discussed here in terms of

- interest in better answers,
- leadership,
- stewardship,
- precedent, and
- compensation.

Interest in Better Answers. The main intellectual justifications for a randomized field test are that it produces an unbiased estimate of relative effectiveness of different treatments and a statistical statement of one's confidence in the results. To the extent that the principals in an organization regard the production of such evidence as desirable, the justification constitutes an incentive for engagement.

That more defensible, less equivocal evidence is indeed an incentive is clear, at times. Gueron (1985), for example, marked this as important in persuading state welfare commissioners to consider controlled tests. Federal law had provided their states with an opportunity to try alternatives to their welfare systems. In the absence of reliable evidence about what would work better, eight commissioners agreed to field testing alternatives. Similarly, in writing about the reasons for controlled tests of pretrial arbitration as a device to reduce burdens on the courts, Judge Irving Kaufman suggested that such tests "may be the only way to settle questions of this nature" (Goldman, 1985, p. 64). A similar spirit appeared to characterize the engagement of one of three federal courts that studied new procedures in experiments that Lind (1985) has described.

The interest in answers may lead to initial agreements at the policy or administrative level of an organization. Management, line staff, and external stakeholders may or may not view the matter similarly. Their engagement must be sought regardless of interest at the level of policymakers.

Petersilia (1989), for example, emphasized enlightened self-interest in explaining why probation officials in various states and jurisdictions agreed to cooperate in field tests of intensive supervision programs for felony offenders. "Having been subject to budget cuts and a loss of public confidence in their ability to rehabilitate offenders, most probation staff were eager to discover whether intensive supervision for probationers really works" (p. 445).

In Minneapolis and Milwaukee, police officers volunteered to be a part of experiments on mandatory arrest in comparison to mediation and other treatments to learn how best to handle misdemeanor domestic violence. Their participation was influenced in part by interest in learning which approach reduced offender recidivism and partly by interest in the workload that arrests could entail (Sherman & Berk, 1985; Sherman et al., 1991).

Better evidence and answers will not, at times, be the only incentive for advocacy groups and other stakeholders supporting a field test. In the Spouse Assault Replication Program, for example, at least some advocacy groups viewed experiments positively because, as a consequence of randomization, more assailants would be arrested than if the experiment had not been undertaken (Sherman & Berk, 1985). In court tests of court-annexed arbitration, randomized field tests were "one of several . . . provisions that the court has used to demonstrate to the local bar its sincerity in testing the effectiveness of arbitration" (Lind, 1985, pp. 75-76).

Interest in answers was not, of course, uniform across police departments, to judge from districtwide field tests of domestic violence projects in Omaha (Dunford et al., 1990), Charlotte (Hirschel et al., 1991), and elsewhere. Police officers varied in their level of cooperation in the tests. One can reasonably expect similar variation in the level of cooperation by individual service providers simply because good evidence is of varying interest to them.

Leadership. Gueron (1985) appears to have been the first to identify an interest in leadership as an incentive for engaging in comparative tests. She stressed the matter in explaining why at least some commissioners of welfare committed to the idea of testing new work and welfare schemes. Similarly, Sherman and Berk (1985) emphasized Minneapolis Police Chief Anthony Bouza's proactive stance in deciding to support tests in the domestic violence arena. Goldman (1985) credits Judge Irving Kaufman with taking an early initiative in tests of court-annexed arbitration.

The leadership view, at times, has been incorporated into organizational culture. Test and Burke (1985, p. 82), for example, depended heavily on A.

M. Ludwig's influence at Mendota State Hospital in mounting controlled tests of treatments for the chronic mentally ill: "Unless clinicians are willing to stick their professional necks out and assume the risks associated with employing and evaluating potentially effective therapeutic techniques, especially when traditional procedures seem so inept, they are derelict in their duties toward patients."

Stewardship. A principal duty of some organizations lies in reducing the vulnerability and enhancing the well-being of their clients. Producing better evidence about what works and for whom is a first line of approach to this goal and so may be considered an incentive. A second line hinges on the idea of fairness to individuals, or ethical propriety.

Relative to some ethical standards, the random assignment of individuals to alternative treatments is fair if resources available for ostensibly beneficial treatments are scarce. That the field test meets this and other standards of ethical propriety (considered in Chapter 3 on ethics) is, for some service providers, a prerequisite for collaborating in a controlled field test. Meeting the ethical standards may also serve as an incentive for service providers insofar as individual rights are protected (e.g., privacy) and risks to participants in the study are minimized. Addressing such issues helps to legitimize efforts to uncover which alternatives work best.

What happens to the control group in tests of new treatments may be important if the new approaches appear more attractive than the old, regardless of any real difference in the efficacy of any treatment. In the Spouse Assault Replication Program, the conventional control treatment of mediating a dispute appeared to some to be less attractive than the new treatment, arresting the assailant. To satisfy the interests of advocacy groups in what happens to the control group, members of the control group were provided with information about legal counsel, victim assistance, and so forth (Sherman et al., 1991). The fact that more offenders would be arrested relative to ambient conditions was, in Sherman and Berk's (1985) judgment, the persuasive incentive in the Minneapolis experiment; whether arrest or other approaches eventually reduced recidivism was of less import to the interest groups.

Precedent. The policymaker and administrator may accede, in principle, to a proposal for a randomized field test. Their reservations, however, may hinge on its feasibility. Furnishing evidence about precedents helps to ensure that an informed decision will be made. At best, the information helps to counter arguments that such tests are infeasible and to provide a kind of empirical benchmark for the prudence of an experiment.

It is because precedent is important to those who are invited to engage in a randomized study and to those who design studies that the illustrations given in this book are numerous. In any given discipline area, it is the responsibility of the research team to identify precedents, understand them, and use them in designing and negotiating the field test at hand. To judge from the six police departments that committed resources to the Spouse Assault Replication Program, for example, the precedent set by the Minneapolis experiment on handling spouse abuse was an important guide to decisions about further studies (Reiss & Boruch, 1991). Similarly, early experiments fostered the undertaking of later, better experiments on evaluating court procedures (Lind, 1985), work and welfare innovations (Gueron, 1985), training and employment programs (Betsey et al., 1985), employment programs for disabled workers (Rupp et al., 1994), and others.

Because one randomized field experiment has been undertaken successfully does not mean that all subsequent efforts will succeed. Nor does the absence of a precedent mean that randomized field tests cannot be done; someone has to set the precedent.

Compensation, Conditional Funding, and Future Benefits. Insofar as a randomized experiment is unusual in a given organizational environment, the study will make unusual demands on the organization's managers, staff members, and perhaps other stakeholders. Some common responsibilities of a service provider that engages in an experiment are outlined in Box 8.3. They can be substantial. Incentives that have been discussed already may be sufficiently rewarding in that no other compensation is warranted; they also may be insufficient.

Tangible compensation has at times been important. State governments that engaged in tests of work-welfare initiatives, for example, arguably did so partly because half the costs of evaluation were borne by an external source, the Ford Foundation (Gueron, 1985). The funding allocated to community-based organizations by the Rockefeller Foundation, for operating new programs, was augmented to cover the costs of their participating in a formal test of the program: outreach efforts to ensure adequate sample size, supplying information required by the test, explaining the randomization procedure, and so on (Cottingham, 1991). In statewide tests of financial incentives to improve school performance, Bickman (1985) and his colleagues developed monetary compensation plans for each school involved in the study. Compensation has been necessary in multischool experiments on substance abuse prevention programs (Ellickson, 1994).

Arrangements in some studies ensure that the organization receives funding for operations and other tasks if and only if the organization actually participates in the study. The responsibility for structuring and

---

BOX 8.3

Service Provider:
Common Responsibilities at the Interface of
Treatment Delivery and the Randomized Field Test

1. Identifying and engaging the target individuals
2. Explaining the treatments and the experiment to individuals
3. Intake screening/eligibility determination of target individuals
4. New treatment delivery
5. Planning for orderly throughput
6. Identifying problems or issues in random assignment or other tasks
7. Contributing to the management information system for the experiment

---

employing this strategy usually lies with the sponsors of a new program and its evaluation. This is in the interest of ensuring that good evidence will be produced on the program's value.

The strategy has been employed, arguably with some success, in the civil and criminal justice sector, notably in Petersilia's (1989) work on intensive supervision for probationers, the Spouse Assault Replication Program, and tests of innovative court procedures (Goldman, 1985). It has been employed in the private foundation sector by the Rockefeller Foundation, Ford Foundation, and Robert Wood Johnson Foundation, among others. In each case, grant or contract monies were tied to the organization's engagement in the field test.

Future funding for public or private agencies depends at times on evidence about the effectiveness of the treatments that they deliver. To the extent that this is true, the prospect of funding constitutes an incentive for engaging in a field test. For a probation system in which budgets are vulnerable because it is not clear which probation system works, the prospect of tests that will show that something works has been attractive (Petersilia, 1989). For welfare systems that encounter difficult and politically controversial problems as a matter of course, the prospect of better evidence on success and the financial support from that success must also be regarded as an incentive.

Credibility

The credibility of the research institution arguably is important in engaging organizations in randomized field studies. Consider, for example,

Test and Burke's (1985) enumeration of reasons why they were able to negotiate cooperation in randomized tests of alternative treatments for the chronic mentally ill:

- the history of the host institution for the tests, the Mendota Mental Health Institute,
- the conscientiousness of the investigators in building new tests on the results of earlier ones,
- prestige, in the sense of the research team's receiving grants for high-quality research,
- the research team's scientific productivity, in the sense of their reporting results in scientific journals, and
- the investigators' willingness to invest time in negotiating the design of the tests, mutual education, and the partnership.

Philadelphia's controlled experiment on a program for children at risk of violence and aggression engaged Head Start families. The latter arguably would not have made a decision to collaborate had the principals, Fantuzzo and Stevenson (1993), not made the effort to establish credibility with the local and regional Head Start organizations, Philadelphia's Department of Human Services, and other groups.

SCOUTING, SELECTING, AND TERMINATING SITES

Scouting and Selection

Generally, the responsibility for selecting sites that might collaborate in field tests lies with the sponsors of the experiment and the research team responsible for its execution. For cases in which the site's participation is voluntary rather than mandatory, and participation must then be negotiated, stakeholders at the site share this responsibility.

Irrespective of specific responsibility, some reconnaissance of sites usually is necessary. The primary functions of scouting are to understand the program sites and the context in which they operate, to determine whether an experiment is appropriate and feasible, and to decide how to tailor the experiment's design to suit the setting. The main functions are put in question form in Box 8.4. Consider these questions in the context of

---

BOX 8.4
Scouting the Sites

1. Is the sample of eligible recipients sufficiently large to sustain a randomized controlled field test? In what senses can sample size be controlled?
2. Is the composition of the eligible target population suitable relative to policy objectives, in terms of economic, ethnic, racial, or other representation?
3. Is the capacity of the service delivery unit sufficient to recruit clients, engage and maintain them in programs, and maintain records?
4. Is the service delivery system willing to engage in formal randomized field tests? Under what conditions? With what incentives?
5. Is on-site coordination feasible?
6. Can staff for data collection be developed within the site? Or can trained staff be transported regularly at reasonable cost to the site?

---

scouting sites prior to experiments in health, education, law enforcement, and welfare.

In pre-field test studies, Hedrick et al. (1991) undertook to understand the workings of U.S. Veterans Administration hospitals, focusing on medical, scientific, and management characteristics that would permit, encourage, or discourage the conduct of controlled experiments on health-related day care. The study team judged that the likelihood of successful implementation of the experiments would be enhanced by some of the hospitals' earlier engagement in tests of various health service procedures. They found differences across hospital sites, however, that engendered problems, notably variation in personnel practices that affected the research team's ability to maintain on-site interview staff.

Scouting in the National Dropout Demonstration project influenced decisions to choose sites for testing new dropout prevention programs. Some schools, for example, with small numbers of students were not targeted for experiments, despite their interest in controlled tests of their innovative programs, partly because the number of students involved was too small to sustain an experiment with sufficient statistical power (see Chapter 4 on power of statistical tests). Other schools had a sufficient sample size, but they were unwilling to engage in randomized tests despite positive incentives. Still other sites were eliminated because dealing with sites at a great distance from the research team posed severe logistical problems.

Large-scale experiments that involve a nationally representative sample of sites, each site being expected to participate in a randomized test, are not common. A recent example, involving controlled tests of Upward Bound Programs for high school students from low-income families, nevertheless is instructive. Myers and colleagues (1993) first identified a target universe of more than 400 programs that were mature (i.e., operating for at least 3 years) and maintained by a postsecondary institution. From these, the research selected a random sample of 200 programs, having first stratified the universe on variables thought to be important to interpretation and policy analysis (e.g., project enrollments and rural versus urban location).

From this sample of 200, 70 program sites were then selected randomly as candidates for participation in controlled experiments. The remaining sites were set aside to be used in passive observational surveys and case studies of local operations. Each of the 70 sites was screened more deeply to determine eligibility, and substitute sites were sampled from a sample of backup sites to keep the sample size at 70.

To the research team's credit, the reasons for rejecting 11 sample sites were documented. Table 8.1 summarizes the reasons for rejection. These include sites being defunded during the planning phase of the experiment. Three of the 11 sites had too few recruits in the program to fill available Upward Bound slots; that is, the flow of clients into system pipeline was too low to justify investing in a local experiment (see Chapter 4 on population, power, and pipeline). Evidently, only one site of the 70 could not adjust random assignment procedures to the local setting. Myers et al. (1993) eventually managed to tailor the procedures for all sites in the sample.

Judgments about the capacity of a site to engage in a controlled field test at times requires dedicating serious attention to the site's political environment. In the New Jersey Negative Income Tax Experiment, for example, Jersey City's "notoriously oppressive political climate" during the 1970s did not dissuade researchers from working with this site. Newark and Camden, however, were eliminated because of the likelihood of race riots (Kershaw & Fair, 1976, p. 25). The Spouse Assault Replication Program, on the other hand, expected no problems in Omaha. The unexpected firing of the police chief and the ensuing organizational turmoil threatened the study seriously. Good data nevertheless were produced as a result of the intense efforts of the research team and, ultimately, the chief's reinstatement (Dunford, 1990; Dunford et al., 1990). It is not clear how political volatility can be explored well, although thorough scouting may suffice. The matter is important nevertheless in the decisions made by an experiment's sponsors and others about where to run the study.

TABLE 8.1
Projects Dropped From the Upward Bound Effectiveness Study

Reasons for Dropping Project	Number of Projects
Not in the universe	5[a]
Too few recruits to fill Upward Bound funded slots	3[b]
Weak relationship between the community and the project	1
Project did not have any openings to be filled	1[c]
Could not sufficiently adjust randomization procedures to accommodate project operations	1
Total	11

SOURCE: Adapted from *The National Evaluation of Upward Bound: Design Report*, Myers, Moore, Schirm, and Waldman, © copyright 1993 by Mathematica Policy Research.
a. Some projects were defunded, and one project was not mature. Although the latter had held an Upward Bound grant for 3 years, it had been operating for only two and one-half years because of difficulties encountered while hiring staff.
b. A backup was not selected for one of these projects.
c. A backup was not selected for this project.

Sites may nominate themselves for participation in a field test by responding to requests for proposals issued by the field test's sponsor. Screening criteria for their selection, constructed by the sponsor, usually accord with the standards implied by Box 8.4. For example, in tests of the Supported Work Program for individuals with severe unemployment problems, 40 operating agencies in as many cities submitted proposals in response to invitations supported by the Ford Foundation and U.S. Department of Labor (Hollister, 1984). Ten of the sites were selected for comparative tests based on criteria similar to those in Box 8.4, including their capacity to recruit target individuals for the program, their willingness to cooperate in random assignment and data collection, and so on.

Termination

Despite good planning and reconnaissance, the attempt to emplace a field test may fail. The site, for example, may be characterized by disorder, volatility, and scarcity of resources that could not be anticipated when the decision was made to engage the site. For example, two of six sites that originally were selected as good candidates in the Rockefeller Foundation's tests of the Minority Female Single Parent Program failed; the community-based organizations responsible for delivery of integrated training at each site did not deliver. These two sites were withdrawn from the tests after considerable debate among the sponsor and its advisers. One of six sites in the Spouse Assault Replication Program failed in the sense that the principal investigator did not produce a final report and data set. The severity of problems was disclosed too late to terminate the site earlier. In experiments on reemployment programs for displaced workers, two of five sites were terminated (Bloom, 1990). At one site, the unexpected installation of a competing program led to cancellation of plans for the program to be tested. Local management problems led to termination at the second site.

The main lesson from these and other experiences (e.g., Conner, 1977) is that the possibility of failure is real. It must be planned for. The responsibility for detecting problems lies jointly with the sponsor and the group responsible for executing the field test. The responsibility for termination and for handling the political or legal untidiness that termination may engender lies heavily with the sponsor.

ON-SITE ADVISORY GROUPS

When a field test is undertaken at a single site, multiple stakeholders may influence its execution. The appointment of a group to advise on local operations is then often essential.

The Spouse Assault Replication Program in Metro-Dade County (1991), for example, engaged a Domestic Violence Committee composed of representatives from six administrative entities including the police department, state attorney's office, victim's advocate office, Department of Human Resources, Police Training Bureau, and Warrants Bureau. Representatives from several divisions within the police department were engaged, notably officers of the particular patrol districts in which the experiment operated.

This group helped to create procedures for handling cases, eligibility criteria for selecting assault cases, special reports for use in the field test, and a training curriculum for officers who would be engaged in the effort. Members of the group also contributed to actual training.

INFORMATION COLLECTION

The group responsible for implementing the experiment generally will have responsibility for designing an information system for the experiment, collecting information, or both, and for ensuring the quality of data, consolidating it, and presenting it in usable form. In small-scale tests, these tasks may be undertaken by a few individuals. In medium- to large-scale efforts, the tasks usually require the cooperation of several independent organizations and the sponsoring agency. The magnitude and diversity of the effort required can be formidable. Even in small experiments such as those conducted by Heller and Fantuzzo (1993) and Fantuzzo et al. (1995) with Head Start children, data were generated through direct observations of children and their playmates, interviews with their mothers and teachers, and administrative and other record systems that helped to register the integrity of the treatments and describe the local context. Medium-scale efforts, such as the multisite Spouse Assault Replication Program, entailed interviews with victims and offenders; police administrative records generated by police, the courts, and other agencies; narrative and statistical description of the process of treatment; biomedical observations (e.g., urine analyses); questionnaires; and direct observation of behavior.

Experiments that involve large samples often must simplify measurement and simultaneously exploit the resources of an existing administrative system. As an example, consider the Social Security Administration's (SSA) experiment on how to enhance the ability of disabled people to work. Project NetWork depended on three information sources to address three kinds of questions (Rupp et al., 1994). To obtain information on individuals' eligibility for the study and on their baseline characteristics, the experiment relied on case managers at more than 20 sites. The managers were provided with personal computers and standard software to do so and to update reports.

In this experiment, it was important to understand who received disability payments, how much they received, why, and when. Because the experiment was designed to learn whether earnings could be enhanced for the disabled, measuring earnings was important. The experiment then relied on the SSA's existing information system to obtain data on all these response variables.

The experiment also was designed to increase understanding of the backgrounds and the state of disabled people who volunteer to participate in such a study. Consequently, the research team's interviewers elicited information on participants' functional limitations, previous education, family support, and other factors that are not part of SSA administrative data systems at the national or regional levels.

One of two strategies generally is employed to obtain data that is not produced by existing administrative data systems. Each depends on interviewers or mail surveys. Small- to medium-scale experiments usually involve localized recruitment and training of data collection staff. University-based studies, for example, have relied on mature graduate students in some experiments that assess preschool programs (Heller & Fantuzzo, 1993; Fantuzzo et al., 1995), criminal justice programs (Dennis, 1988), juvenile diversion initiatives (Lipsey, Cordray, & Berger, 1981), and others. When students are unavailable or their use is inappropriate, studies on this scale usually rely on local recruitment, training, and monitoring. The objective usually has been to capitalize on local talent to develop a reliable and productive cadre of interviewers or telephone/mail survey specialists. The individuals' familiarity with neighborhoods from which the experiment draws participants and with local cultures has been important in experiments and survey research more generally (see Chapter 7 on measurement).

The second strategy involves hiring firms known to have high standards of performance. No firm, of course, can always perform well. There are, nevertheless, entities that have acquired a reputation for their ability to obtain high-quality data in multiple projects or over a sustained period. They usually are employed in large-scale experiments. These organizations include employee-owned, family-owned, and corporate entities that specialize in survey research. Their survey efforts are reported routinely in the *Proceedings of the American Statistical Association* and at the meetings of professional societies such as the American Evaluation Association, Association for Policy Analysis and Management, Criminal Justice Society, and American Educational Research Association. Some of them are identified elsewhere in this text because of their contributions to field experiments.

OVERSIGHT AND COORDINATION
OF MULTISITE FIELD EXPERIMENTS

A multisite experiment refers here to a study in which independent randomized experiments are undertaken simultaneously in each of two or more sites. The study involves deliberate planning and coordination among the sites so as to enhance understanding within each site and across sites. The first justification for a study of this kind is the need to replicate, that is, to understand how often the treatments work and for whom, in different settings. A second justification for multisite tests is ensuring that sample size is sufficient to discern small treatment effects, the results from each site being pooled in final analyses (see Chapter 4 on statistical power).

Multisite experiments are not common in the social and behavioral sciences but have increased in frequency over the last decade. For example,

18 service locations (sites) were employed in a massive study of project NetWork's effect on employment activities of 8,000 disabled people (Rupp et al., 1994). The U.S. Department of Education's study of the effects of Upward Bound Programs on academic careers of students involved 70 sites selected so as to be representative nationally (Myers et al., 1993). In police research, the Spouse Assault Replication Program engaged six cities; each city's police department undertook tests of methods for handling domestic violence (Berk et al., 1992; Garner et al., 1995). The National Institute on Alcohol Abuse and Alcoholism sponsored experiments in more than 10 sites in a coordinated effort to understand the effectiveness of treatment programs for the homeless (Orwin, Cordray, & Huebner, 1994).

Strategies that have been employed to coordinate multisite experiments vary considerably. Consider polar illustrations. The Spouse Assault Replication Program was sponsored by a federal grant agency, the National Institute of Justice (NIJ), whose specific interest lay in replicating an earlier experiment in Minneapolis (Sherman & Berk, 1984). A program announcement was issued to invite independent investigators to undertake a replication study under the condition that each must cooperate in a collaborative effort. No formal coordination mechanism was created until the NIJ awarded grants to enable the work. Instead, a program review team was created later to convene quarterly meetings of site representatives, reach agreement on choice of measures and imposition of treatments, and check on the quality of products issued by each site. In most respects, each site's research team had considerable autonomy in data collection, design, and analysis. The sites reported directly to the NIJ in each quarter of the year, as did the program review team (Reiss & Boruch, 1991). A more intensive variation on this strategy has been employed in multisite experiments on treating homeless individuals who are alcoholic or are substance abusers. Monitoring, some coordination, and substantial technical assistance were provided to 14 independent studies by a national evaluation team (Orwin, Cordray, & Huebner, 1994).

The arrangement in SARP and in evaluations of treatments for the homeless were less centralized than other multisite experiments. In Project NetWork, an evaluation sponsored by the Social Security Administration, for example, the responsibility for the experiments' design, much of the data collection, and analysis lay with a single contractor (Abt, 1992). Similarly, a single contractor undertook to tailor randomization procedures, data collection plans, and so on in each site involved in the evaluations of Upward Bound Programs (Myers et al., 1993), intensive supervision programs in California (Petersilia, 1989; Petersilia & Turner, 1990), and others.

The Spouse Assault Replication Program illustrates an approach that involves principal investigators working independently but under negotiated agreements to cooperate, each being responsible for local staff, budget, design, and so on, and for cooperation in the general effort. This strategy involves less administrative control and influence by the sponsor of the experiment than the approach taken in Project NetWork, Upward Bound, and others. As a consequence, the experiments in each SARP site differed somewhat. This made cross-site analyses complicated (Garner et al., 1995). Procedures, data collection, protocols, and so forth are far more uniform across sites in the centralized experiments that are typical of contracted experiments. This means that analysis across sites also will be supplied. On the other hand, the more centralized approach arguably leads to less opportunity to generate and act on original ideas because it does depend on centralized control. It confines the opportunity to one research cadre rather than to several.

TRAINING AND TRAINING MATERIALS

Training and education of the research team, sponsor, treatment providers, and stakeholders are palpably important to mounting a high-quality field experiment. Obviously, the targets for training include individuals who are responsible for data collection. Training also may be warranted for the individuals who implement the programs being tested, referral agency staff, and others. At best, the education is mutual insofar as the experimenters themselves learn from each of the groups targeted for training.

Two factors argue for a broad strategy of continuous mutual education. First, turnover of program staff or research staff is inevitable in longitudinal experiments. Second, the experimenter and other stakeholders will learn as the experiment unfolds. Ensuring that all are informed about the learning is essential to success, judging from multisite experiments of the kind described by Ellickson (1994), for example.

Data Collectors

The task of eliciting information or making observations in medical clinical trials is sufficiently demanding that data collectors are at times certified officially (Meinert, 1986). Certification is not yet a practice in experiments in social and education programs, although intensive training is. This training often will be similar to training undertaken in survey (nonexperiment) settings. Most survey organizations include education in the use of interview protocols, ground rules for handling difficult situations (e.g., interviewing spousal assault victims outside the house), responsibility for identifying and discussing problems, quality ensurance, and so on. There normally is considerable stress on nondirective questioning, especially when the data collector cannot be blinded as to the group to which the respondent has been randomly assigned, and on probing when responses are ambiguous. Insofar as it is possible, the interaction between interviewer and interview protocol has to be taken into account; interviewers cannot be expected to do well when interview protocols are poorly designed.

The skills required of an interviewer and the kinds of training that enhance interviewing are covered in specialized texts. Lavrakas (1993), for example, summarizes considerable experience in recruiting, training, and supervising telephone interviewers. Groves (1989) handles the topic of interviewers, their training, and their adherence to training guidelines based on a substantial body of research on interviewer variance. The training resources that can be exploited include reports of research on interview methods that appear in the professional literature, such as *Public Opinion Quarterly*, and texts, such as Bradburn and Sudman (1979).

Treatment Providers

When new procedures must be introduced into a service provider's operation, training and education need to be directed at several levels. In the Spouse Assault Replication Program, for example, each member of the police department's communications staff had to be informed about changes in procedures for identifying domestic violence calls. Dispatchers needed to know the kinds of calls to be so designated and to which officers the calls would be directed. Supervisors and police officers were trained in how to determine the eligibility of cases for the experiment and to recognize, for example, that only those cases for which arrest (on one hand) or simple restoration of order (on the other hand) were pertinent to the test. They were trained in how to access their headquarters for the random assignment of cases and in how to use a standard protocol to inform the victim and offender about the offense. Police officers were trained in how to activate some other treatment once the assignment was made, should this be necessary. An offender who was assigned randomly to the "mediation" treatment and who then assaults the officer would, for example, be arrested under the treatment protocol. Training sessions were enlarged as the experiment proceeded. Questions about officer discretion and legal liability, for example, that emerged early in the experiment helped to inform officers and the researchers responsible for the field test. Training also has been a fundamental strategy in gaining acceptance for randomization in some experiments. Stevens (1994), for example, reports that applicants for new positions in a prevention program were informed about the experiment as part of screening interviews; they were hired on the condition of their willingness to participate in the tests of the program. The staff training included continuous education about the benefits of the study's design, notably random assignment, in ensuring high-quality evidence, and about the use of the study design in other research.

Manuals and Protocols

Written manuals, protocols, and so on commonly are developed in controlled field experiments in research in civil and criminal justice, mental health, education, social services, and medicine. The "question and answer" (Q and A) pamphlet or the "concern and response" letter of the sort given in this chapter's appendix represent a small part of this body of training material. The internal memos bearing on new ideas, issues, and options; the oral briefings on such topics; and the written sequelae of each also fall within the mutual education effort. To the extent that events unfold quickly in a field test and not all are anticipated, the need to update materials periodically becomes important.

Videotapes in Training

Some research teams have produced videotapes that cover the need for randomization in field tests, debates over the political acceptability of randomization, the ethical protection of human subjects in experiments, and other topics. The tapes have been used to introduce and explain randomization to managers and staff in the settings in which controlled tests are planned, notably in civil and criminal justice, welfare reform, and health. They have been used in graduate-level training at the University of Pennsylvania, Harvard, and elsewhere.

The National Institute of Health's (1986) videotapes constitute a basic primer for researchers whose work must be screened for its ethical propriety and for educating the institutional review boards (IRBs) that are authorized to review the ethics of a field test. The tapes describes IRB criteria for ethical practice and their use in behavioral and biomedical studies, including randomized clinical trials. The contents are covered in Chapter 3 in this volume.

The Rockefeller Foundation's (1988) videotapes were based on a multisite randomized field test of specialized programs for low-income single parents. The tests, undertaken in Georgia, Rhode Island, Washington, D.C., and California, generated some concerns among community-based training programs, such as the Atlanta Urban League. The tapes were produced to document and address the concerns. Explaining the purpose of random assignment often is difficult, for example, and the tapes illustrate how the task was done at each of the sites and the kinds of questions broached by program managers and staff who were asked to participate in experiments.

Some tapes have been developed by individual researchers to better understand and diagnose local obstacles to controlled randomized tests. Sherman and colleagues (1991, 1992) and the Crime Control Institute (1986), for example, capitalized on the Milwaukee City Council's routine practice of videotaping council meetings to record, analyze, and inform debate about experiments in the domestic violence arena. Replication experiments in Georgia, North Carolina, Nebraska, Wisconsin, and Florida capitalized on the Milwaukee tapes to develop randomization plans. The tape extends major early work on the development of training tapes for police research by the National Institute of Justice (1987).

Similarly, Metzger (1993) produced a videotape to inform prospective participants in experiments on clinical trials of AIDS vaccines. In this tape, as in others, the content focuses on actual participants in experiments, as well as prospective participants, and on eliciting questions. The tape has been used in training program staff, research staff, and graduate students at the University of Pennsylvania.

Such tapes set a fine precedent for training in field research generally and controlled tests in particular. The costs of local production appear to have been sufficiently low and the benefits sufficiently great that production of such tapes can be regarded as (uncommonly) good practice in field research.

APPENDIX

UNITED STATES DEPARTMENT OF EDUCATION
Washington, DC 20202
March 24, 1992

Dear Colleague:

The purpose of this note is to respond to concerns raised by some Upward Bound project directors in recent meetings with ED and Mathematica Policy Research (MPR) staff. Most of these concerns relate to the use of one element of the study design—random assignment—to document the effectiveness of Upward Bound.

ED considers an exactly matched comparison group—as can be generated by only random assignment—to be critical to assessing the impact of Upward Bound. Previous evaluations of this program have been suspect because program participants differed significantly from students in the comparison group. Our design will establish comparable groups of students, thereby ensuring that subsequent educational differences can be attributed to participation in Upward Bound.

We must also consider the fact that Upward Bound is an ongoing program. We recognize that our evaluation should do nothing to damage program operations and good will at the local level. Thus, we must work to identify a strategy that allows us to implement a rigorous evaluation and accommodate local needs.

Five specific concerns have been raised about the evaluation:

Concern: Random assignment is unethical because students in the comparison/control group cannot enter Upward Bound at a later date.

Response: We have adjusted our procedures so that all students in the comparison group have a chance of participating in Upward Bound. The original plan called for all students selected as part of the comparison group to be permanently denied Upward Bound services. Under normal circumstances, most Upward Bound projects must also deny services to students; however, some of these students are placed on a waiting list, and the others may reapply at a later date. To reflect this feature of Upward Bound, ED and MPR have adjusted the way in which the evaluation design is implemented.

All students identified as eligible applicants by the Upward Bound project directors will have the same, fair chance of participating in Upward Bound. The names of eligible applicants will be placed on a list in random order. Project directors will take names from the list, starting with the first name, and then fill program slots. Students not initially selected for Upward Bound will be placed on a waiting list. As vacancies in the program become available, project directors will fill slots by taking names in random order from the waiting list. These procedures ensure that students on the waiting list have a fair chance of participating in Upward Bound. Some projects may want to maintain a separate waiting list of students who applied after the initial selection. These students may enter Upward Bound at the discretion of the project directors and by using the project directors' own selection criteria. Finally, some projects will want to maintain a specific mix of students when filling vacancies. This requirement can also be accommodated by adjusting our procedures.

Concern: Project directors will need to increase recruitment beyond normal levels to implement the evaluation.

Response: Our original plan called for an equal number of students in Upward Bound and in the comparison group. While many projects have a surplus of eligible applicants, some projects do not. We do not plan to place additional burden on projects to recruit more applicants where this may be infeasible. When there are too few applicants to fill all program openings and create a comparison group, it will not be possible to implement our design. Under these circumstances, a project in the sample will be replaced.

In some cases, there may be enough total applicants, but not enough applicants from certain subgroups. Some programs may have so few male applicants, for example, that they normally accept all who apply. In projects where this arises, the subgroups will not be included in the evaluation.

Concern: Project directors will not be given the opportunity to identify students with unique characteristics who would benefit all students in the program.

Response: Project directors will be given the opportunity to identify unique characteristics that must be included in the pool of students selected to participate in Upward Bound. Many projects select one or two students with unique characteristics (e.g., leadership skills) each year. In effect, this selection forms part of the treatment provided by Upward Bound. Our plan allows project directors to identify students in the applicant pool who fill this role and guarantees that one or two such students will be admitted into Upward Bound.

Concern: Parents and students will be upset if they are not informed about the evaluation prior to completing application forms.

Response: It is our intention to inform students and parents about the evaluation before they fill out applications for Upward Bound. Experience in other studies suggests that recruitment will not be adversely affected when students understand the reason for the evaluation and the way in which program participants will be chosen.

Concern: Staff in target high schools may believe that the evaluation will place too great a burden on them and that the procedures are unethical.

Response: MPR staff will be available to work with target high school staff and other concerned parties to explain the procedures, to listen to their concerns, and to show why the approach is fair for the students who participate in the study.

These are the ways in which we will accommodate concerns that have been raised so far. Other issues may arise after we draw the project sample and consult with each of the project directors. We are committed to addressing those issues as well.

Sincerely,

David Goodwin, Ph.D.   David Myers, Ph.D.
Planning and   Project Director
  Evaluation Service   Mathematica Policy
U.S. Department of Education   Research

9

Analysis

Analyze them as you've randomized them.
—R. A. Fisher (attributed)

Four classes of analysis are important in experiments for planning and evaluating programs:

- Analyses of study quality
- Core analysis
- Understanding estimates of treatment differences
- Assessing generalizability and concordance

Analyses of a study's quality can cover a large range of complex activity. Here, the focus is on what the data imply about the integrity of the study. Core analysis refers to the experiment's primary questions and the evidence used to address them. It often involves formal statistical tests of hypotheses that are specified beforehand about differences among treatments, the construction of confidence intervals to characterize the reliability of the findings, and the examination of other evidence that will help readers to understand the results.

Statistical analyses for quality and for producing an estimate of the differences among treatment effects both can be fairly straightforward. Understanding the results thoroughly and making a scientifically defensible case for a particular interpretation are rather more complicated, given the inevitable imperfections that appear. The focus here is on how quality in measurement, imposition of treatments, context, and pipeline affect the interpretation of an experiment's results.

Finally, it behooves the conscientious analyst to consider the generalizability of results and the concordance between the results of the experiment at hand and the results of other studies. This topic is also considered in what follows.

ANALYSES OF STUDY QUALITY

At a minimum, assessing the quality of the experiment involves examining data on the way treatments were assigned to individuals or entities and the way they were delivered, examining baseline data on the individuals or entities, and conducting a preliminary core analysis. Each is considered in what follows.

Treatments: Assigned Versus Delivered

One of the benefits of a randomized experiment hinges on the fact that groups are constructed through a random assignment process. The groups will then not differ systematically, so that comparisons of the groups will be fair. In most experiments, the treatment that is assigned randomly will not always be the treatment that is delivered. Medical clinical trials, for example, draw a distinction between the "treatment intended," that is, the one that is assigned randomly, and the treatment that is actually received by the patient (e.g., Friedman et al., 1985).

Table 9.1 illustrates the point and directs attention to periodic tabulation during the course of the study. Such a tabulation usually reveals departures from the randomized allocation plan that indicate the need for corrective measures. In the extreme case, such data may suggest terminating the experiment.

The table shows how, early in an experiment, half of the individuals who were assigned randomly to one treatment (T) instead wound up in the second treatment group, the control condition (C). Furthermore, half of the individuals who were randomly assigned to the control group actually received the special treatment, which was not assigned to them. For example, some individuals who were randomly assigned to be arrested (the treatment) in a police experiment on handling misdemeanor violence may instead have been mediated (the control condition). In a particular case, the police officer in charge may have adjudged that arrest would put the offender's job and his family at risk. The individuals assigned to the mediation (control) condition, on the other hand, who were instead arrested (the new treatment) may have been arrested because they became obstreperous. The offender may, for example, have assaulted the police officer in charge of the case.

The second panel of Table 9.1 shows that adherence to the assigned treatments in this experiment improved in the second quarter. Adherence

TABLE 9.1

Treatments Randomly Assigned and
Treatments Actually Delivered:
A Simple Analysis

	Treatment Randomly Assigned	Treatment Actually Delivered		
		T	C	
First quarter	T	25	25	50
	C	25	25	50
		50	50	100
Second quarter	T	65	35	100
	C	35	65	100
		100	100	200
Third quarter	T	115	35	150
	C	35	115	150
		150	150	300
Fourth quarter	T	265	35	300
	C	35	265	300
		300	300	600

NOTE: The exhibit covers four quarters in the course of a year of a randomized experiment. T represents a treated group; C represents a control group. The exhibit illustrates how a randomized test is implemented gradually in accord with the experiment's design. In the first quarter, half of those assigned to T actually get T; the remainder get C. In the fourth quarter, the majority of those assigned to T actually receive the T treatment.

to the randomization protocol was perfect in the third and fourth quarter of the experiment. Each of the individuals who entered the system in each quarter received the treatment that was randomly assigned.

One of the reasons for such an improvement lies with the analysis of data from the first quarter. Such information triggered steps in the police experiments to enhance adherence to the random assignment protocol. Improvement would also come about through efforts to determine why discrepancies occurred between the treatments assigned and those delivered and through efforts to generate information and incentives to enhance the likelihood that the treatments assigned would be delivered. In the Spouse Assault Replication Program, this involved repeated and diverse reminders to police officers about why adherence to the experiment's design was in their interest. The incentives included peer recognition and rewards as well as sanctions, such as elimination from the experiment's team of police officers for those who consistently failed to adhere to the design. See Sherman et al. (1992), Dunford et al. (1990), Hirschel et al. (1991), and Garner et al. (1995).

Baseline Data

Researchers obtain baseline data on the individuals or entities selected to participate in an experiment so as to ensure that the groups that are composed randomly are indeed similar. It has become good practice to monitor the comparability of groups, using the baseline data over the entire course of a controlled field test.

The simplest comparison of differences among treatment groups involves laying out the statistics associated with each baseline variable for each group. Some analysts usually undertake formal statistical tests to determine if differences among the groups are within the limits that one would expect on the basis of random variation. For example, it is common to conduct simple t tests of the null hypothesis that the mean age of each group does not differ. It is customary to undertake a series of such tests to understand whether groups differ with respect to prior work history, level of education, health status, criminal record, and so forth, under the assumption that these variables influence response to treatment.

Consider Table 9.2, excerpted from a report on the Perry Preschool experiment (Schweinhart et al., 1993). The study, undertaken during the 1960s, continues with contemporary follow-ups of individuals who were preschoolers at that time. The table provides evidence that the groups are indeed similar in composition. It further provides p values, the probabilities that the differences observed across the Perry Preschool group and the control group are attributable to ordinary chance variation if indeed the participants are taken randomly from the same target population.

Undertaking separate tests on each baseline variable or providing p values is an imperfect strategy in that the variables within any group are correlated. A series of ostensibly independent tests fails to take into account their relatedness. A generalization of the conventional t statistic for evaluating a null hypothesis that the groups do not differ with respect to all variables is available and is described in textbooks such as Morrison's (1990).

Baseline data also are a vehicle for ensuring that the kinds of people who are targeted for the experiment eventually participate. Consider again the Perry Preschool experiment on intensive services for children in impoverished families. Table 9.3 lays out characteristics of the families served. It puts the experiment in one kind of social context, presenting available data

TABLE 9.2
Categorical Background Variables at Study Entry: High/Scope Perry Preschool Project

Variable	Program Group (percentage)	No-Program Group (percentage)	p	Effect Size
Participant's gender				
Male	57	60	.869	0.06
Female	43	40		
Family configuration at study entry				
Two-parent	55	51	.625	0.09
Single-mother	45	49		
Nuclear	15	20	.433	0.14
Extended	85	80		
Employment status of parents				
Father and mother employed	5	9	.018	0.44
Father alone employed	44	35		
Single mother employed	4	22		
No parent employed	47	34		
Father's employment level				
Managerial or skilled	3	2	.279	0.29
Semiskilled	9	3		
Unskilled	28	40		
Family welfare status at study entry				
On welfare	58	45	.230	−0.25
Not on welfare	42	55		
Family in public housing	40	32	.396	−0.15

SOURCE: From *Significant Benefits: The High/Scope Perry Preschool Study Through Age 27*, in Categorical Background Variables at Study Entry: High/Scope Perry Preschool Project, Schweinhart, Barnes, and Weikart, p. 49, © copyright 1993 by High/Scope Press. Reprinted with permission.
NOTE: Program group n = 56 to 58, no-program group n = 63 to 65. The data source is the initial parent interview. The p values are based on Pearson chi-square statistics.

on African Americans and the U.S. population for the census year (1970) closest to the period in which the study was run. The table helps to make the point that the families served in the experiment were indeed at considerable disadvantage relative to both African Americans and the U.S. more generally. That is, the experiment appears to have engaged children that it intended to engage. Parents have far lower rates of high school completion than the U.S. population. Their employment levels and income are lower,

TABLE 9.3

Demographic Status of Perry
Preschool Parents and U.S. Families

Variable	Perry Parents in 1963-1965	African Americans in 1970	U.S. Population in 1970
Schooling of mothers/women			
Median years of school	9.7	10.0	12.1
Completed high school	21%	33%	53%
Schooling of fathers/men			
Median years of school	8.0	9.6	11.8
Completed high school	11%	32%	54%
Family composition			
Husband-wife families	53%	69%	86%
Single-head families	47%	33%	14%
Employment of parents/adults			
Not employed or looking for work	40%	25%	17%
Mothers employed	20%	47%	38%
Fathers employed	47%	60%	74%
Family on welfare	49%	18%	5%
Household density			
Median persons	6.7	3.1	2.7
Median persons per room	1.40	0.66	0.56

SOURCE: From *Significant Benefits: The High Scope Perry Preschool Study Through Age 27*, Schweinhart, Barnes, and Weikart, p. 28, © copyright 1993 by High/Scope Press. Reprinted with permission.

and their reliance on welfare assistance is far greater. Such data are helpful in making judgments about the generalizability of the experiment's results, a topic considered later in this chapter.

Preliminary Core Analysis

In high-quality sample surveys, it is customary to capitalize on the first 5-10% of observations to

- refine the primary (core) questions or hypotheses,

- obtain estimates of mean response for each group,
- construct the confidence intervals for estimates of important parameters,
- conduct quality control checks on the data, and
- lay out the tables that would summarize final analyses.

A similar strategy can be, and often is, exploited in field experiments. The conscientious analyst would employ the first 10% of the individuals (or other entities) enrolled in the experiment to produce a preliminary core analysis that serves as a model for final analyses. Additional products include count data on the treatments that are randomly assigned and delivered, comparisons of groups on the basis of baseline data, and estimates of the reliability and validity of observations. Preliminary analyses then help to ensure that the mechanics of the final core analysis are appropriate and feasible.

The preliminary analyses suggest nothing about the substance of a final analysis. The former are based on small samples that alone cannot be used to make decisions about the relative differences among treatment groups. They form a part of the scientific log on the experiment, being accessible eventually to other scientists perhaps, but are not exploited in scientific forums.

CORE ANALYSIS

Core analysis refers to the formal statistical investigation of hypotheses that are framed at the start of the experiment. These hypotheses can be put into interrogatory form. Is there any difference in the average effectiveness of the treatments? Does the effectiveness depend on the kind of person or entity to which the treatments are directed? How does the effect vary over time?

This section outlines the desirable features of such an analysis and some technical resources on which the analyst may rely. It covers a fundamental rule for a core analysis and the statistical models on which conventional analyses depend.

Desirable Features of a Core Analysis

Understanding how to design a controlled experiment and how to analyze its results occupied the attention of Fisher (1935), Kempthorne (1952),

Campbell and Stanley (1966), and others who have contributed remarkably to this arena. Their lessons include the following.

First, the core analysis ought to exploit the protection against error afforded by the randomization process. Why do a controlled experiment, in the interest of fair comparison and making statistically defensible statements about results, if the analyst does not depend on the randomization in the analysis?

Second, the core analysis must be driven by the process that is assumed to underlie the resultant data. For the conscientious experimenter, this means that the results must be expressed in a way that makes it clear how an individual's (or entity's) response to treatment depends on the treatment that was assigned, on the individuals' (or entities') characteristics, and on ordinary variation in human behavior. This, at the least, means specifying the statistical model that is presumed to underlie the data.

Third, the comparisons among treatments that are regarded as important for decisions ought to be specified as part of the experiment's design. This specification helps to ensure that the objectives of the study are met in a core analysis. It also ensures that exploratory analyses (fishing expeditions) are identified as such and that the findings from these are marked for deeper examination in later stages of research.

Fourth and finally, the core analysis should be simple. The simplicity is important to science. It also can be bracing for the policy audience to which results of controlled field tests must be presented. The simplicity also sustains economy of the effort.

Resources for Core Analysis

To understand whether one treatment group fares better than others based on simple numerical counts in a randomized experiment, the analyst can rely on standard methods described in Hollander and Wolfe (1973), and Mosteller and Rourke (1973), among others. The statistical methods applicable to more complex data have been described by Haberman (1978), Clogg and Shockey (1988), and Magidson (1978).

Many controlled field tests involve count data that depend partly on time. A police study, for example, may focus on the time lapse, counted in days, between the initial arrest of an offender and the offender's later arrest. Each of the experiments in the Spouse Assault Replication Program, for example, analyzed such data to determine if initial arrest delayed the onset of a subsequent assault and arrest. Increasing the time that students spend in school may be an objective of some dropout prevention programs. Delaying infection is the objective of health education programs that are tested in some experiments. The statistical analysis of count data on success or failure that depend on time (and on other factors) falls under the general rubric of survival analysis. Allison (1984) and Willett and Singer (1991) are valuable resources.

Count data are sturdy grounds for understanding some phenomena. Admitting that a mortality rate is important, however, one may also detect improved health status as measured on some continuous scale. Enumerating dropouts from a school or program is important, but one may go further to understand whether the performance of those who have not dropped out has improved as a consequence of a particular project, program, or policy.

A variety of textbooks handle the technical aspects of analyzing data based on measures of continuous response variables, rather than count data, in experiments. They include Neter, Wassermann, and Kutner (1990), Ferguson and Takane (1989), and Kirk (1982). Textbooks that integrate explanations of the statistical methods with personal computer software also are available. Darlington (1990), Lindman (1992), Dowdy and Weardon (1991), and Neter et al. (1990) use SAS as a vehicle for illustration. The Darlington text also exploits SYSTAT; Lindman's also exploits SPSS. A separate chapter in Popham and Sirotnik (1992) provides programs and outputs to illustrate most topics handled in this basic text on statistics in education.

The Fundamental Rule for Core Analysis

In a randomized experiment, the proper core analysis involves comparing the groups that are assigned randomly to alternative treatments regardless of which treatments were actually delivered. Put bluntly, the relevant rule is: *Analyze them as you have randomized them.* There are two reasons for the rule, one bearing on science, the other on policy.

Scientific Rationale. For the statistician and scientist, the main justification for the rule is that groups composed randomly do not differ systematically. On this account, comparisons among the groups will yield unbiased estimates of differences in treatment effectiveness and legitimate statistical statements about the reliability of the results. Furthermore, the analysis will be "simple" in the sense that conventional statistical technology can be exploited to understand what works better and for whom, despite considerable variation in human behavior.

By way of contrast, one may argue that the groups composed randomly are not relevant. Rather, one ought to compare those who actually received one treatment against those who actually received another. The problem with comparing groups on the basis of the treatment that is delivered, rather the treatment that is assigned randomly, is that this approach abandons the guarantee engendered by the random assignment. Groups to which treatments are delivered are not covered by a guarantee that they will not differ systematically; that is, such groups are likely to differ in observable and unobservable ways. To the extent that they do, a comparison will not yield unbiased estimates of the relative effectiveness of the treatments. Rather, the analysis will yield estimates of effects that are tangled with whatever factors caused the migration from the treatment assigned to the treatment delivered.

The counsel to "analyze the units as randomized" is then reiterated here for experiments in mental health, education, justice, and so forth. It accords with what is regarded as good scientific practice in other arenas. In medical clinical trials, for example, eligible individuals who have been assigned randomly to a particular drug regimen may or may not comply with the regimen. The core procedure in such cases is to compare the groups that are constructed on the basis of random assignment, that is, intended treatments (e.g., Meinert, 1986; Friedman et al., 1985).

The analyst need not stop with this core analysis. Most good analysts go further, albeit cautiously, to understand the results of the experiment. The matter is considered later in this chapter.

Policy Rationale. Comparing treatment groups that are randomly constituted, despite the fact that some treatments assigned may not be delivered, has a policy-based justification. In particular, any regimen prescribed by law, rule, or policy will not always be delivered. The departures from specification in a controlled field experiment arguably can be taken as evidence of what would happen if the prescribed treatments were adopted as law, rule, or policy.

In the Spouse Assault Replication Program, for example, a number of offenders who had been randomly assigned to the mediation treatment became offensive to police or to the victim after the random assignment. They were then arrested. That is, the treatment that was randomly assigned was not delivered. The experiment included an arrest condition to which they might also have been assigned randomly. In a sense, this departure from the treatment that was randomly assigned, mediation, can be regarded as "natural." The departure was an indicator of what happens normally when a participant in a violent episode is questioned by police. Police officers' efforts to restore order, a mediational enterprise, will not always result in the restoration of order. On account of the offender's behavior, the offender invites arrest.

Similarly, some offenders in the Spouse Assault Replication Program experiments were assigned randomly to the arrest treatment. Of those who were supposed to be arrested, some were not. Again, this occurrence and the reasons for it in the field experiment arguably are a reflection of what would happen if a policy of *mandatory* arrest for misdemeanor domestic violence assaults was adopted. That is, some people who are supposed to be arrested, under a strict interpretation of the law, are not.

The rationale, then, is that comparing the intended treatments—the treatments randomly assigned—is sensible on policy grounds. There will always be some departures from what is intended. Those departures are taken into account when the core analysis compares the performance of the individuals who are randomly assigned to one treatment against individuals who are assigned to other treatments.

A similar justification often is used in clinical trails in medicine. For example, some individuals who are assigned randomly to a particular drug may regurgitate it. The treatment, in some sense, is rejected. The comparison of this group against a randomized placebo group is nevertheless fair insofar as one can expect that a fraction of those to whom the drug is prescribed would do the same.

The Statistical Model
Underlying a Core Analysis

The core analysis of data from a randomized controlled field test is driven by a statistical model of the structure presumed to underlie the data. In the simplest case, the statistical model is an assertion about how an observation on an individual or entity, a child's well-being, for example, depends on the treatment in which the child engages and on the ordinary random variability in the child's behavior. This model, put in a common symbolic form, is:

$$Y_{ij} = u + T_j + e_{ij}$$

Here, Y_{ij} represents a measurement, Y, made on a particular child, i, on the child's well-being. The child is a member of a treatment group, j. The model posits that the state of child i depends partly on an overall mean (u) the level of children's well-being averaged across all groups involved in the experiment. The model assumes also that the child's state depends on an effect of the particular treatment that is provided to the child, T_j, and on random error, e_{ij}. This last element, e_{ij}, represents ignorance and random variation. It reflects the fact that individuals ordinarily will depart from a simple scenario in which children on average respond to different treatments in a simple additive way.

The model is a formal assertion, one that is made in the interest of making explicit the statistical evidence that underlies the comparison of programs. Furthermore, the model invites the question, Does treatment T_1 or treatment T_2 work better, taking into account the way children ordinarily vary?

Any such statistical model contains parameters, that is, population characteristics that cannot be observed directly but must be estimated from the sample at hand. These parameters bear on the question that the field test is designed to answer, on the assertion that is made in the statistical model.

The T_j, for example, reflects the relative differences among treatments, j, and must be estimated from the data at hand. In the simple experiment involving two treatment conditions, the parameter for treatment j often is estimated using the difference between the average well-being of children in the treated group and the overall mean. The difference in welfare of children treated, as against those not treated, is of paramount importance and is a focus of the analysis. The element of the model denominated as e_{ij}, the random variation associated with a particular child who is engaged in a particular treatment, is summarized as the variance within the treatment groups. Whether average treatments that are found are reliable in a statistical sense is judged against indicators of this normal variability among children.

This statistical model that underlies analysis depends on the analyst's prior knowledge, theory, and the experiment's design. For example, the model implies that the treatments are known or supposed to have a simple additive effect. It says that, on average, an increment will be added to a child's well-being as a consequence of the treatment. The treatments are known to have been assigned randomly and are thn characteristics of children, the characteristics being encompassed by the error term, e_{ij}. More elaborate models and analyses, of course, can be built to recognize how different kinds of people or entities are affected differently by treatments. See the textbooks referenced earlier.

Making the statistical model explicit for a core analysis is a matter of good practice for the experimenter. The specification helps to ensure that

- all major relevant factors are taken into account,
- mistakes in the statistical model and the ensuing analysis will be discernible if indeed there are any,
- alternative statistical models can be distinguished from the one posited, and

- the structure that is assumed to underlie the data is made plain.

The model drives analysis, notably estimation of parameters, formal tests of hypotheses, and the specification of one's confidence in results. The estimates of parameters such as a treatment difference, for example, usually are constructed so that the discrepancy between model and data is minimized relative to a conventional statistical standard. In effect, this produces analyses that are as precise as possible and exploit the available information to the maximum extent possible.

UNDERSTANDING ESTIMATES
OF TREATMENT DIFFERENCES

Randomization provides a partial guarantee of unbiased estimates. The process prevents systematic differences among the groups that are compared. Randomization is not a complete guarantee insofar as statistical biases in estimates of treatment effects stem from imperfections in the study's execution. Furthermore, an estimate of a program effect may be unbiased but complicated to interpret on account of the influence of extraneous factors.

The influences on biased estimates and complications include the quality of measurement of the response variable, contaminated treatments, and the social context of the experiment. Deep handling of such matters can be found in Lipsey (1992) on psychology experiments and Dennis (1990) on substance abuse program evaluations. Cook and Campbell (1979), Reichardt and Gollob (1989), and Campbell and Stanley (1966) discussed the topic thoughtfully in terms of "threats to validity." Yeaton and Sechrest (1986, 1987a, 1987b) and Julnes and Mohr (1989) examined the topic within the framework of "no difference" findings; this too is discussed below.

Quality in Measuring the Response Variable

In a simple experiment involving two groups, the level of validity in measuring the state of treatment group members may differ from the level of validity in measuring the state of the control group members. If there is a remarkable difference, then estimates of treatment effects will be affected.

TABLE 9.4

How Differences in the Validity of Measurement
Across Treatment Groups in an Experiment
Might Affect an Estimated Treatment Difference

		T	C	Total
Panel 1	Success	500	500	1000
	Failure	500	500	1000
	Total	1000	1000	2000
Panel 2	Success	500	600	1100
	Failure	500	400	900
	Total	1000	1000	2000

NOTE: Panel 1 shows no treatment effect, with perfect measurement in each group. The implication is that the treatment's effect or success does not differ from the control conditions. Panel 2 shows no treatment effect, with imperfect validity of measurement in the control group (exaggerated reports of success) and perfect validity of measurement in the treatment group. The ostensible implication is that the treatment has a negative effect, relative to the control condition.

As an illustration, consider Table 9.4, which shows hypothetical counts of "successes" and "failures" in a randomized test of a drug treatment program of the sort described by McLellan et al. (1993). A success is indexed by asking an individual whether he or she has abstained from drugs, a "yes" being counted as success.

Panel 1 of the table shows the state of affairs when the accuracy of reporting is perfect or uniform across the treatment and control groups. The data suggest that the treatment has no discernible effect. That is, the rates at which the treated group and control group admit drug abstention are identical at 50%.

Panel 2 illustrates the same scenario: There is no treatment difference. The data are modified so as to incorporate the fact that 20% of drug-using members of the control group report falsely that they are abstainers. This imperfect validity in response may stem from the respondents' distrust of the interviewer, a failure to recall accurately one's drug use, or other reasons. A higher validity in response might be expected of treatment group members for various reasons; this is ignored in the panel display. These respondents may be more inclined to trust interviewers, to monitor their drug use conscientiously, and so on, on account of their familiarity with and trust in the program staff.

Panel 2 suggests that there is a real treatment effect when, in fact, there is none. The rate of abstinence appears to differ across each treatment group. Moreover, the difference is negative, $-.10$, making the treatment appear harmful relative to the second treatment, the control group, when in fact it has no effect on actual abstinence. The difference is solely on account of the imperfect measurement.

This scenario is oversimplified, of course. Members of each treatment group in any field experiment arguably will report with imperfect validity. The point here is that differences in validity across groups are a potential problem that needs to be recognized in the interpretation of an experiment's results.

Differential validity is plausible, to judge from empirical data and theory. Aiken and West (1990), for example, reviewed the matter in the context of therapeutic experiments. They unbundled the problem by classifying four major sources of invalidity in response and how these sources might produce biased estimates of differences in treatment effect in an experiment. The sources that they identify include:

Experiment Limitation: For example, experience in a training group may increase the validity of self-reported behaviors, including undesirable ones. This can lead to negative biases in estimates, when compared to an otherwise equivalent control group.

Condition Justification: Individuals seeking a desirable treatment may exaggerate symptoms to obtain it, then desist from exaggeration. This may produce positively biased estimates of a treatment's effects over time.

Altered States: Individuals forced to seek treatment may understate their problems initially but state them more accurately later relative to a control group.

Self-Presentation: Individuals may exaggerate problems to stay hospitalized or minimize problems so as to exit more quickly from enforced treatment.

Aiken and West (1990) provide examples from the published literature. Related problems, described in Cook and Campbell (1979), include ceiling and floor limits in experiments on programs designed to improve academic ability or achievement.

The problem of differential validity can be addressed best at the design stage of the experiment, rather than at the analysis stage. For example, one may depend on blind independent ratings rather than self-ratings. Instead of self-reports of drug use, one may employ physical measures such as urine testing in drug studies, and so on. When side studies on the validity of self-reports can be done, these can help at the analysis stage to provide evidence that the problem is important, trivial, or uncertain.

When data or theory suggest that the problem is important, one can produce several estimates of treatment differences. Each estimate would be based on a different assumption about the magnitude of the plausible differences in validity, for example, no difference and a difference of 2%, 5%, and so on. Plausibility depends on the local experiment's context and topic, and local knowledge needs to be exploited in such a sensitivity analysis.

Contaminated Treatments and Estimates of Treatment Differences

An important reason for conscientiously observing what happens in each treatment condition, including the condition in an experiment, is to ensure that one understands the activities being compared. Establishing which treatment is assigned through the randomization is simple. Characterizing treatment implementation so as to ensure sensible interpretation of an experiment's results is not. Partly for this reason, it has become common to present descriptions of each treatment's implementation and to analyze the data.

Johnson and Geller (1992), for example, summarized the class time spent on computer-assisted instruction in a large experiment on the effectiveness of limited computer-assisted instruction (CAI) in Job Corps training. They were able to verify that 35% of class time, on average, was exploited in CAI instruction. The reader further learns that this targeted use rate was not sufficient to generate remarkable effects on performance relative to comparison with conventional classes. The data on CAI use rate helped to sustain a conclusion that the dose was insufficient, given that the dose was delivered more or less as planned.

Social Context

How can data about the social context of a field experiment be exploited to better understand estimates of treatment differences that are generated in an experiment? Or to avoid misleading interpretation? No formal rules have been invented to address the question, but illustrations can be helpful.

In employment and training experiments, the regional job market is part of the context. If no jobs are available locally, as might be and has been the case in some contemporary experiments, then *no* training program will lead to employment. That is, the size of the possible program effect is constrained by local environmental conditions. It has become common for researchers in human resources experiments to obtain and present job market information in the interest of understanding whether, indeed, the market is a constraint on achievable differences between treatments. Also in the training and employment arena, the phenomenon of displacement affects estimates of the effects of treatment differences. The idea is that, over the course of the experiment, those who are treated may get jobs faster than those untreated *within a particular time period* (Dynarski, 1993). The net impact of a special treatment on the waiting time for jobs, however, is zero because the time period remains stable. Some people—members of the control group, for example—merely wait longer to get a job as a consequence of the treatment groups' pursuit and earlier acquisition of jobs. A simple difference estimate of employment rate is then a misleading indicator of the effect of treatment.

More generally, social, behavioral, or education theory can help to make explicit the external conditions that are thought to influence the effects of treatments. For example, in describing evaluations of rehabilitation programs, Keith and Lipsey (1993) argued that external factors such as family, community support, health care funding, and government regulations ought to be taken into account in any conscientious evaluation of particular programs. Rudimentary theory suggests which factors must be present for particular treatments to work. Measures of these factors can then help researchers to understand why it was possible for a treatment difference to emerge or not to emerge. At the analysis stage, a rudimentary theoretical framework of this sort can be used to understand the results at hand and the cross-site variations in multisite experiments.

Finding No Differences in Effects of Treatments

Treatments may indeed differ in their effects, but the data generated in a controlled experiment may not reflect the fact. In particular, a finding of "no difference" among treatments in a formal statistical test may occur because

- measurement of the response to treatment, Y, is insufficiently valid,
- measurement of Y is insufficiently relevant to treatment,
- the statistical power of the experiment is too low, or
- the wrong population was targeted for treatment.

Any combination of these may produce a finding of "no difference." Analyses and interpretations of so-called null results must take these influences into account.

At the experiment's analysis stage, the evidence collected at earlier stages can be exploited to provide information about the influence of imperfect validity in measurement. This evidence may take the form of empirical estimates of the validity of measuring response to treatment based on a side study. It may involve describing procedures, such as blind ratings and measurement, that support an a priori judgment that the measures of response are valid even though numerical indicators of validity are not available. In the absence of such evidence, the case that the actual treatment differences are negligible cannot be sustained well. That is, a failure to find differences among treatments may be due to invalid measures of response to treatment.

The measure of the response variable may be a valid indicator of a construct that is important, but the variable and the method of measuring it may be irrelevant to treatments. A finding that there are no differences in the treatments' effects is then specious. Recall the examples given in the chapter on measurement. The "relevance" of the measure to what the treatments are designed to affect may be justified on empirical grounds. That is, prior research in which the measure has been shown to reflect treatment effectiveness should be employed to sustain the case. Similarly, theory can be employed to argue the case. Again, in the absence of theory or data to show "relevance," a conclusion that treatments do not differ is suspect.

The able analyst recognizes that a failure to detect treatment differences also may be attributable to the experiment's low statistical power. As a practical matter, power depends heavily on sample size. In particular experiments, other characteristics of the experiment's design may be important. At the data analysis stage, nothing can be done to increase the study's initial sample size so as to enhance power. The analyst nevertheless can make plain whether certain differences are detectable with the sample size at hand, the experiment's design, and the statistical analyses that are employed. Interpretation of results might be enhanced if confidence intervals are used instead of a strict threshold condition. Relying on confidence limits arguably is sensible inasmuch as it avoids naive dependence on a single cutoff point. Partly as a consequence of this line of reasoning, scholarly publications such as the *New England Journal of Medicine* routinely require authors to present statistical power results.

Finally, consider the eligibility criteria used to select individuals (or entities) for the experiment. The theory underlying the construction of mental health treatments and programs in other areas usually must specify who is eligible for and might benefit from the treatments. An experiment designed to test the relative effects of programs for people who are seriously mentally ill may, if it engages people who are not seriously ill, produce data that show that treatments are not effective. Verifying that participants met eligibility requirements helps to establish that, if the treatments produced no difference, the finding of "no difference" relates to the treatments rather than to failure to meet eligibility criteria.

A distinctive advance in some contemporary experiments lies in the fact that the analyst went beyond the finding that treatments did not differ appreciably in their effect. In particular, the contribution lies in the analysts' reanalysis of who was engaged in the program and the eligibility criteria that were thought essential for engagement.

For example, in evaluating Family First programs in Illinois, Schuerman et al. (1994) found no differences in the foster care placement rates between Family First and normal procedures for handling children "at risk" of being assigned to foster families. The issue appears to have been that children and families who were selected into the experiment by social service workers were not really at risk of separation from their natural families. A program designed to reduce risk of separation, such as Family First, could not then affect separation rate.

Similarly, in evaluating the effect of prenatal ultrasound screening on prenatal outcome, Ewigman et al. (1993) found no effect of screening on neomortality or morbidity. The absence of an effect appears to lie in a failure to include women who were at any real risk in the trial. That is, women were deemed ineligible for the experiment on the basis of risk factors found on their screening for the experiments. Some critics would argue that a study of the effectiveness of ultrasound screening could not show appreciable effects of ultrasound screening simply because the women selected for the experiment were at a low risk.

ASSESSING GENERALIZABILITY
AND CONCORDANCE

When properly executed, randomized studies yield trustworthy estimates of the relative effectiveness of treatments that have been applied to the target sample. It is to this sample—individuals or entities who were eligible for treatments, were accessible, and who agreed to participate— that statements about treatment effectiveness are most easily directed.

Such a sample may have been drawn from a larger target population based on a probability sample design, or it may be conceived of as having been drawn from some hypothetical target population to which inferences about treatment effects based on the sample might be made.

In either case, the analyst needs to understand the generalizability of the study's results beyond the sample at hand. There are three broad approaches to this (U.S. GAO, 1992):

- Assessment of procedures for selecting the sample
- Analysis of baseline data
- Analysis of representativeness using outcomes data

Similar approaches are helpful in determining whether the results in a study at hand fit with results from other experiments, that is, in determining concordance.

**Assessment of Procedures
for Selecting the Sample**

Understanding a study's generalizability or its concordance with other studies involves focusing on the ways the members of the study sample were

- identified and screened under explicit eligibility criteria,
- recruited,
- rejected, even if they met the eligibility criteria, and
- willing or able to participate (or refuse to participate) in the study.

Earlier chapters of this book considered each of these from the point of view of the experiment's design.

From the analyst's vantage point, understanding the eligibility criteria is essential for delimiting generalization of the study's results. The Spouse Assault Replication Program (SARP), for example, excluded juveniles from experiments on police handling of domestic violence. The SARP results, without strong theory or other information, were not expected to be generalizable to juveniles based on the adult sample that was used. Similarly, the Minority Female Single Parent Program experiments excluded single fathers from training and support samples. A variety of heart disease studies have excluded women from experiments. Generalizations about the effectiveness of treatments for one group—the study sample— may not be made about an excluded group without considerably more information about the latter.

A subtler matter concerns how individuals or entities were recruited into a study. Using friendship networks to attract adolescents into a substance abuse prevention program arguably would lead to a study sample that differs from one that is produced by, say, parent, teacher, and school recruitment efforts. Each approach may yield samples of adolescents who meet nominal eligibility requirements for a test of abuse prevention programs, such as age, absence of a criminal felony record, or full-time student status. The sample engaged through friendship networks may differ appreciably in knowable and in unknowable ways from those who were encouraged to participate by adults. The effects of alternative treatment approaches may, then, also differ.

Some individuals or entities eligible for treatments in a study may be eliminated from the study sample for reasons other than explicit eligibility criteria. Exclusions on the basis of vague criteria apparently are not uncommon in some medical trials, for example. Two thirds of breast cancer trials prior to 1984 evidently did not maintain logs on those rejected for the trial (U.S. GAO, 1992). Whether the experiment's results, based on the sample at hand, could be generalized to the rejected sample demands additional data or strong theory on why the rejections occur. Neither may be sufficient to permit generalization.

When participation in an experiment is voluntary, rather than mandatory, the individual or organization invited to be randomly assigned to alternative treatments may decline the invitation. Those who choose not to participate may or may not differ from those who choose to do so. A treatment found effective (or ineffective) for the participant group may be ineffective (or effective) for those who choose not to be a part of the study. For example, a school-based health program may have little discernible effect on adolescents' knowledge of sexual health based on a randomized experiment involving a volunteer sample of children. Many such volunteers already may be oriented toward learning about sexual health. Nonparticipants, on the other hand, may differ in the sense that an education program may help, as determined by an experiment, if nonparticipants are less well-informed. Alternatively, the program might have no effect if nonparticipants are as well-informed as their peers who participated in the study.

Determining why the study at hand differs in its results from earlier studies usually requires attention to factors such as identification and screening of eligible participants, the study's recruitment methods and rejection rules, and variations in willingness to participate. Only two of six independent experiments on handling misdemeanor domestic violence, for example, showed that arrest reduced recidivism. Among the reasons one might posit for differences are that police in different jurisdictions use different criteria in designating a misdemeanor domestic violence case as such. Further, victims in different jurisdictions may vary in the reasons they are willing to call police. In the two sites in which an effect was found, for example, it could be the case that the women who called were more likely to break up the relationship (leading to a reduction in couples and recidivism) when the partner was arrested. An arrest is a threshold condition that works only if the women are oriented toward separation. This orientation influences their willingness to call.

Assessment of Baseline Data

Recall, from Chapter 7 on observation and measurement, that baseline data obtained in a randomized study usually include demographic information such as age, race, gender, and other characteristics of the sample that are regarded as important in the particular study. Such information might include the number of prior pregnancies among women in a study of drug use prevention methods in fertility control trials, work experience in an experiment on employment programs, and so on. These data presumably are important to understanding for whom the treatments are most effective.

To understand the generalizability of the study's results or concordance with other studies, the analyst might then compare the baseline data obtained in the study at hand with the data that are available in administrative record systems or research data archives and that are pertinent to the study's target population. In the civil and criminal justice arena, a variety of resources can be helpful in putting the particular experiment into a larger context and making an empirically based judgment about generalizability of the experiment's result with respect to baseline data. They include the publications of the Bureau of Justice Assistance and research data archived with the support of the National Institute of Justice. In the education arena, the U.S. Department of Education's Planning and Evaluation Service, National Center for Education Statistics, and the Office of Educational Research and Improvement, among others, produce regular reports on the national and state level that assist in understanding how a local experiment's sample is similar to or different from a sample of the national or a regional population.

The reports and public use data archives produced by other federal agencies can be exploited similarly. These agencies include the Bureau of Labor Statistics, and the National Center for Health Statistics, among others. See Cordray et al. (1991) and Fienberg, Martin, and Straf (1985) for details on what data are accessible to whom from specific studies in the social and behavioral sciences and economics. See the U.S. GAO report (1992) for illustrations from health program evaluations.

Insofar as the study's sample differs appreciably from samples or populations examined in other studies, or from the groups that are often used as a basis for informing policy decisions, generalizing from the study's results to some larger population can be difficult. The differences that matter most are characteristics of the sample that are arguably or empirically related to the effects of the treatments being compared. Neither male nor female preschoolers may differ in their response to a specialized education program. The exclusion of males from a sample that is enrolled in an experiment may, then, be unimportant. On the other hand, if a baseline characteristic such as gender is important, then it must be taken into account by the analyst who is concerned about generalizing a study's results. The absence of preschool girls from a study of a particular education program for young children may be unimportant; the girls' absence from a study of science programs may be crucial. To understand the matter, the analyst might draw on earlier studies to assay whether the effects of some education efforts depend on the child's gender or on theory.

Assessment of Outcomes

Consider a multischool experiment on a school dropout prevention program in which the rate of dropout from schools in the control condition is 20%. Suppose further that the schools having a prevention program reduced this rate to 5%. A natural way to gauge the generalizability of results is to compare this outcome with outcomes in other schools, including schools that are similar to those in the sample used in the experiment.

If the average dropout rate for metropolitan high schools in the United States generally is 20%, then one may argue that the schools in the field experiment are similar to metropolitan schools more generally. That is, the effect of employing the same program in other schools, a change in dropout rate from 20% to 5%, might reasonably be expected.

Another experiment might focus only on schools with 50% dropout rates. Suppose that a prevention program managed to reduce the rate to 35%. If ambient levels of dropout in metropolitan schools are 20%, it is not clear how the results from this second experiment might be generalized or whether they should be generalized. The experiment's schools in both the treatment and control conditions appear different enough from metropolitan schools, on account of differences in ambient dropout rate, to justify caution and deeper inquiry.

These two examples are "simple"; matters often are more complicated. Base rates and outcomes in a particular study may or may not differ in magnitude from rates and outcomes in earlier studies, from experience in different geographic regions, and so on. For example, when field experiments in disparate contexts are virtually identical except for results, it is sensible to try to understand the ostensible lack of concordance in statistical terms. One can imagine that, on average, a uniformly implemented preschool program has an effect size of .20. It is reasonable to imagine that there will be chance departures from this average effect size across all possible studies on the identical treatment. This generates a distribution of effect sizes; that is, the treatment works on average, but it works to a greater or lesser extent depending on ordinary variability in behavior of preschool children, the ability of staff, and the contexts in which the preschool program operates. In effect, this line of thinking implies that a meta-analytic framework is useful in understanding how well results of one study accord with others. For more thorough handling of the matter, see Lipsey (1992), Cook et al. (1992), and U.S. GAO (1992).

10

Reporting

*By examination and mathematical computation I find
that the proportion of the spoken lie to others is as 1 to 22,894.
Therefore the spoken lie is of no consequence,
and it is not worth while to go around fussing about it.*
—Mark Twain, *The Man That Corrupted Hadleyburg* (1900)

Chartas meas omnes in tabulam ponam.
—Beard (Barbatus) (1990)

This chapter concerns the reports that are often produced in the course of a controlled experiment. It addresses the following questions:

- To whom are the reports addressed?
- At what times are reports produced?
- What kinds of reports are produced, and what are their contents?
- What proprieties should be observed?

The examples given below illustrate what can be regarded as good practice. They also accord well with the guidelines that have been developed to assist in reporting.

AUDIENCES FOR THE REPORTS

The results of experiments designed to test policy-relevant programs ought to be useful. Indeed, some have argued that unless there is a real prospect that results will be used, the experiment is unethical at worst and pointless at best (Federal Judicial Center, 1981; Ginsburg et al., 1992).

It is incumbent on the experiment's design team to identify the audiences for results. How the information is reported and what is reported depends heavily on characteristics of these potential users.

219

Direct Sponsors

The sponsor of the experiment normally requires a final report on all aspects of the experiment, including, at times, machine-readable data files that are generated by the study. For example, the U.S. Department of Education required its contracted research team to produce detailed final reports on the Even Start Adult Literacy Experiments that included results, machine-readable micro-records, questionnaires, case studies, and other information (St. Pierre, Swartz, Murray, Deck, & Nickel, 1995). In this case, as with other sizable experiments, both written and oral interim reports of various kinds are required as part of contract or grant agreements. Each principal investigator in the multisite experiments on police handling of domestic violence, for example, was required by the National Institute of Justice to present quarterly interim reports on progress.

Indirect Sponsors

There often will be indirect sponsors. A legislature, for example, may direct a government agency to engage in controlled field tests. The audiences for final reports, then, include legislative staff or legislative committee as well as the agency that sponsors the work directly. In the private foundation sector, a foundation's board of directors is an analogous indirect sponsor and may have similar expectations. Oral briefings by the sponsoring agency to these indirect sponsors or clients are an integral part of contemporary reporting in federal agencies. The focus is on ensuring that the work stays on course and that unexpected problems or changes in executing the study are understood by the community, such as a legislature or administrative office, that will depend on the data. Briefings also are devices to sustain the interest of such communities in the study, especially when their portfolio of responsibilities is large and diverse. Generally speaking, these audiences must receive *brief* summaries of the experiment, inasmuch as brevity and timeliness are valued by policymakers. Full reports are supplied to their staff.

Service Providers

The third potential audience for certain reports comprises individuals who are responsible for providing the treatment services that are being examined in the field test. In the Spouse Assault Replication Program (SARP), for example, the stakeholders who received interim and final reports of a variety of kinds included the street police who cooperated in the field tests for handling domestic violence, the sergeants and lieutenants who provided immediate leadership, and the captains, commanders, and chiefs who made the tentative decision to cooperate in the field tests (Reiss & Boruch, 1993). Providing a draft of an important report to these stakeholders was justified partly on quality control grounds. Treatments, for example, must be described. These individuals were positioned well to ensure accuracy in description. The justification also lies in a pragmatic courtesy and mutual education. Given their assistance in the work, service providers arguably have a right to learn about the full contents of a final report and to quarrel with its conclusions.

Special Interest Groups

The cooperation of advocacy groups, including groups that represent the study's participants, often is necessary for the successful conduct of an experiment. Regardless of their cooperation, the members of such groups are potential users of reports or experiments. For example, reports on experiments in the SARP were provided to the members of victim assistance groups who also served on advisory panels for the studies. Reports on experiments sponsored by the U.S. Department of Education and other federal agencies routinely are made available to such groups through similar arrangements or more generally through distribution systems such as ERIC and the Government Printing Office. Here, as in the case of indirect sponsors, summaries of results often will suffice, rather than full-blown reports.

To accommodate specialized audiences and functions, some sponsors of field tests lay out general requirements for reports beyond the final one. The additional products expected by the National Institute of Justice, for example, have included a summary of findings that can be published in the institute's practitioner-oriented *Research in Brief* and *Focus on Research* series.

Researchers and Other Scholars

The potential audiences for the results of controlled tests may include members of the larger community of researchers. Publication of excerpts of final reports in academic journals, for example, is a partial check on and verification of the quality of the enterprise. It also is a device for informing these communities about results, the problems that were encountered in executing the field test, and the solutions that others might exploit. The references to published articles ced in this book reflect the wide array of scholarly journals in which experiments are reported. Generally, these articles involve considerable abbreviation and reworking of final reports. Complete multivolume final reports for the SARP, the Rockefeller Foundation Experiments on Minority Female Single Parents, and others, for example, each ran to hundreds of pages. The summaries that appear in the published literature are considerably more terse and of necessity provide far less information. This is one reason for depending on the final reports here.

The General Public

Finally, the potential audiences for results of experiments include the general public. Journalists usually are the primary intermediaries between the research group and the public, and the better ones usually capitalize on oral information from a variety of sources. Press coverage can be substantial. For example, results of the Minneapolis experiment on the use of arrest in misdemeanor domestic violence cases were reported in more than 300 U.S. newspapers (Sherman & Cohn, 1989). Press clippings on the manpower and welfare experiments run by the Manpower Demonstration Research Corporation (1994) for 1993 and 1994 cover 500 pages. It is partly as a consequence of potential public interest that some research units or the experiment's sponsors compose press releases that summarize the study's results.

Audiences for Machine-Readable Data Files

The main audiences for machine-readable data files are the sponsoring agency and researchers with serious interest in using the data. Other data users include university faculty who employ the data for pedagogical or research purposes, and oversight agencies such as the U.S. General Accounting Office that have a mission of ensuring quality.

Federal agencies that sponsor applied research, including experiments on programs and projects, and that routinely require the development of machine-readable data files include the National Science Foundation, the National Institute of Justice, the U.S. Department of Education, and parts of the U.S. Department of Health and Human Services. The files received from the study team are maintained by the agency or, more commonly, by independent entities such as the U.S. National Archives or the Inter-University Consortium for Political and Social Research (1990). The consortium, for example, currently maintains and distributes data files generated in the SARP experiments on domestic violence (Sherman &

Berk, 1984; Dunford et al., 1990) and experiments on postprison income supports (Rossi et al., 1980), among others.

Not all federal or private sponsors of experiments require producing such public use data files. Nevertheless, their production has helped to ensure that data are exploited well and that analyses can be verified by a variety of independent investigators (Fienberg et al., 1985; Cordray et al., 1991). As a consequence, it has been possible for Garner et al. (1995) and Berk, Campbell, Klap, and Western (1992), among others, to undertake critical reanalyses of the data generated in the experiments in the SARP.

TIMELINESS OF REPORTS

As suggested earlier, deciding when reports need to be produced and for whom is basic to good practice in experiments. Planning for report distribution then becomes part of the overall evaluation design. The decisions regarding reports must, at times, be influenced heavily by the schedule of the clients for the results. For example, agencies such as the Department of Agriculture's Food and Nutrition Service, the U.S. Department of Education's Planning and Evaluation Service, and the General Accounting Office usually are obliged to produce final reports in time for them to be used by Congress, the client, in making decisions about authorization or appropriations for programs.

Failures to produce timely reports have occurred and have been criticized vigorously by legislatures, government agencies, and scholars (Ginsburg et al., 1992). These failures have had two consequences. First, late reports will not be used or will be less useful after decisions have been made. Second, the agency or others responsible for producing the evaluation becomes vulnerable to losing resources on account of failure to report well. As a practical matter, reports should be planned so that they are in step with authorization, appropriation, and other decisions.

Results of randomized field tests of different approaches to facilitate employment of food stamp recipients, for example, were used periodically by both the sponsoring agency and Congress, partly because they were available for scheduled discussions about how to reduce the costs and increase the value of the programs (Wargo, 1989). Field experiments to discern how to better reduce high school dropout rates similarly were designed to produce results between 1991 and 1996 that would be used to inform debate at the congressional, state, and regional levels (U.S.

Department of Education, Planning and Evaluation Service, 1991b, 1991c).

Decisions about when to produce a report on a field test may, at times, be driven less by the need to meet a client's schedule than by other factors. Each test in the SARP was sponsored through a grant that required a report within several months of the project's end. The reports' timing was determined by agency program policy that involved no assumptions about their use in time-constrained decision processes. Rather, each site's results were used locally by police departments and advocacy groups as the final reports appeared.

THE KINDS AND CONTENTS OF REPORTS

Executive Summary

A succinct summary typically includes text on why the experiment was undertaken, what the experiment was designed to do, characteristics of the target samples and treatments, and a dozen or fewer important results. A few charts or graphs are included at times.

Such a document is considerably briefer than a final full report. The Perry Preschool study's 20-year follow-up of participants in a preschool experiment is reported in a 250-page volume; the summary is about 5 pages (Schweinhart et al., 1993). The report on the National JTPA Program experiments summarizes a 400-page document in about 30 pages (Bloom & Orr, 1993).

No uniform standards have been adopted for the construction of an executive summary; consequently, the variation in length and character is substantial. How to tailor the summary to the needs of audiences for the report usually demands considerable attention from the research team and other stakeholders, notably sponsors.

It is difficult to overstate the importance of an executive summary. The summary, often issued apart from the main final report, often is the only report read by some stakeholders. In any case, it is far easier to distribute than the main reports.

Final Reports

Box 10.1 contains a checklist of topics that generally are considered in a final report on a controlled experiment. The topical coverage is identical to that given in this book; see the text for definitions. The list is sufficiently

---

BOX 10.1
A Checklist of Contents of the
Final Report on a Controlled Experiment

0. Executive summary
1. The question

   Authorization/justification for addressing the question
   Related studies

2. Description of treatments, including control group treatments
3. Experiment design

   Sponsor of the experiment
   Target units and population
   Statistical power and intended sample sizes
   Pipeline
   Eligibility criteria
   Randomization procedures
   Specification of models and hypotheses
   Outcome variables and measurement methods

4. Experiment integrity

   Treatments assigned versus delivered
   Baseline data comparisons
   Eligibility-related data
   Treatment adherence/compliance
   Validity and reliability evidence
   Attrition and missing data

5. Analysis and results

   Comparisons among groups: what works, for whom?
   Analysis methods
   Results
   Limits and sensitivity analysis
   Special problems such as missing data

6. Conclusions
7. Recommendations (when applicable)
8. References
9. Appendices

   Survey questions, inventories, and administrative reporting forms
   Informed consent forms
   Supporting statistical tables
   Changes in design during the course of the study

10. Public use data file

---

lengthy to justify, at times, a number of separately bound final reports. Each volume might handle a different topic or objective of the test and, as a consequence, the separate volumes might be directed toward somewhat different audiences. A detailed technical description of the test's design, for example, is likely to be of small interest to the decision makers who must attend primarily to the implications of results, but it may be of considerable interest to a legislative office, the sponsor's staff, or others whose responsibility lies heavily in understanding the quality of the evidence.

For example, the Rockefeller Foundation distributed the results of field tests on the Minority Female Single Parent Program through separate reports on the child care aspects of the training programs being tested (Maynard, Kisker, & Kerachsky, 1991), program costs (Handwerger & Thornton, 1988), target population and local context (Burghardt & Gordon, 1990), short-term economic impacts of the programs being tested (Gordon & Burghardt, 1990), program operations (Hershey, 1988), and a cross-site synthesis of how the integrated programs compared with traditional programs (Burghardt & Gordon, 1990).

At the U.S. Department of Education's Planning and Evaluation Service, undertaking studies with multiple objectives is essential to meet the needs of diverse constituencies for evaluative information (Ginsburg et al., 1992). As a result, separate reports were issued on the Even Start Family Literacy Experiments (St. Pierre et al., 1995). A summary covered items 1 through 8 of the checklist briefly; item 7 on recommendations was excluded. One volume of the final report covered each of these topics in detail. A second final volume of appendices included case studies of various projects that were examined, supplementary data, and copies of administrative record forms and questionnaires.

Inasmuch as the printed word is a limited vehicle for provoking interest in an experiment and for explaining results, some sponsors and investigators have explored the use of videotape. The Rockefeller Foundation (1988), for example, supported the production and distribution of a specialized videotape to illustrate why a randomized test was deemed essential in evaluating the foundation's program for minority female single parents, and how staff and management at community-based organizations handled the problems engendered by the randomization procedure. Other tapes were developed to provide information about the program and its effects on the Hispanic community.

At least one federal agency has integrated videotape reports into a broad dissemination program: the National Institute of Justice. The tapes are oriented toward practitioners, notably criminal and civil justice administrators and police executives and officers, who may use the tapes to educate themselves and their colleagues about new research results.

Full-blown final reports usually build on earlier interim work and are preceded by a draft whose review often is required by the experiment's sponsor. This review may entail critical reading by an oversight board, a project monitor appointed by the project's sponsor, executives at the sponsoring agency, or other stakeholders such as the managers of programs that are being compared. Any or all of these reviews may be used in the interest of ensuring the quality of the final report.

The checklist in Box 10.1 was constructed on the basis of the contents of reports cited in this volume. No formal standards of this sort have been adopted by, say, professional organizations with an interest in experiments, but the list accords with guidelines that have been generated by scholars, such as Mosteller, Gilbert, and McPeek (1980), and special advisory panels, such as the Standards of Reporting Trials Group (1994) in medicine.

Interim Reports

The contents of interim reports vary over time as the field test staff and service providers complete tasks required by the experiment, encounter problems, and try to resolve them. Such reports generally bear on the quality of the study.

Box 10.2, based on experience in multisite tests of methods for handling domestic violence, illustrates one scenario (Reiss & Boruch, 1991). Early discussions and quarterly reports concerned issues in the design of the experiments, randomization procedures, and eligibility requirements. Pipeline studies were a routine part of interim reports until the magnitude of caseflow into the experiments became clear. Later reports attended more to baseline characteristics of individuals enrolled in the study, the difficulties of following up on victims, and discrepancies between the treatments assigned and those delivered. Reports issued much later in the course of the study covered issues of ensuring quality—including updated data on baseline and caseflow, treatments delivered, and interview rates—and new problems, such as the employment of analytic methods beyond those specified in original proposals.

Regardless of their periodicity, interim reports may include machine-readable data files. For example, each principal investigator involved in the SARP provided oral and written quarterly reports to the SARP's sponsor and to an oversight panel, as well as providing interim data files. These data were used during each subsequent quarter to confirm the analyses produced earlier and to generate new ideas.

BOX 10.2
An Outline of Topics That
Interim Reports Might Cover

Early in the Experiment

Design issues
Pipeline-related data and power estimates
Treatments assigned versus delivered: pilot stage or run-in stage

Mid-Course or Periodic Reports

Problems encountered in random assignment and possible solutions
Design, pipeline, and power updates
Baseline data comparisons
Treatments assigned versus delivered
Follow-up survey of treatment recipients: cooperation rates
Machine-readable data files

Later in the Experiment

Preliminary analyses
Routine quality assurance analysis
Reporting options
Publication options
Machine-readable data files
Final analyses

Generally, interim reports are produced quarterly or less frequently. As suggested above, they are designed to inform the experiment's sponsor about the conduct of the experiment and to facilitate the research team's efforts to keep the experiment on track. These reports usually do not include analyses of the effects of treatments, partly because the statistical power of such analyses increases as the sample size increases over the course of the experiment. That is, preliminary findings that treatments do not differ are likely to be wrong, and disclosure of such analyses to a naive audience can seriously disrupt the experiment. Similarly, a chance difference that appears early may be misunderstood and disappear by the experiment's end.

Preliminary analyses do form part of interim reports when the experiment involves hazardous treatments, as in medical trials. Practice in this latter arena involves, at times, the construction of specialized statistical stopping rules and always involves special groups charged with monitoring observable risks to patients (see Friedman et al. [1985] for a review).

Machine-Readable Data Files: Contents and Quality

The contents of machine-readable files issued as a product of a controlled experiment normally are determined through an agreement between the sponsor of the study and the research team responsible for its implementation. These agreements are at times delimited by law and standards of ethics bearing on privacy. They also will be determined by laws that encourage the disclosure of information in the public interest. The work product may include all statistical data used in developing the interim and final reports. This includes files of micro-records on (anonymous) individuals or organizations who are the target of the experiment, such as their responses to interview questions.

General standards for preparing machine-readable files based on field research data can be tailored to the special case of interim or final data sets that are generated in experiments. The standards employed by the National Center for Education Statistics (1992) are illustrative. Among other things, they advise the data file preparer to generate descriptions of

- the study,
- data collection and editing procedures,
- frequency counts and response rates,
- file structure and contents,
- record length, format, and count, and
- data element definitions.

The study description may, for example, follow the outline in Box 10.1.

A variety of conventions usually are employed in preparing data files, and these need to be made explicit. Making a distinction among nonresponse, legitimate response, and legitimate skips, for example, is customary for defining data elements in a file and is critical to the user of the files. Similarly, record conventions require unique identifiers for each unit of observation, a uniform format for each record, and rectangular structure. The NCES standard for record layout requires conventional handling of record layouts, notably ensuring that the blocking factors, block size, and record counts are documented and that record types are defined. Diskettes must be formatted to ensure that MS-DOS file structures can be used; ASCII and files compatible with readily available statistical software such as SAS are a standard.

A Note on Standards
for the Contents of Reports

There have been notable gaps over the last 20 years in the information reported on experiments. The reader of a report may be told, for example, that the study is a randomized field experiment but be given no details about the randomization procedure. There may be little or no account of the eligibility requirements and recruitment of individuals for the study. The reasons for choosing a particular response variable, the treatments, and so forth also may not be discussed. Finally, treatments that occur naturally in the control group condition often go unmeasured and unreported despite the fact that this is the standard against which other treatments are judged.

Lacunae in reports on experiments and on evaluations more generally make these reports difficult for a thoughtful reader to understand. They may lead to a well-conducted experiment being ignored because the information that is reported is insufficient to regard the experiment as trustworthy. They can lead to decisions to adopt an innovation based on reports that were incomplete. The reporting gaps also complicate efforts to develop quantitative syntheses of multiple experiments so that researchers can anticipate how the effects of new programs vary over subgroups and time, and so that researchers can learn how to design better experiments. See, for example, Farrington (1983), Light and Pillemer (1984), Cordray & Fisher (1994), and Cook et al. (1992) on meta-analysis and the problems that poor reporting engenders.

The quality of reporting on controlled experiments has improved over the last decade, partly as a result of the episodic development of reporting standards. Chalmers et al. (1981), DerSimonian, Charette, McPeek, and Mosteller (1982), and the Standards of Reporting Trials Groups (1994) in the medical clinical trials arena; Dennis (1990) in evaluation of drug programs; and Betsey et al. (1985) on tests of employment and training programs are among those on whom this book relies. Guidelines for ensuring quality in reporting in related areas also have been worked out by some professional organizations and government agencies. *Standards for Evaluations of Educational Programs, Projects, and Materials* (Joint Committee on Standards for Educational Evaluation, 1981), for example, covers reporting briefly and focuses on candor. The standards of the U.S. Department of Education's National Center for Education Statistics (1991) standards were designed primarily to enhance the quality and usefulness of statistical education surveys rather than controlled tests. They are nevertheless relevant to any experiment in which information is elicited periodically from individuals who are the targets for various services.

PROPRIETIES

When controlled field tests are undertaken to inform public policy, the proprieties of reporting often will be determined by law, administrative rule, or legal contract. They also will be influenced by professional standards of practice that have less force behind them than law but are nevertheless crucial.

Authority for Releasing Reports

The authority for release or disclosure of a report to any community depends heavily on agreements between the sponsor of the experiment and those responsible for its execution. In general, if the study is sponsored through a government or foundation *grant*, the authority resides with the principal investigator. Most grants are made to nonprofit organizations, including universities. Federal agencies, such as the National Science Foundation and National Institute of Justice, and some private foundations normally require that the grantee produce a report at the end of the project that will be disclosed to the public. The agencies have no authority to prevent its release.

If the study is sponsored through a *contract* rather than a grant, then the contracting agency specifies when reports are due and often takes responsibility for the contractor's (or agency's) public disclosure of reports. Arrangements vary as a function of the organizational vehicle used to implement the work.

Universities, for example, may contract to undertake randomized experiments, based on proposals by faculty and staff. The university's charter and operating rules are normally such that the university-based investigator must be free to distribute a report. The custom is one driven by the university's mission of free inquiry and dissemination of scientific knowledge. A contract with a university then will normally contain no provisions that prevent distribution of a report by an investigator. Sponsors, however, may require that reports be reviewed by the sponsoring agency prior to the formal release of the report to the public. The requirement is sound in the sense that the sponsoring agency ought to be apprised early about results that may demand considerable attention once they are introduced into combative public forums.

Nonprofit research groups and for-profit organizations other than universities undertake sizable field experiments. Government contracts with these organizations usually require submission of a final report to the sponsor that will (or will not) be released formally by the sponsor. The sponsor then is vested with authority for disclosure.

Regardless of whether the agreements between sponsor and the research entity are based on grants or contracts, the "authority" for release is a bit ambiguous once the report is submitted to some sponsors. For example, reports that are submitted to the federal government frequently fall within the ambit of the Freedom of Information Act. In effect, citizens can elicit and obtain reports that are not formally released by the government and, within limits, government agencies will be compelled to disclose them. Private foundations and corporations are not covered by such laws.

Sponsorship and Conflict of Interest

Conscientious sponsors are interested, of course, in understanding the results of comparative experiments. This is one reason for a sponsor's ensuring that the study is run independently and at a level of quality that is reasonable.

The potential for unseemly influence on an independent field test by a sponsor and by those who exercise influence on a sponsor is sufficiently great, however, that the reports on a field test should acknowledge the source of financial support for the test. This is notwithstanding the integrity of the sponsoring agency and the system for ensuring quality that underlies the well-designed field experiment.

Individual Privacy and Textual Reports

There usually is no need, in a report on the substantive results of an experiment, to disclose the identity of individuals who received different treatments. The analysis usually consists of statistical summaries that preclude disclosure of information on individuals. Furthermore, standards for good ethical practice, of the kind described earlier in this book, demand that individual privacy be protected. As a consequence, no individual identifiers appear in interim or final reports of randomized controlled experiments.

Individual participants often are quoted anonymously in good reports, however, as part of an ethnographic description or case study. The individual who is quoted normally will have been assured, in the interest of respondent candor and privacy, that his or her identity will not be disclosed to the reader of reports. There is a possibility, nevertheless, of deductive disclosure. That is, the report's description of context and the specific quotation may contain enough information for some readers to deduce the identity of the individual being quoted.

The problem of deductive disclosure in narrative reports is sufficiently important in principle and practice to have attracted the attention of scholars: Margaret Mead, William Kruskal and others have advised caution on this account (Boruch & Cecil, 1979). The remedy is to vet reports containing descriptive information so as to ensure that a reader cannot deduce the identity of a respondent and educe more information about the individual from the report. For example, the reader of a report in which an individual parent who happened to participate in the field test is described as "a Native American author of a book on his experience in crossing the country in a van" might deduce that the parent was William Least Heat Moon (author of *Blue Highways*) and learn about opinions that the individual might have regarded as a private matter. The vetting involves ensuring that the report does not contain information that is sufficiently collateral with public information to permit deductive disclosure.

Individual Privacy and
Machine-Readable Data Files

The machine-readable statistical data provided as part of a final report generally contain no individually identified records. There usually is no need for identifiers, in that the purpose of making the files available to others is to facilitate independent statistical analyses, not to enhance information about individuals. Beyond this, identifiers are excluded in the ethical interest of protecting the privacy of the individuals who participated in the research.

Deleting identifying information from micro-records on individuals is a sturdy device for ensuring their privacy. It is insufficient to the extent that deductive disclosure is possible. As with ethnographic reports, the files must be reviewed so as to reduce to a reasonable level the possibility that the inquisitor of "anonymous" records will deduce the identity of the individual on whom the record is maintained. Consequently, any vetting of files to be released for use by the scientific community would involve deletion of data from a record that, when used with collateral information based on local directories or a visit to the neighbors, for example, would permit unique identification of an individual's record. Procedures for reviewing machine-readable data files so as to prevent deductive disclosure have been described by, among others, Boruch and Cecil (1979).

Candor

The pronouncement given in Latin at the start of this chapter means "I'll put all my cards on the table" (Beard, 1990, p. 49). Standards in reporting research ask for full and frank disclosure of findings (Joint Committee on Standards for Educational Evaluation, 1981). However gratuitous this counsel or cynical its reception, the goal is easy to achieve in some respects and difficult in others. The ease in meeting this standard comes about partly by undertaking research in which quality is an explicit theme. Individuals who aspire to conduct high-quality field tests then avoid sponsors that are likely to bring overpowering influence to bear on the results of the test. The sponsor with a reputation for honesty and an interest in quality is likely to be no less sensitive to a relationship with individuals or firms that are easy to corrupt.

Beyond the broad interests of a sponsor or those who engage in a field test, explicit rules and contractual agreements that stress quality, when taken seriously, are important. That is, the quality assurance required by sponsors, the peers who may select a particular group to conduct the field test, oversight committees, and so on normally will demand disclosure of as much relevant information as possible. At their best, the inquisitors are thorough and, in effect, assist the experimenter in producing a honest report.

A more difficult aspect of meeting a standard of full and frank disclosure stems from mistakes, perceived or real, in conducting the field test. To abide well by the standard, the research team must remember the mistakes, at least the remarkable ones. Memory is frail in this and other settings; the research diary, quarterly reports, and so on must sustain the effort. The acknowledgment of a mistake also should take into account the context at the time decisions were made, including the local obstacles to producing evidence.

No randomized field test is perfectly run, just as services are never perfectly provided. Mistakes ought to be expected and, when understood, exploited: They are a vehicle for building new knowledge. Candor in reporting the failures of randomization procedures, for example, has been the basis for analytic reviews of the problem by Conner (1977), Rossi et al. (1987), Boruch and Wothke (1985), and Betsey et al. (1985). These reviews, in turn, have led to more conscientious attention to centralizing the randomization procedure and preventing its subversion (see Chapter 5 on randomization). Similar candor about imperfections has led to considerable emphasis on good management, to resolving the ethical problems that may be encountered in field tests, and to more thoughtful anticipation of the problems and how they may be resolved. In a volatile arena such as experiments on AIDS prevention programs, for example, the need to understand the mistakes of research and attempts at rectification is critical (Coyle et al., 1991).

References

Abt Associates. (1992). *Project NetWork: Draft evaluation data collection guide*. Cambridge, MA: Author.

Aiken, L. H., & Kehrer, B. H. (Eds.). (1985). *Evaluation studies review annual 10*. Beverly Hills, CA: Sage.

Aiken, L. S., & West, S. G. (1990). Invalidity of true experiments: Self-report pretest bias. *Evaluation Review, 14*(4), 374-390.

Allison, P. (1984). *Event history analysis: Regression for longitudinal event data*. Newbury Park, CA: Sage.

Aplasca, M. R., Siegel, D., Mandel, J. S., Santana-Arciaga, R. T., Paul, J., Hudes, E. S., Monzon, D. R., & Hearst, N. (1995). Results of a model AIDS prevention program for high school students in the Philippines. *AIDS, 9*(Supplement 1), 7-13.

Arkin, C. F., & Wachtel, M. S. (1990). How many patients are necessary to assess test performance? *Journal of the American Medical Association, 263*(2), 275-278.

Auspos, P., Cave, G., Doolittle, F., & Hoerz, G. (1989). *Implementing JOBSTART*. New York: Manpower Demonstration Research Corporation.

Bangser, M. R. (1985). *Lessons from transitional employment: The STETS demonstration for mentally retarded workers*. New York: Manpower Demonstration Research Corporation.

Barnes, C. J. (1984). Impediments to recruitment in the Canadian National Breast Screening Study. *Controlled Clinical Trials, 5*, 129-140.

Beard, H. (1990). *Latin for all occasions*. New York: Villard Books.

Bejar, I. (1983). *Measurement*. Beverly Hills, CA: Sage.

Bell, S. H., Orr, L. L., Blomquist, J. D., & Cain, G. (1995). *Program applicants as a comparison group in evaluating training programs: Theory and a test*. Kalamazoo, MI: W. E. Upjohn Institute for Employment Research.

Berk, R. A., Campbell, A., Klap, R., & Western, B. (1992). The deterrent effect of arrest in incidents of domestic violence: A Bayesian analysis of four field experiments. *American Sociological Review, 57*, 698-708.

Berk, R. A., Smyth, G. K., & Sherman, L. W. (1988). When random assignment fails: Some lessons from the Minneapolis Spouse Abuse Experiment. *Journal of Quantitative Criminology, 4*(3), 209-223.

Berlin, M., Mohadjer, L., Waksberg, J., Kolstad, A., Kirsch, I., Rock, D., & Yamamoto, K. (1992). An experiment in monetary incentives. In *1992 Proceedings of the Section on Survey Research Methods: American Statistical Association* (pp. 393-398). Alexandria, VA: American Statistical Association.

Bermant, G., Kelman, H. C., & Warwick, D. P. (1978). *The ethics of social experimentation*. New York: Wiley.

Betsey, C., Hollister, R., & Papagiordiou, M. (Eds.). (1985). *Youth employment and training programs: The YEDPA years*. Washington, DC: National Academy of Sciences Press.

Beyer, W. H. (1988). *CRC handbook of tables for probability and statistics* (2nd ed.). Boston: CRC Press.

Bickman, L. (1985). Randomized field experiments in education: Implementation lessons. *New Directions for Program Evaluation, 28,* 39-54.

Bickman, L. (Ed.). (1990). *Advances in program theory.* San Francisco: Jossey-Bass.

Bickman, L., Guthrie, P. R., Foster, E. M., Lambert, E. W., Summerfelt, W. T., Breda, C. S., & Heflinger, C. A. (1994). *Final report of the outcome and cost/utilization studies of the Fort Bragg evaluation project* (Vol. 1). Nashville, TN: Vanderbilt Institute for Public Policy Studies.

Bloom, H. S. (1990). *Back to work: Testing reemployment services for displaced workers.* Kalamazoo, MI: W. E. Upjohn Institute for Employment Research.

Bloom, H., & Orr, L. (1993). *The Job Training Partnership Act Experiment: Final report.* Cambridge, MA: Abt Associates.

Bohrnstedt, G. W. (1983). Measurement. In P. H. Rossi, J. D. Wright, & A. B. Anderson (Eds.), *Handbook of survey research* (pp. 70-122). New York: Academic Press.

Borenstein, M., & Cohen, J. (1990). *Statistical power analysis.* Hillsdale, NJ: Lawrence Erlbaum.

Boruch, R. F., & Cecil, J. S. (1979). *Assuring the confidentiality of social research data.* Philadelphia: University of Pennsylvania Press.

Boruch, R. F., & Cordray, D. S. (1980). *An appraisal of education program evaluations: Federal, state, and local agencies* (Contract #300-79-0467). Washington, DC: U.S. Department of Education.

Boruch, R. F., Dennis, M., & Carter, K. (1988). Lessons from the Rockefeller Foundation's experiments on the Minority Female Single Parent Program. *Evaluation Review, 12,* 396-426.

Boruch, R. F., & Wothke, W. (1985). Seven kinds of randomization plans for designing field experiments. *New Directions for Program Evaluation, 28,* 95-118.

Bowman, K. O., & Kastenbaum, M. A. (1975). Sample size requirement: Single and double classification experiments. In H. L. Harter & D. B. Owen (Eds.), *Selected tables in mathematical statistics* (Vol. 3, pp. 000-000). Providence, RI: American Mathematical Society.

Bradburn, N., & Sudman, S. (1979). *Improving interview method and questionnaire design.* San Francisco: Jossey-Bass.

Breger, M. (1983). Randomized social experiments and the law. In R. F. Boruch & J. S. Cecil, (Eds.), *Solutions to legal and ethical problems in applied social research* (pp. 97-144). New York: Academic Press.

Brent, E., Mirielli, E., & Thompson, A. (1993). *Ex-Sample (Version 3): User's guide and reference manual.* Columbia, MO: Idea Works.

Brooks-Gunn, J., McCormick, M. C., Gunn, R. W., Shorter, T., Wallace, C. Y., & Heagarty, M. C. (1989). *Medical Care, 27*(2), 95-102.

Bunker, J. P., Barnes, J. P., & Mosteller, F. (1977). *Costs, risks, and benefits of surgery.* New York: Oxford University Press.

Burghardt, J., & Gordon, A. (1990). *More jobs and higher pay: How an integrated program compares with traditional programs.* New York: The Rockefeller Foundation.

Campbell, D. T., & Boruch, R. F. (1976). Making the case for randomized assignment treatments by considering the alternatives: Six ways in which quasi-experimental evaluations in compensatory education tend to underestimate effects. In C. A. Bennett & A. A. Lumsdaine (Eds.), *Central issues in social program evaluation* (pp. 195-297). New York: Academic Press.

Campbell, D. T., & Stanley, J. S. (1966). *Experimental and quasi-experimental designs for research.* Chicago: Rand McNally.

Cantor, D. (1989). Substantive implications of selected operational longitudinal design features: The National Crime Survey as a case study. In D. Kasprzyk, G. Duncan, G. Kalton, & M. P. Singh (Eds.), *Panel surveys* (pp. 25-51). New York: John Wiley and Sons.

Cecil, J. S. (1993). Confidentiality legislation and the United States federal statistical system. *Journal of Official Statistics, 9*(2), 519-536.

Cecil, J. S., & Boruch, R. F. (1988). Compelled disclosure of research data: An early warning and suggestions for psychologists. *Law and Human Behavior, 12*(2), 181-189.

Chalmers, T. C., Smith, H., Blackburn, B., Silverman, B., Schroeder, B., Reitman, D., & Ambroz, A. (1981). A method for assessing the quality of a randomized controlled trial. *Controlled Clinical Trials, 2*(1), 31-50.

Chen, H. T., & Rossi, P. H. (1980). The multi-goal, theory driven approach to evaluation: A model linking basis and applied social science. *Social Forces, 59*(1), 106-122.

Christopherson, G. (1983). *Administration of the Seattle-Denver Income Maintenance Experiment.* Princeton, NJ: Mathematica Policy Research.

Clogg, C. C., & Shockey, J. W. (1988). Multivariate analysis of discrete data. In J. R. Nesselroade & R. B. Cattell (Eds.), *Handbook of multivariate psychology* (pp. 337-366). New York: Plenum.

Cochran, W. G. (1983). *Planning and analysis of observational studies.* New York: Wiley.

Cochran, W. G., & Cox, G. M. (1950). *Experimental designs.* New York: Wiley.

Cohen, J. (1988). *Statistical power analysis for the behavioral sciences.* (2nd ed.). New York: Academic Press.

Cohen, J. (1992). A power primer. *Psychological Bulletin, 112*(1), 155-159.

Cohen, P. G. (1982). *A calculating people: The spread of numeracy in early America.* Chicago: University of Chicago Press.

Collins, J. F., & Elkin, I. (1985). Randomization in the NIMH treatment of depression collaborative research program. *New Directions for Program Evaluation, 28,* 27-38.

Committee on Evaluating Medical Technologies in Clinical Use, Institute of Medicine. (1985). *Assessing medical technologies.* Washington, DC: National Academy of Sciences Press.

Conner, R. F. (1977). Selecting a control group: An analysis of the randomization process in twelve social reform programs. *Evaluation Quarterly, 1*(2), 195-243.

Conrad, K. (Ed.). (1994). Critically evaluating the role of experiments [Special Issue]. *New Directions for Program Evaluation, 63*(Fall).

Cook, T. D., & Campbell, D. T. (1979). *Quasi-experimentation: Design and analysis issues for field settings.* Chicago: Rand McNally.

Cook, T. D., Cooper, H., Cordray, D. S., Hartmann, T., Hedges, L. V., Light, R. J., Louis, T. A., & Mosteller, F. (Eds.). (1992). *Meta-analysis for explanation: A casebook.* New York: Russell Sage.

Cordray, D. S., Dion, G., & Boruch, R. F. (1991). Sharing research data: With whom? How much? In *Proceedings of the Conference on Data Management in Biomedical Research* (pp. 39-85). Washington, DC: U.S. Department of Health and Human Services.

Cordray, D. S., & Fischer, R. L. (1994). Synthesizing evaluation findings. In J. S. Wholey, H. H. Hatry, & K. Newcomer (Eds.), *Handbook of practical program evaluation* (pp. 198-231). San Francisco: Jossey-Bass.

Cordray, D. S., & Orwin, R. G. (1983). Improving the quality of evidence: Interconnections among primary evaluation, secondary analysis, and quantitative synthesis. In R. J. Light (Ed.), *Evaluation studies review annual* (Vol. 8, pp. 91-119). Newbury Park, CA: Sage.

Corsi, J. R., & Hurley, T. L. (1979). Pilot study report on the use of the telephone in administrative fair hearings. *Administrative Law Review, 31*(4), 484-524.

Cottingham, P. H. (1991). Unexpected lessons: Evaluation of job training programs for single mothers. *New Directions for Program Evaluation, 50,* 59-70.

Cox, D. R. (1958). *Planning of experiments.* New York: Wiley.

Coyle, S. L., Boruch, R. F., & Turner, C. F. (Eds.). (1991). *Evaluating AIDS prevention programs.* Washington, DC: National Academy of Sciences Press.

Crain, R. L., Heebner, A. L., & Si, Y. (1992). *The effectiveness of New York City's career magnet schools: An evaluation of ninth grade performance using an experimental design.* Berkeley, CA: National Center for Research in Vocational Education.

Crime Control Institute. (1986). *The Milwaukee City Council debate on the Spouse Assault Replication Program.* (Available from Dr. L. Sherman, Crime Control Institute, 1063 Thomas Jefferson Street, Washington, DC 20007)

Darlington, R. B. (1990). *Regression and linear models.* New York: McGraw-Hill.

Dennis, M. L. (1988). *Implementing randomized field experiments: An analysis of criminal and civil justice research.* Unpublished doctoral dissertation, Northwestern University, Department of Psychology, Evanston, IL.

Dennis, M. L. (1990). Assessing the validity of randomized field experiments. *Evaluation Review, 14*(4), 347-373.

Dent, C. W., Sussman, S., & Flay, B. R. (1993). The use of archival data to select and assign schools in a drug prevention trial. *Evaluation Review, 17*(2), 159-181.

DerSimonian, R., Charette, L. J., McPeek, B., & Mosteller, F. (1982). Reporting on methods for clinical trials. *New England Journal of Medicine, 306*(22), 1332-1337.

Devine, J., Wright, J. D., & Joyner, L. (1994). Issues in implementing a randomized experiment in a field setting. *New Directions for Program Evaluation, 63*(Fall), 27-40.

Dolittle, F., & Traeger, L. (1990). *Implementing the National JTPA study.* New York: Manpower Demonstration Research Corporation.

Dowdy, S., & Weardon, S. (1991). *Statistics for research.* New York: Wiley.

Droitcour, J., Silberman, G., & Chelimsky, E. (1993). Cross design synthesis. *International Journal of Technology Assessment in Health Care, 9*(3), 440-449.

Duffer, A., Lessler, J., Weeks, M., & Mosher, W. (1994). Effects of incentive payments on response rates and field costs in a pretest of a national CAPI survey. In *1994 Proceedings of the Section on Survey Research Methods: American Statistical Association* (Vol. 2, pp. 1386-1391). Alexandria, VA: American Statistical Association.

Duncan, G. T., Jabine, T. B., & de Wolf, V. A. (Eds.). (1993). *Private lives and public policies: Confidentiality and accessibility of government statistics.* Washington, DC: National Academy of Sciences Press.

Dunford, F. W. (1990). System-initiated warrants for suspects of misdemeanor domestic assault: A pilot study. *Justice Quarterly, 7*(4), 631-653.

Dunford, F. W., Huizinga, D., & Elliott, D. S. (1990). The Omaha Domestic Violence Experiment. *Criminology, 28,* 183-206.

Dynarski, M. (1993). The effects of displacement on measures of reemployment bonus impacts. *Evaluation Review, 17*(1), 47-59.

Ellickson, P. L. (1994). Getting and keeping schools and kids for evaluation studies. *Journal of Community Psychology* (Special Issue), 102-116.

Ellickson, P. L., & Bell, R. M. (1992). Drug prevention in junior high: A multi-site longitudinal test. *Science, 247,* 1299-1306.

Ellickson, P. L., Bianca, D., & Schoeff, D. C. (1988). Containing attrition in school based research: An innovative approach. *Evaluation Review, 12*(4), 331-351.

Ewigman, B. G., Crane, J. P., Frigoletto, F. D., LeFevre, M. L., Bain, R. P., McNellis, D., & the Radius Study Group. (1993). Effects of prenatal ultrasound screening on perinatal outcome. *New England Journal of Medicine, 329*(12), 821-827.

Fairweather, G. W., & Tornatsky, L. G. (1977). *Experimental methods for social policy research.* New York: Pergamon.

Fantuzzo, J., Davis, G., & Ginsburg, M. (1995). Effects of parent involvement in isolation or in combination with peer tutoring on student self concept. *Journal of Educational Psychology, 87,* 271-281.

Fantuzzo, J. F., Jurecic, L., Stovall, A., Hightower, A. D., Goins, C., & Schachtel, D. (1988). Effects of adult and peer social initiations on the social behavior of withdrawn, maltreated preschool children. *Journal of Consulting and Clinical Psychology, 56*(1), 34-39.

Fantuzzo, J., & Stevenson, H. (1993). *Observations on the design, initiation, and conduct of tests of a program for high risk children in Philadelphia* (Research Report). Philadelphia: Center for Research on Evaluation and Social Policy.

Farrington, D. P. (1983). Randomized experiments on crime and justice. *Crime and Justice: An Annual Review of Research, 4,* 257-308.

Federal Judicial Center. (1981). *Social experimentation and the law.* Washington, DC: Author.

Feldt, L., & Brennan, R. (1993). Reliability. In R. L. Linn (Ed.), *Educational measurement* (3rd ed., pp. 105-146). Washington, DC: American Council on Education/Oryx Press.

Ferber, R., & Hirsch, W. (1982). *Social experimentation and economic policy.* Cambridge, UK: Cambridge University Press.

Ferguson, G. A., & Takane, Y. (1989). *Statistical analysis in psychology and education.* New York: McGraw-Hill.

Fetterman, D. M. (1989). *Ethnography step by step.* Newbury Park, CA: Sage.

Fienberg, S. E., Martin, M. E., & Straf, M. L. (Eds.). (1985). *Sharing research data.* Washington, DC: National Academy of Sciences Press.

Fienberg, S. E., Singer, B., & Tanur, J. M. (1985). Large-scale social experimentation in the United States. In A. C. Atkinson & S. E. Fienberg (Eds.), *A celebration of statistics: The ISI centenary volume* (pp. 287-325). New York: Springer-Verlag.

Finn, J. D., & Achilles, C. M. (1990). Answers and questions about class size: A statewide experiment. *American Educational Research Journal, 27*(3), 557-577.

Fisher, R. A. (1935). *The design of experiments.* Edinburgh: Oliver and Boyd.

Flay, B. R. (1986). Efficacy and effectiveness trials and other phases of research in the development of health promotion programs. *Preventive Medicine, 15,* 451-474.

Fleiss, J. L. (1986). *The design and analysis of clinical trials.* New York: Wiley.

Fraker, T., & Maynard, R. (1987). Evaluating comparison group designs with employment related programs. *Journal of Human Resources, 22,* 195-227.

Friedman, L. M., Furberg, C. D., & DeMets, D. L. (1985). *Fundamentals of clinical trials* (2nd ed.). Littleton, MA: PSG Publishing.

Garner, J., Fagen, J., & Maxwell, C. (1995). Published findings from the Spouse Assault Replication Program: A critical review. *Journal of Quantitative Criminology, 11*(1), 3-28.

Gilbert, J. P., McPeek, B., & Mosteller, F. (1977). Assessing medical innovations. In J. P. Bunker, B. A. Barnes, & F. Mosteller (Eds.), *Costs, risks, and benefits of surgery* (pp. 124-169). New York: Oxford University Press.

Ginsburg, A. (1992). Reinvigorating program evaluation: U.S. Department of Education experience. *Evaluation Review, 13*(6), 579-597.

Ginsburg, A. L., McLaughlin, M., Pliska, V., & Takai, R. (1992). Revitalizing program evaluation at the U.S. Department of Education. *Educational Researcher, 18,* 24-27.

Glass, G. V, & Hopkins, K. D. (1984). *Statistical methods in education and psychology.* Englewood Cliffs, NJ: Prentice-Hall.

Goerge, R. M. (1991). *An integrated data base on children's services.* Chicago: Chapin Hall Center for Children, University of Chicago.

Goerge, R. M., Osuch, R., & Costello, J. (1991). *The evaluation of family assistance law for mentally disabled children in Illinois.* Chicago: Chapin Hall Center for Children, University of Chicago.

Goldman, J. (1985). Negotiated solutions to overcoming impediments in a law-related experiment. *New Directions for Program Evaluation, 28,* 63-72.

Goldstein, R. (1989). Power and sample size via MS/PC-DOS computers. *American Statistician, 43,* 253-260.

Gordon, A., & Burghardt, J. (1990). *The Minority Female Single Parent Demonstration: Short term economic impacts.* New York: The Rockefeller Foundation.

Gordon, G., & Morse, E. V. (1975). Evaluation research. *Annual Review of Sociology, 1,* 339-361.

Gottfried, A. W. (Ed.). (1984). *Home environment and early cognitive development: Longitudinal research.* New York: Academic Press.

Gramlich, E. M. (1990). *A guide to benefit cost analysis.* Englewood Cliffs, NJ: Prentice-Hall.

Gray, J. N., & Melton, G. B. (1985). The law and psychosocial research on AIDS. *University of Nebraska Law Review, 64,* 637-688.

Greenberg, D. H., & Mandell, M. (1991). Research utilization in policy makings. *Journal of Policy Analysis and Management, 10*(4), 633-656.

Groves, R. M. (1989). *Survey errors and costs.* New York: Wiley.

Guenzel, P. J., Berckmans, T. F., & Cannell, C. F. (1983). *Economic survey methods.* Ann Arbor, MI: Institute for Social Research.

Gueron, J. M. (1985). The demonstration of work/welfare initiatives. *New Directions in Program Evaluation, 28,* 5-14.

Gueron, J. M., & Pauly, E. (1991). *From welfare to work.* New York: Russell Sage Foundation.

Haberman, S. J. (1978). *Analysis of qualitative data: Vol. 1. Introductory Topics.* New York: Academic Press.

Handwerger, S., & Thornton, C. (1988). *The Minority Female Single Parent Demonstration: Program costs.* New York: The Rockefeller Foundation.

Hansen, W. B., & Graham, J. W. (1991). Preventing alcohol, marijuana, and cigarette use among adolescents: Peer pressure resistance training versus establishing conservative norms. *Preventive Medicine, 20,* 414-430.

Hansen, W. B., Johnson, C. A., Flay, B. R., Graham, J. W., & Sobel, J. (1988). Affective and social influence approaches to the prevention of multiple substance abuse among seventh grade students: Results from Project SMART. *Preventive Medicine, 17,* 135-154.

Harskamp, E., & Suhre, C. (1995). Mathematics programs and means to improve job qualifications for women. *Evaluation Review, 19*(5), 523-544.

Hausman, J. A., & Wise, D. A. (Eds.). (1985). *Social experimentation*. Chicago: University of Chicago Press.

Hawkins, J. D., Catalano, R., Jones, G., & Fine, D. (1987). Delinquency prevention through parent training. In J. Q. Wilson & G. C. Loury (Eds.), *Families, schools, and delinquency prevention: Vol. 3. From children to citizens* (pp. 186-204). New York: Springer-Verlag.

Hawkins, J. D., Jenson, J. M., Catalano, R. F., & Wells, E. A. (1991). Effects of skills training intervention with juvenile delinquents. *Research on Social Work Practice, 1*(2), 107-121.

Heckman, J. J., & Hotz, V. J. (1989). Choosing among alternative nonexperimental methods for estimating the impact of social programs: The case of manpower training. *Journal of the American Statistical Association, 84*, 862-874.

Hedrick, T. E., Bickman, L., & Rog, D. J. (1993). *Applied research design: A practical guide*. Newbury Park, CA: Sage.

Hedrick, S. C., Sullivan, J. H., Ehreth, J. L., Rothman, M. L., Connis, R. T., & Erdly, W. W. (1991). Centralized versus decentralized coordination in the adult day health care evaluation study. *New Directions for Program Evaluation, 50*, 19-32).

Heller, L. R., & Fantuzzo, J. W. (1993). Reciprocal peer tutoring and parent partnership: Does parent involvement make a difference? *School Psychology Review, 22*, 517-534.

Hershey, A. (1988). *Program processes: The Minority Female Single Parent Demonstration*. New York: The Rockefeller Foundation.

Hirschel, J. D., Hutchison, I. W., & Dean, D. W. (1992). The failure of arrest to deter spouse abuse. *Journal of Research in Crime and Delinquency, 29*, 7-33.

Hirschel, J. D., Hutchison, I. W., Dean, C. W., Kelley, J. J., & Pesackis, C. E. (1991). *Charlotte Spouse Assault Replication Project: Final report*. Charlotte: University of North Carolina at Charlotte.

Holland, P. W., & Rubin, D. B. (1988). Causal inference in retrospective studies. *Evaluation Review, 12*(3), 203-231.

Hollander, M., & Wolfe, D. A. (1973). *Nonparametric statistical methods*. New York: John Wiley and Sons.

Hollister, R. G. (1984). The design and implementation of the Supported Work evaluation. In R. G. Hollister, P. Kemper, & R. A. Maynard (Eds.), *The National Supported Work Demonstration* (pp. 12-49). Madison: University of Wisconsin Press.

Hollister, R. G. (1990). *The Minority Female Single Parent Demonstration: New evidence about effective training strategies*. New York: The Rockefeller Foundation.

Hollister, R. G., Kemper, P., & Maynard, R. (Eds.). (1984). *The National Supported Work Demonstration*. Madison: University of Wisconsin Press.

Ibn Khaldun. (1978). *Muqadimmah*. (N. J. Dawood, Ed., F. Rosenthal, Trans.). London: Routledge and Kaegan Paul. (Original work published 1377)

Inter-University Consortium for Political and Social Research. (1990). *Guide to resources and services*. Ann Arbor, MI: Author.

Jason, L. A., Johnson, J. H., Danner, K. E., Taylor, S., & Kuraski, K. S. (1993). A comprehensive, preventive, parent based intervention for high risk transfer students. *Prevention in Human Services, 10*(2), 27-38.

Jason, L. A., Weine, A. M., Johnson, J. H., Warren-Sohlberg, L., Filippelli, L. A., Turner, E. Y., & Lardon, C. (1992). *School transfer: A strategic time to help children*. San Francisco: Jossey-Bass.

Johnson, T. R., & Geller, D. M. (1992). Experimental evidence on the impacts of computer assisted instruction in the Job Corps program. *Evaluation Review, 16*(1), 3-22.

Joint Committee on Standards for Educational Evaluation. (1981). *Standards for evaluations of educational programs, projects, and materials.* New York: McGraw-Hill.

Julnes, G., & Mohr, L. B. (1989). Analysis of no difference findings in evaluation research. *Evaluation Review, 13*(6), 628-655.

Kaftarian, S. J., & Hansen, W. B. (Eds.). (1994). Community Partnership Program [Special Issue]. *Journal of Community Psychology.*

Kasprzyk, D., Duncan, G., Kalton, G., & Singh, M. P. (Eds.). (1989). *Panel surveys.* New York: John Wiley and Sons.

Keith, R. A., & Lipsey, M. W. (1993). The role of theory in rehabilitation, assessment, treatment, and outcomes. In H. Gluekauf et al. (Eds.), *Improving assessment in rehabilitation and health* (pp. 33-58). Newbury Park, CA: Sage.

Kelling, G. L., Pate, A., Dieckman, D., & Brown, C. E. (1974). *The Kansas City Preventive Patrol Experiment.* Washington, DC: Police Foundation.

Kempthorne, O. (1952). *The design and analysis of experiments.* New York: Wiley.

Kerachsky, S., Thornton, C., Bloomenthal, A., Maynard, R., Stephens, S., Good, T., & Fox, D. (1985). *Impacts of transitional employment on mentally retarded young adults: Results of the STETS demonstration.* Princeton, NJ: Mathematica Policy Research.

Kershaw, D., & Fair, J. (1976). *The New Jersey Income Maintenance Experiment* (Vol. 1). New York: Academic Press.

Killen, J. D., & Robinson, T. N. (1988). School based research on health behavior change: The Stanford Adolescent Heart Health Program as a model for cardiovascular disease risk reduction. *Review of Research in Education, 15,* 171-202.

Kirk, R. E. (1982). *Experimental design: Procedures for the behavioral sciences.* Belmont, CA: Wadsworth.

Knerr, C. R. (1982). What to do before and after the subpoena arrives. In J. E. Sieber (Ed.), *The ethics of social research* (pp. 191-206). New York: Springer-Verlag.

Kraemer, H. C., & Thiemann, S. (1987). *How many subjects? Statistical power analysis in research.* Newbury Park, CA: Sage.

Kruskal, W. (1980). The significance of Fisher. *Journal of the American Statistical Association, 75*(372), 1019-1030.

Kulik, J., & Bell, S. (1992). *Project NetWork evaluation: Random assignment and survey sampling plan.* Cambridge, MA: Abt.

Lally, R. J., Mangione, P. L., & Honig, S. A. (1988). The Syracuse University Family Development Program. In D. R. Powell (Ed.), *Advances in applied developmental psychology: Vol. 3. Parent education as early childhood intervention: Emerging directions in theory, research, and practice* (pp. 79-104). Norwood, NJ: Ablex.

LaLonde, R. J. (1986). Evaluating the econometric evaluations of training programs with experimental data. *American Economic Review, 76*(4), 604-619.

Land, K. C., McCall, P. L., & Williams, J. R. (1990). Something that works in juvenile justice: An evaluation of the North Carolina court counselors' Intensive Protective Supervision Randomized Experimental Project. *Evaluation Review, 14,* 574-606.

Land, K. C., McCall, P. L. & Williams, J. R. (1991). Intensive supervision of status offenders. In J. McCord & R. Tremblay (Eds.), *The interaction of theory and practice: Experimental studies of intervention* (pp. 172-188). New York: Guilford Press.

LaPrelle, J., Bauman, K. E., & Koch, G. G. (1992). High inter-community variation in adolescent cigarette smoking in a ten community experiment. *Evaluation Review, 16*(2), 115-130.

Lavrakas, P. J. (1993). *Telephone survey methods: Sampling, selection, and supervision.* Newbury Park, CA: Sage.

Levin, H. M. (1991). Cost effectiveness at the quarter century. In M. W. McLaughlin & D. C. Phillips (Eds.), *Evaluation and education at quarter century: Ninetieth yearbook of the National Society for the Study of Education* (pp. 189-209). Chicago: University of Chicago Press.

Leviton, L., & Schuh, R. (1991). Evaluation of outreach as a project element. *Evaluation Review, 15,* 533-554.

Light, R. J., & Pillemer, D. B. (1984). *Summing up: The science of reviewing research.* Cambridge, MA: Harvard University Press.

Light, R. J., Singer, J. D., & Willett, J. B. (1990). *By design: Planning research on higher education.* Cambridge, MA: Harvard University Press.

Lind, E. A. (1985). Randomized experiments in the federal courts. *New Directions for Program Evaluation, 28,* 73-80.

Lindman, H. R. (1992). *Analysis of variance in experimental design.* New York: Springer-Verlag.

Lippmann, W. (1963). The Savannah speech. In C. Rossiter & J. Lare (Eds.), *The essential Lippman* (pp. 495-497). New York: Random House. (Originally published 1933)

Lipsey, M. W. (1990). *Design sensitivity: Statistical power for experimental design.* Beverly Hills, CA: Sage.

Lipsey, M. W. (1992). Juvenile delinquency treatment: a meta-analysis inquiry into the variability of effects. In T. D. Cook, H. Cooper, D. S. Cordray, H. Hartmann, L. V. Hedges, R. J. Light, T. A. Louis, & F. Mosteller (Eds.), *Meta-analysis for explanation* (pp. 83-127). New York: Russell Sage.

Lipsey, M. W. (1993). Theory as method: Small theories of treatments. *New Directions for Program Evaluation, 57,* 5-38.

Lipsey, M. W., Cordray, D. S., & Berger, D. E. (1981). Evaluation of a juvenile diversion program: Using multiple lines of evidence. *Evaluation Review, 5*(3), 283-306.

Littell, J. H., Schuerman, J. R., & Rzepnicki, T. L. (1991). *Preliminary results from the Illinois Family First Program.* Chicago: Chapin Hall Center for Children, University of Chicago.

Little, R. J. A., & Rubin, D. B. (1987). *Statistical analysis with missing data.* New York: John Wiley.

Magidson, J. (Ed.). (1978). *Analyzing qualitative/categorical data: Log linear models and latent structure analysis.* Cambridge, MA: Abt.

Manpower Demonstration Research Corporation. (1980). *Summary and findings of the National Supported Work Demonstration.* Cambridge, MA: Ballinger.

Manpower Demonstration Research Corporation (1994). *Press coverage of MDRC experiments in employment and training* (Research Report). New York: Author.

Mastroianni, A. C., Faden, R., & Federman, D. (Eds.). (1994). *Women and health research: Vol. 2. Ethical and legal issues of including women in clinical studies.* Washington, DC: National Academy of Sciences Press.

Maynard, R. (1991). *Proposal for evaluating dropout demonstration programs.* Princeton, NJ: Mathematica Policy Research.

Maynard, R. A., Kisker, A., & Kerachsky, S. (1991). *Child care in the Single Female Parent Program.* Princeton, NJ: Mathematica Policy Research.

McCormick, M. C., et al. (1989). Outreach as case finding: Its effect on enrollment in prenatal care. *Medical Care, 27*(2), 103-111.

McKay, H., Sinisterra, L., McKay, A., Gomez, H., & Lloreda, P. (1978). Cognitive growth in Colombian malnourished preschoolers. *Science, 200*(4339), 270-278.

McLaughlin, M. W. (1987). Learning from experience: Lesson from policy implementation. *Educational Evaluation and Policy Analysis, 9*(2), 171-178.

McLellan, A. T., Arnat, I. O., Metzger, D. S., Woody, G., & O'Brien, C. P. (1993). The effects of psychological services in substance abuse treatment. *Journal of the American Medical Association, 269*(15), 1953-1959.

Meier, P. (1972). The biggest public health experiment ever: The 1954 field trial of the Salk poliomyelitis vaccine. In J. M. Tanur, F. Mosteller, W. H. Kruskal, R. F. Link, R. S. Pieters, & G. Rising (Eds.), *Statistics: A guide to the unknown* (pp. 2-13). San Francisco: Holden-Day.

Meinert, C. L. (1986). *Clinical trials: Design, conduct, and analysis.* New York: Oxford University Press.

Messick, S. (1993). Validity. In R. L. Linn (Ed.)., *Educational measurement* (3rd ed., pp. 13-104). Washington, DC: American Council on Education/Oryx Press.

Metzger, D. (1993). *Trials on trial* [Videotape]. Philadelphia: University of Pennsylvania/VAMC Center for Studies of Addiction.

Meyer, H. J., & Borgotta, E. F. (1959). *An experiment in mental patient rehabilitation.* New York: Russell Sage.

Meyer, M., & Fienberg, S. E. (Eds.). (1992). *Assessing evaluation studies: The case of bilingual education strategies.* Washington, DC: National Academy of Sciences Press.

Miles, M. B., & Huberman, A. M. (1984). *Qualitative data analysis.* Newbury Park, CA: Sage.

Morrison, D. F. (1990). *Multivariate statistical methods.* New York: McGraw-Hill.

Moses, L. E. (1995). Measuring effects without randomized trials? Options, problems, challenges. *Medical Care, 33*(4, Suppl.), AS8-AS14.

Mosteller, F. (1978). Nonsampling errors. In W. H. Kruskal & J. M. Tanor (Eds.), *International encyclopedia of statistics* (pp. 208-299). New York: Free Press.

Mosteller, F., Gilbert, J. P., & McPeek, B. (1980). Reporting standards and research strategies for controlled trials: Agenda for the editor. *Controlled Clinical Trials, 1,* 37-58.

Mosteller, F., & Rourke, R. E. K. (1973). *Sturdy statistics: Nonparametric and other order statistics.* Reading, MA: Addison-Wesley.

Murarka, B. A., & Spiegelman, R. G. (1978). *Sample selection in the Seattle and Denver Income Maintenance Experiment* (SRI Technical Memorandum No. 1). Menlo Park, CA: SRI International.

Murray, D., McKinlay, S. M., Martin, D., Donner, A. P., Dwyer, J. H., Raudenbush, S., & Graubard, B. I. (1994). Design and analysis issues in community trials. *Evaluation Review, 18*(4), 493-514.

Myers, D., Moore, M., Schirm, A., & Waldman, Z. (1993). *The national evaluation of Upward Bound: Design report.* Princeton, NJ: Mathematica Policy Research.

National Academy of Sciences, Panel on Bilingual Education Studies, Committee on National Statistics. (1992). *Bilingual education studies.* Washington, DC: National Academy of Sciences Press.

National Center for Education Statistics. (1992). *Standards and guidance* (Draft). Washington, DC: U.S. Department of Education, NCES.

National Center for Health Statistics. (1984). *NCHS staff manual on confidentiality.* Washington, DC: Public Health Service.

National Institute of Health, Office of Protection from Research Risks. (1986). *Balancing society's mandates: IRB review criteria* [Videotape]. (Available from OPRR, NIH, Building 31, Room 4B09, 9000 Rockville Pike, Bethesda, MD 20892)

National Institute of Justice. (1978). *Confidentiality of research and statistical data.* Washington, DC: U.S. Department of Justice.

National Institute of Justice. (1987). *What works* [Videotape]. Washington, DC: Author.

Neter, J., Wasserman, W., & Kutner, M. H. (1990). *Applied linear statistical models: Regression analysis and experimental designs.* Homewood, IL: Irwin.

Newhouse, J. P., Marquis, K. H., & Morris, C. N. (1979). Measurement issues in the second generation of social experiments: The Health Insurance Study. *Journal of Econometrics, 11,* 117-130.

Newman, R. G. (1977). *Methadone treatment in narcotic addiction.* New York: Academic Press.

Neyman, J. (1977). Experiments with weather control and statistical problems generated by it. In P. R. Krishnaiah (Ed.), *Applications of statistics* (pp. 1-26). New York: North-Holland.

Nordle, O., & Brantmark, B. (1977). A self adjusting randomization plan for allocation of patients into two treatment groups. *Clinical Pharmacology and Therapeutics, 22,* 825-830.

Oden, S. (1993). *Strategies for subject identification, location, and interviewing.* Ypsilanti, MI: High/Scope Educational Research Foundation.

Orwin, R. G., Cordray, D. S., & Huebner, R. B. (1994). Judicious application of randomized designs. *New Directions for Program Evaluation, 63,* 73-86.

Orwin, R. G., Sonnefeld, L. J., Garrison-Mogren, R., & Smith, N. G. (1994). Pitfalls in evaluating the effectiveness of case management programs for homeless persons. *Evaluation Review, 19*(2), 153-207.

Perng, S. S. (1985). The Accounts Receivable Treatments Study. *New Directions for Program Evaluation, 28,* 55-62.

Petersilia, J. (1989). Implementing randomized experiments. *Evaluation Review, 13*(5), 435-459.

Petersilia, J., & Turner, S. (1990). *Intensive supervision for high risk probationers.* Santa Monica, CA: RAND.

Peterson, P. L., Hawkins, J. D., & Catalano, R. F. (1992). Evaluating comprehensive drug risk reduction interventions. *Evaluation Review, 16*(6), 579-602.

Polit, D. F., & Sherman, R. E. (1990). Statistical power in nursing research. *Nursing Research, 39*(6), 365-369.

Popham, W. J., & Sirotnik, K. A. (1992). *Educational statistics.* New York: Harper and Row.

Porter, A. C. (1988). Comparative experimental methods in educational research. In R. M. Jaeger (Ed.), *Complementary methods for research in education* (pp. 391-417). Washington, DC: American Educational Research Association.

Puma, M., et al. (1989). *Study of the impact of WIC on the growth and development of children.* Bethesda, MD: Abt.

Puma, M., DiPietro, J., Rosenthal, J., Connell, D., Judkins, D., & Fox, M. K. (1991). *Study of the impact of WIC on the growth and development of children: Field Test. Final report of the feasibility assessment.* Bethesda, MD: Abt.

Reichardt, C. S., & Gollob, H. F. (1989). Ruling out threats to validity. *Evaluation Review, 13*(1), 3-17.

Reiss, A. J., & Boruch, R. F. (1991). The program review team approach to multi-site experiments: The Spouse Assault Replication Program. *New Directions for Program Evaluation, 50*(Summer), 33-44.

Reiss, A. J., & Roth, J. A. (Eds.). (1993). *Understanding and preventing violence.* Washington, DC: National Academy of Sciences Press.

Ricchio, J., & Friedlander, D. (1992). *GAIN: Program strategies, participation, patterns, and first year impacts in six counties.* New York: Manpower Demonstration Research Corporation.

Ricketts, E. R., & Sawhill, I. V. (1988). Defining and measuring the underclass. *Journal of Policy Analysis and Management, 1*(2), 316-325.

Riecken, H. W., Boruch, R. F., Campbell, D. T., Caplan, N., Glennanu, T. K., Pratt, J. W., Rees, A., & Williams, W. W. (1974). *Social experimentation: A method for planning and evaluating social programs.* New York: Academic Press.

Robert Wood Johnson Foundation. (1992). *Call for proposals: No place like home—providing supportive services in senior housing.* Princeton, NJ: Author.

Robins, P. K., Spiegelman, R. G., Weiner, S., & Bell, J. G. (1980). *A guaranteed annual income: Evidence from a social experiment.* New York: Academic Press.

Rockefeller Foundation. (1988). *Irrefutable evidence: Lessons from research funded by the Rockefeller Foundation* [Videotape]. New York: Author.

Rockefeller Foundation. (1990). *Into the working world* [Videotape]. New York: Author.

Roos, L. L., Roos, N., & McKinley, B. (1977). Implementing randomization. *Policy Analysis, 3*(4), 547-559.

Rosenbaum, D., Ringwalt, D., Curtin, T. R., Wilkinson, D., Davis, B., & Tarnowski, C. (1991). *The second year evaluation of D.A.R.E. in Illinois.* Chicago: Center for Research in Law and Justice, University of Illinois at Chicago.

Rosenbaum, P. R. (1987). A nontechnical introduction to statistical power and the control of bias. In J. A. Steinberg & M. S. Silverman (Eds.), *Preventing mental disorders: A research perspective* (pp. 43-48). Rockville, MD: National Institute of Mental Health.

Rosenbaum, P. R. (1995). *Observational studies.* New York: Springer-Verlag.

Rosenbaum, P. R., & Rubin, D. B. (1983). The central role of the propensity score in observational studies for causal effects. *Biometrika, 70*(1), 41-55.

Rosenthal, R., & Rosnow, R. L. (1985). *Contrast analysis.* New York: Cambridge University Press.

Rosenthal, R., & Rosnow, R. L. (1991). *Essentials of behavioral research* (2nd ed.). New York: McGraw-Hill.

Ross, R. T., Begab, M. J., Dondis, E. H., Giampiccolo, J. S., & Meyers, C. E. (1985). *Lives of the mentally retarded: A forty year follow-up.* Palo Alto, CA: Stanford University Press.

Rossi, P. H. (1969). Practice, method and theory in evaluating social action programs. In D. P. Moynihan (Ed.), *On understanding poverty* (pp. 217-234). New York: Basic Books.

Rossi, P. H., Berk, R. A., & Lenihan, K. J. (1980). *Money, work and crime: Experimental evidence.* New York: Academic Press.

Rossi, P. H., & Freeman, H. F. (1989). *Evaluation.* Newbury Park, CA: Sage.

Rossi, P. H., Wright, J. D., Fisher, G. A., & Willis, G. (1987). The urban homeless: Estimating composition and size. *Science, 235*(4794), 1336-1341.

Roth, J. A., Scholz, J. T., & Witte, A. D. (Eds.). (1989). *Paying taxes: An agenda for compliance research* (Report of the Panel on Research on Tax Compliance Behavior, National Academy of Sciences). Philadelphia: University of Pennsylvania.

Rubin, D. (1987). *Multiple imputation for non-response in surveys.* New York: Wiley.

Rupp, K., Bell, S., & McManus, L. (1994). Design of the Project NetWork return to work experiment for people with disabilities. *Social Security Bulletin, 57*(2), 3-20.

Rutstein, D. D. (1969). The ethical design of human experiments. *Daedalus, 98*(2), 523-541.

SAS/Stat. (1990). *User's guide* (Vol. 2). Cary, NC: SAS Institute.

Schalock, R. L., & Thornton, C. V. D. (1988). *Program evaluation: A field guide for administrators.* New York: Plenum.

Schuerman, J. R., Rzepnicki, T. L., & Littell, J. (1994). *Putting families first: An experiment in family preservation.* New York: Aldine DeGruyter.

Schuster, J. J. (1990). *CRC handbook of sample size guidelines for clinical trials.* Boston: CRC Press.

Schwartz, R. D., & Orleans, S. (1967). On legal sanctions. *University of Chicago Law Review, 34*(274), 282-300.

Schweinhart, L. J., Barnes, H. V., & Weikart, D. P. (1993). *Significant benefits: The High Scope Perry Preschool study through age 27.* Ypsilanti, MI: High/Scope Press.

Sherman, L. W., & Berk, R. A. (1984). The specific deterrent effects of arrest for domestic assault. *American Sociological Review, 49*, 261-272.

Sherman, L. W., & Berk, R. A. (1985). The randomization of arrest. *New Directions for Program Evaluation, 28*, 15-26.

Sherman, L., & Cohn, L. (1989). The impact of research on legal policy: The Minneapolis Domestic Violence Experiment. *Law and Society Review, 23*, 117-144.

Sherman, L. W., & Hamilton, E. (1984). *The impact of the Minneapolis Domestic Violence Experiment.* Washington, DC: Police Foundation.

Sherman, L. W., Schmidt, J. D., & Rogan, D. P. (1992). *Policing domestic violence: Experiments and dilemmas.* New York: Free Press.

Sherman, L. W., Schmidt, J. D., Rogan, D. P., Gartin, P. R., Cohn, E., Collins, D. J., & Bacich, A. R. (1991). From initial deterrence to long term escalation. *Criminology, 29*(4), 821-849.

Sieber, J. E. (1992). *Planning ethically responsible research: A guide for students and institutional review boards.* Newbury Park, CA: Sage.

Silverman, W. A. (1977). The lesson of retrolental fibroplasia. *Scientific American, 236*(6), 100-107.

Snedecor, G. W., & Cochran, W. G. (1989). *Statistical methods.* Ames: Iowa State University Press.

Social Security Administration. (1992). *Project NetWork: Clients' rights, responsibilities, and informed consent* (CMOP.0620.000). Washington, DC: Author.

Social Security Administration. (1994). *Excerpts from program operations manual system: Potential suicidal/homicidal behavior* (DI 23030.005, DI 13005.070). Washington, DC: Author.

Solomon, P., & Draine, J. (1995a). The efficacy of a consumer case management team: Two year outcomes of a randomized trial. *Journal of Mental Health Administration, 22*(2), 135-146.

Solomon, P., & Draine, J. (1995b). One year outcome of a randomized trial of case management with seriously mentally ill clients leaving jail. *Evaluation Review, 19*, 256-273.

St. Pierre, R. G., Cook, T. L., & Straw, R. B. (1981). An evaluation of the Nutrition Education and Training Program: Findings from Nebraska. *Evaluation and Program Planning, 4*, 335-344.

St. Pierre, R., Swartz, J., Murray, S., Deck, D., & Nickel, P. (1995). *National evaluation of Even Start Family Literacy Program* (Contract LC 90062001). Washington, DC: U.S. Department of Education.

Standards of Reporting Trials Group. (1994). A proposal for structural reporting of randomized clinical trials. *Journal of the American Medical Association, 272*(24), 1926-1931.

Stanley, B., & Sieber, J. E. (Eds.). (1992). *Social research on children and adolescents: Ethical issues*. Newbury Park, CA: Sage.

Stevens, S. (1994). Common implementation issues in three large scale social experiments. *New Directions for Program Evaluation, 63*, 45-54.

Stigler, S. M. (1978). Mathematical statistics in the early states. *Annals of Statistics, 6*, 239-265.

Stouthamer-Loeber, M., & Van Kammen, W. B. (1995). *Data collection and management: A practical guide*. Thousand Oaks, CA: Sage.

Stromsdorfer, E., & Farkas, G. (Eds.). (1980). *Evaluation studies review annual 5*. Beverly Hills, CA: Sage.

Taylor, K. M., Margolese, R. G., & Soskolne, X. X. (1984). Physicians' reasons for not entering eligible patients in a randomized clinical trial of surgery for breast cancer. *New England Journal of Medicine, 310*, 1363-1367.

Test, M. F., & Burke, S. (1985). Random assignment of chronically ill persons to hospital or community treatment. *New Directions for Program Evaluation, 28*, 81-94.

Thornton, C., & Decker, P. (1989). *The Transitional Employment and Training Demonstration (TETD): Analysis of program impacts*. Princeton, NJ: Mathematica Policy Research.

Tremblay, R. E., McCord, J., Boileau, H., Charlebois, P., Gagnon, C., LeBlano, M., & Larivee, S. (1991). Can disruptive boys be helped to become competent? *Psychiatry, 54*, 148-161.

Turner, A. G. (1982). What subjects of survey research believe about confidentiality. In J. E. Sieber (Ed.). *The ethics of social research* (pp. 151-166). New York: Springer-Verlag.

Turner, C. F., Miller, H. G., & Moses, L. E. (Eds.). (1989). *AIDS: Sexual behavior and intravenous drug use*. Washington, DC: National Academy of Sciences Press.

Turpin, R. S., & Sinacore, J. N. (Eds.). (1991). Multi-site evaluation [Special issue]. *New Directions for Program Evaluation, 50*.

Tyler, R. (1991). General statement on program evaluation. In M. W. McLaughlin & D. C. Phillips (Eds.), *Evaluation and education at the quarter century* (pp. 3-17). Chicago: University of Chicago Press.

U.S. Department of Agriculture, Food and Nutrition Service. (1992). *Request for proposal: WIC Child Impact Study*. Arlington, Virginia: Author.

U.S. Department of Education, National Center for Education Statistics. (1991). *Standards for education data collection and reporting*. Washington, DC: Author.

U.S. Department of Education, Planning and Evaluation Service. (1991a). *Request for proposals: Evaluation of Upward Bound programs*. Washington, DC: Author.

U.S. Department of Education, Planning and Evaluation Service. (1991b). School Dropout Demonstration Assistance Program: Notice inviting applications for new awards for fiscal year FY 1991 (CFDA No. 84.201). *Federal Register, 56*(23), 4364-4369.

U.S. Department of Education, Planning and Evaluation Service. (1991c). School Dropout Demonstration Assistance Program: Notice of final priorities for FY 1991. *Federal Register, 56*(23), 4384-4387.

U.S. General Accounting Office. (1986). *Teenage pregnancy: 500,000 births a year but few tested programs* (GAO/PEMD-86-16BR). Washington, DC: Author.

U.S. General Accounting Office. (1987). *Federal evaluation* (PEMD-87-9). Washington, DC: Author.

U.S. General Accounting Office. (1988a). *Education issues: Transition series* (GAO OCG-89-8TR). Washington, DC: Author.

U.S. General Accounting Office. (1988b). *Program evaluation issues: Transition series* (GAO OCG-89-8TR). Washington, DC: Author.

U.S. General Accounting Office. (1992). *Cross-design synthesis: A new strategy for medical effectiveness research* (GAO/PEMD-92-18). Washington, DC: Author.

Valdiserri, R. O., Lyter, D. W., Leviton, L. C., Callahan, C. M., Kingsley, L. A., & Rinaldo, C. R. (1989). AIDS prevention in gay and bisexual men. *AIDS, 3*(1), 21-26.

Vinokur, A., Price, R. H., & Schul, Y. (1995). Impact of the JOBS intervention on unemployed workers varying in risks for depression. *American Journal of Psychology, 23*(1), 39-73.

Walker, G., & Vilella-Velez, F. (1992). *Anatomy of a demonstration: The Summer Training and Education Program from pilot through replication and post program impacts.* Philadelphia: Public/Private Ventures.

Wargo, M. J. (1989). Characteristics of successful program evaluation. In J. S. Wholey & K. E. Newcomb (Eds.), *Improving government performance* (pp. 71-82). San Francisco: Jossey-Bass.

Wegman, E. J., & DePriest, D. J. (Eds.). (1980). *Statistical analysis of weather modification experiments.* New York: Marcel Dekker.

Willett, J. B., & Singer, J. D. (1991). From whether to when: New methods for studying student dropout and teacher attrition. *Review of Educational Research, 61*(4), 407-450.

Winer, B. J., Brown, D. R., & Michaels, K. M. (1991). *Statistical principles in experimental design.* New York: McGraw-Hill.

Wortman, P. M., & Marans, R. W. (1987). Reviving pre-evaluation research. *Evaluation Review, 11*(2), 197-215.

Wright, J. D., Allen, T. L., & Devine, J. A. (1995). Tracking non-traditional populations in longitudinal studies. *Evaluation and Program Planning, 18*(3), 267-277.

Yates, B. T. (1996). *Analyzing costs, procedures, processes, and outcomes in human services.* Thousand Oaks, CA: Sage.

Yeaton, W. H., & Sechrest, L. (1986). Use and misuse of no difference findings in eliminating threats to validity. *Evaluation Review, 10*(6), 836-852.

Yeaton, W. H., & Sechrest, L. (1987a). Assessing factors influencing acceptance of no difference research. *Evaluation Review, 11*(1), 131-142.

Yeaton, W. H., & Sechrest, L. (1987b). No difference research. *New Directions for Program Evaluation, 34*, 67-82.

Yin, R. K. (1989). *Case study research.* Newbury Park, CA: Sage.

Zaslow, M. (1995). *Proposal for research on the children of young working mothers.* Washington, DC: Child Trends.

Author Index

Subject Index

About the Author

Robert Boruch is University Trustee Chair Professor in the Graduate School of Education and the Statistics Department of the Wharton School of the University of Pennsylvania. He is a member of the board or of statutory advisory committees in three sectors: private foundations, research corporations, and federal agencies. He has been a principal author for more than 120 articles in scholarly journals and a dozen books. His primary interests lie in the methods of producing evidence, their use in evaluation and public policy, and the managerial, ethical, and institutional contexts in which evidence can be produced. The topics that he has addressed include controlled experiments, privacy, confidentiality and access to data, and innovative approaches in difficult settings. The disciplinary contexts include education, civil and criminal justice, health services, energy, welfare, child abuse and neglect, and defense.

APPLIED SOCIAL RESEARCH
METHODS SERIES
Series Editors
LEONARD BICKMAN, Peabody College, Vanderbilt University, Nashville
DEBRA J. ROG, Vanderbilt University, Washington, DC

Other volumes in this series are listed on the series page